The Inkwell Dictionary of Business and Economics

The Inkwell Dictionary of Business and Economics

James A. Barham

Editor

Inkwell PRESS

Description

The Inkwell Dictionary of Business and Economics contains articles covering the fields of business, industry, entrepreneurship, finance, and economics. In all, this volume contains 162 entries, from "absolute advantage" to "zombie company." Most entries consist of three sections. The first section discursively defines the term or phrase under consideration. The second section provides a complete etymology of each entry. We provide an unusually full etymology for a dictionary of this type in the conviction that knowing the history of an idea and of the terminology through which it is expressed promotes a more fully rounded understanding. Finally, the third section discusses the manner and the circumstances in which the entry is used in practice.

Library Cataloging Data

The Inkwell Dictionary of Business and Economics edited by James A. Barham
Trim size: 7 × 10 inches
Library of Congress Control Number: 2026936186
ISBN: 979-8-89946-031-9 (Paperback), 979-8-89946-030-2 (Kindle)
BISAC: BUS055000 BUSINESS & ECONOMICS / Reference
BISAC: BUS024000 BUSINESS & ECONOMICS / Education
BISAC: EF008000 REFERENCE / Dictionaries

Book Cover Design

By Chloe Dembski. The image is a detail of Marinus van Reymerswale's *The Banker and His Wife* (16th century).

Inkwell
PRESS

2321 Sir Barton Way
Suite 140-1032
Lexington, KY 40509
https://press.inkwell.net

Why This Dictionary?

Every field of human endeavor has its jargon. In this respect, the business world is no different from any other.

However, business, economics, and allied fields do have one unique feature. They have a large number of technical terms that at first glance appear to be ordinary words and phrases. I am thinking of terms like "goodwill," "headhunter," "inflation," "interest," "invisible hand," "margin," "poison pill," and numerous others.

This can create confusion. For example, any lay person encountering the word "ionized" will know he or she is dealing with a scientific term of art, whereas someone encountering the word "rainmaker" may have no idea that they are dealing with a term of art in the business world.

For this reason, we at Inkwell Press decided it would be useful to provide a succinct volume devoted to some of the most misleading terms of this type, as well as others that are frankly esoteric—whose meaning is simply inscrutable, rather than misleading. The result is *The Inkwell Dictionary of Business and Economics.*

Our dictionary provides definitions, etymologies, and examples of usage for 162 words and phrases that constitute terms of art commonly encountered in the fields of business, finance, economics, and entrepreneurship. We hope you will find it both useful and enjoyable.

—James A. Barham

Table of Contents

1. Absolute Advantage

DEFINITION: The phrase "absolute advantage" refers to the capacity of an economically productive entity—whether an individual, a firm, or a nation—to manufacture a greater number of units of a given product or service within a particular time span than any rival entity can produce in the same time span.

A company may acquire an absolute advantage in one of two ways: (1) by producing a greater quantity of unit-goods within the given time span using the same quantity of resources as its rivals; or (2) by producing the same quantity of unit-goods within the given time span using fewer resources than its rivals.

In other words, absolute advantage is the superiority enjoyed by the *most-efficient* producer of a given product over all other producers of that product in the world.

Absolute advantage should not be confused with **comparative advantage**.

Both types of advantage have to do with relative productive efficiency. However, in the absolute case, the advantage is absolute, meaning that the country in question is more efficient in producing a particular product than any other country in the world, while in the comparative case, the advantage is relative to two or more specific countries with respect to a specific product.

The notion of comparative advantage involves the phenomenon of opportunity cost.

If a country enjoys an absolute advantage with respect to some good or service, it is obvious that it ought to pursue the production of that good or the provision of that service.

However, a country that enjoys a comparative advantage over another country in the manufacture of a given good should still look at alternative lines of production. The reason is that it is always possible the country may enjoy a *greater* comparative advantage in one good rather than another.

ETYMOLOGY: The phrase "absolute advantage" was originated by the Scottish moral philosopher **Adam Smith** in his classic 1776 treatise, foundational for economics, *The Wealth of Nations*.

The English adjective "absolute" is attested from the fourteenth century. It derives, via Middle English *absolut,* from the Latin past participle *absolūtus*, meaning "unfettered," "unconditioned," "complete," "perfect," or "absolute," from the verb *absolvo, absolvere,* meaning "to loosen," "to free," "to finish," or "to complete."

The English noun "advantage" is attested from the fourteenth century. It derives, via Middle English *avantage,* from the identical form in Middle French.

The French noun *avantage,* in turn, is closely related to the preposition and adverb *avant,* meaning "before" (thus "advantage" implies "beforeness," that is, priority or superiority). *Avant* itself derives from the Latin adverbial phrase "*ab ante*" (from before).

USAGE: Adam Smith introduced the concept of absolute advantage to illustrate how nations can benefit from trade by focusing on producing and exporting goods they can produce more efficiently than other nations.

Nations possessing an absolute advantage may opt to specialize in the production and trade of particular goods or services. They may then utilize the resulting proceeds to procure various products and services from other nations.

Smith argued that nations which specialize in the manufacture of goods in the production of which they enjoy an absolute advantage, and which then trade in those goods, can make all countries better off, so long as each one enjoys an absolute advantage in the production of at least one product.

In the next couple of generations, Smith's basic idea was refined by **David Ricardo** and others into the more-realistic and -flexible idea of comparative advantage, as discussed above.

2. Acquisition

DEFINITION: The term "acquisition" refers to the purchase by one company of a majority (or total) share in another company's stock, thereby ending the latter's existence as an independent entity.

By owning more than half of a target company's stocks and other assets, the acquiring company becomes entitled to manage the assets of the acquired company without consulting the latter's management team.

ETYMOLOGY: "Acquisition" is derived from the Middle English *acquisicioun,* via Middle French *acquisition* and ultimately the Latin noun *acquisitio,* derived from the past participle, *acquisitus,* of the verb *acquirere.*

USAGE: Acquisitions are a routine in the business world and may take place with or without the acquired company's consent. When the acquired company approves the purchase, the process usually includes a no-shop clause—an agreement that prevents the acquired company from getting an offer from another potential buyer.

While acquisitions involving large, well-known companies often make the newspaper headlines, small and medium-sized companies in fact make up the majority of mergers and acquisitions (M&A).

Firms purchase other businesses for a host of reasons. They may be hoping to achieve economies of scale, otherwise reduce costs, broaden their portfolio, increase their market presence, explore new product lines, or increase synergy.

The following is a list of additional reasons for acquisitions:

1. To enter a foreign market

If a company seeks to extend its operations to a foreign nation, acquiring an existing company in that country might be the most effective method of market entry. The acquired company would already have a workforce that speaks the language and is familiar with local supply chains, as well as a recognizable brand and other non-physical assets.

2. As a strategy for growth

A company may encounter certain physical or logistical limitations to its continued growth. In such situations, it can be more economically efficient to purchase another company than to expand one's own operations. If the company can find a flourishing business to purchase, it may instantly create a new revenue stream, and thus a new means for generating profits.

3. To reduce competition or avoid overcapacity

In scenarios where competition is excessive or physical capacity is underutilized, a company might undertake an acquisition to eliminate a competitor or to diminish surplus capacity.

4. To acquire new technology

Given that developing new technological capabilities in-house can require a very substantial investment of both time and financial resources, it may be more cost-effective to acquire another company that has already successfully developed the needed technology.

What is the Difference Between Acquisitions, Mergers, and Takeovers?

Acquisition: Voluntary sale leading to the demise of the acquired company

In the case of voluntary acquisitions, the acquired company's board of directors consents to the purchase. Such deals are commonly structured to be mutually advantageous to both parties.

The acquired company will typically assist the acquiring company by providing financial statements and other valuations relevant to the acquired company's assets and liabilities.

Merger: Voluntary sale leading to the demise of both the acquired and the acquiring companies and the creation of a third, new company

A merger is a sort of mutual acquisition between equal companies. Both parties must of course agree to the merger.

As a result of a merger, both of the parties entering into the agreement cease to exist, and a brand-new, third entity comes into existence.

For a merger to be mutually desirable, both parties must be approximately equal. However, this rough equality can take a variety of forms, from size, scale of operations, and customer base to stock market valuation, income generated, profitability, etc.

In a merger, each company's management will believe that the new consolidated entity will generate more value for its own stakeholders than the company is capable of doing by operating independently.

Takeover: Involuntary sale of the acquired company by the acquiring company

Hostile acquisitions, also known as "hostile takeovers," happen when the acquired company's management does not want the company to be acquired.

Since the acquired company does not want to be purchased, the managers of the acquiring company are obliged to aggressively pursue the takeover.

Typically, they will seek to buy the acquired company's shares in any way they can, until they have achieved a controlling interest, whereupon they can force the purchase by outvoting the original company's board members.

Assessing Potential Acquisition Targets

A number of factors must be taken into account when one company is considering acquiring another company, including assessing an appropriate price for the target company, its debt burden, and any litigation it may be subject to.

3. Action (Human)

DEFINITION: Human action is the totality of the goal-directed, or purposive, acts in the behavioral repertoire of the human animal.

The capacity for human action lies at the foundation of political economy as a science. Therefore, the study of human action (called "praxeology") is conceptually prior to the study of economics.

ETYMOLOGY: The noun "action," and the related noun and verb, "act," derive, via Middle English, from the Latin substantive *actum*, meaning a "thing done," which derives in turn from the past participle, *actus*, of the verb *ago, agere*, meaning "to set in motion," "to drive," "to do," or "to perform."

"Action" is attested in English beginning in the fourteenth century.

The word "human" derives, via Middle English and Middle French, from the Latin adjective *hūmānus*, meaning "human," which is related to the noun *homo, hominis*, meaning a "human being."

USAGE: The study of human action views the human being, first and foremost, as an animal or, indeed, as a generic organism.

Certain things about the nature of life itself are still little understood and may be quite contentious.

However, no one can dispute the fact that living systems behave in such as way as to maintain themselves in existence, both as "tokens" (individuals) and as "types" (kinds).

Biological tokens, or individuals, are perpetuated through action, while biological types are perpetuated through reproduction.

However, reproduction in all cases consists in a sequence of actions. Therefore, individual action is the logically prior category.

The upshot of this foray into the still-murky conceptual foundations of biology is that action is an intrinsic feature of life itself. A living thing that does not act is inconceivable.

Given this background, economists who pursue the conceptual foundations of political economy—such as, above all, **Ludwig von Mises** in his 1949 classic, *Human Action: A Treatise on Economics*—look at the basic concepts of economics through the lens of human action.

A number of economic principles can be directly derived from the perspective of the theory of human action:

1. Purpose is at the heart of all human action and of life itself.
2. Purposive actions ultimately subserve the goal of the preservation of life.
3. However, most purposive actions consist of sequences of multiple steps.
4. This means that "proximate" (or "instrumental") actions may have their own subsidiary goals.
5. According to the second law of thermodynamics, living systems cannot exist unless they manage to replenish their sources of energy.
6. Therefore, some instrumental actions will involve incorporating external molecules (at the cellular level), or, generally speaking, "food" and other necessary resources.
7. This means that all purposive actions involve distinguishing between external resources that further the attainment of instrumental goals from those that do not.
8. Such a capacity for distinguishing between necessary and neutral (or harmful) resources is the source of all valuing in nature.

One can readily see that the last point, #7, directly implies the truth of the subjective theory of value, which was only achieved by economists after a long period of theoretical struggle during the second half of the nineteenth century.

Similarly, the universality of the reliance of living systems on external resources—or, in a word, *property*—may be seen to follow from point #5.

Moreover, the simple fact that all human life rests upon the foundation of action goes to show the wisdom of basing economic arrangements upon natural human propensities, motivations, and intentions, including private property.

The laws of supply and demand also arise directly out of the phenomenon of human action.

Finally, the praxeological perspective on the human condition emphasizes the fact that the world is not ready-made for our convenience. Rather, we human beings must wrest our livelihood from the world. (See the definition of "**scarcity**" for discussion related to this point.)

Taken together, all these considerations reveal the fallacy at the heart of socialism, **communism**, and similar ideologies.

Namely, they overlook the unconditional necessity for human beings to extract the conditions of their survival through action.

In addition, they ignore the entire psychological structure of rewards, satisfactions, virtues, duties, and other moral imperatives that have grown up around the phenomenon of action over the course of human history.

These blind spots in socialistic thinking amount to what one might call "cornucopianism"—namely, the idea that the goods necessary to support human life do not have to be produced by anyone in particular, but just appear out of thin air, so that they can be "distributed" in an equal manner to all.

But cornucopianism is a sort of childish fantasy, which flies in the face of what human beings are as finite, material beings.

All such utopian thinking studiously averts its gaze from the nature of human action, as well as from its iron necessity, if human life is to continue at all.

4. Ad Valorem Tax

DEFINITION: *Ad valorem* is a Latin phrase meaning "according to value." An *ad valorem tax* is imposed on the basis of the assessed value (the dollar value assigned for tax purposes) of the item being taxed. The most common ad valorem tax is the municipal property tax assessed on the real estate of property owners, but it may also be levied on other property that is owned, such as cars and recreational vehicles.

5. Animal Spirits

DEFINITION: The phrase "animal spirits" refers to the fact that much of **human action** in general, and economic action in particular, is motivated by factors such as instincts, proclivities, and emotions, rather than "pure reason."

ETYMOLOGY: The word "animal" derives from the Latin noun, *animal, animālis,* meaning "animal."

The Latin *animal* is formed from the adjective, *animālis, animāle,* meaning "living," which is itself connected to the noun, *anima,* meaning "soul."

The noun "spirit" derives, via Middle English and Old French, from the Latin noun *spīritus, spīritūs,* meaning 'breeze," "breath," the "breath of life," "divine inspiration," "high spirits," or "pride."

The word *spīritus,* in turn, is connected with the verb *spīro, spīrare,* meaning "to blow" or "to breathe."

USAGE: The phrase "animal spirits" entered economic parlance in 1936 with the publication of *The General Theory of Employment, Interest and Money,* by **John Maynard Keynes**.

However, the phrase became known far beyond the bounds of the academic economics world in the wake of the international financial crisis of 2008, when **Alan Greenspan**, who had served as Chairman of the US Federal Reserve from 1987 until 2006, began to use the expression in his public comments on the crisis.

Consciously borrowing from Keynes, Greenspan explained that he had had to revise his own earlier conviction that a human being was primarily a rational actor—a sort of glorified calculating machine.

Instead, he had changed his mind and now believed that Keynes was right that much of human behavior, including economic behavior, could only be explained by non-rational factors, such fear, hope, greed, impatience, and euphoria.

Greenspan was asked why he thought everyone had "missed" the fact that the startling increase in real estate prices prior to 2008 amounted to an unsustainable "**bubble**."

Greenspan replied that the bankers, Wall Street traders, and other investors at that time *did know* they were in a bubble. The problem was that they *didn't care.*

Why did they not care?

Greenspan said they did not care because they were no longer acting according to reason, but rather were being driven by animal spirits.

More specifically, they were helpless to bail out of the bubble in time because they were overwhelmed by feelings of sheer exuberance, unjustified optimism, and fear of missing out the chance to make still more profits before the music stopped.

Finally, they were driven by the herd effect: When everyone else is running in a stampede, it is not easy to turn away and strike out on one's own.

Analogously, in the run-up to 2008, everyone was getting rich and this made it nearly impossible for anyone to break ranks and go his own way.

All the foregoing psychological factors are encompassed by the phrase "animal spirits," which play a much greater role in real-world economic behavior than most theoretical economists would like to think.

Recently, though, a new economic subdiscipline has grown up, which attempts to do just that—namely, "**behavioral economics**."

6. Appreciation

DEFINITION: "Appreciation" is an increase in the market value of a good over time. It is the opposite of "**depreciation**."

ETYMOLOGY: The noun "appreciation" and the related verb "appreciate" derive from the Late Latin past participle, *appreciatus,* of the verb *appretio, appretiare,* meaning "to appreciate."

The Late Latin term was assembled from the classical Latin preposition *ad,* meaning "towards," and noun *pretium, pretii,* meaning "worth," "value," or "price."

USAGE: The term "appreciate" entered English around the turn of the seventeenth century. It is thus closely associated with the development of long-distance trade routes and the consequent take-off of the market economy that occurred during the Renaissance.

These historic trends began somewhat earlier south of the Alps, in the Mediterranean countries, especially in Italy, and then moved north of the Alps over the course of the sixteenth and seventeenth centuries.

The phenomenon of appreciation must be understood in the context of the **subjective theory of value.**

In a nutshell, appreciation occurs whenever demand increases for a type of commodity whose supply is being held steady or is growing more slowly than the demand.

The classic example of appreciation is real estate. Homes appreciate within a particular market when an increase in demand for housing in that market outpaces any increase in the supply of housing stock.

For example, a population influx into an area that occurs at a faster rate than new housing stock can be produced would lead to appreciation of the existing housing stock.

Other common examples of commodities that may appreciate include precious metals, such as gold, art objects, and other goods for which demand tends to increase over time but whose supply is severely limited.

7. Asset

DEFINITION: An *asset* is anything of monetary value owned by an individual, corporation, or organization.

8. Asset Management

DEFINTION: Asset management involves the purchase and trading of assets for clients. The goal of this trading is the preservation and increase of the assets.

Asset management companies provide their services to affluent individuals or families, as well as to major banks and institutional investors.

Individuals offering asset management services are often referred to as "financial advisors" or "portfolio managers." Such advisor and managers may operate independently or be employed by a financial establishment like an investment bank.

ETYMOLOGY: "Asset" is from Anglo-French *asetz*—meaning a quantity of property sufficient to pay a debt—via Old French *assez* (enough) and ultimately Vulgar Latin *ad satis*.

"Management" is from Italian verb *mannegiare,* which derives from the noun *mano,* which in turn derives from Latin *manus,* both meaning "hand."

USAGE: The twin objectives of asset management are augmenting worth and limiting risk.

The foremost consideration is the client's risk appetite. For example, a retired person subsisting on his portfolio income, or a pension fund manager supervising retirement assets, should proceed in a risk-averse manner.

On the other hand, younger or more-adventurous individuals may be more comfortable with a riskier investment strategy.

However, most individuals fall somewhere in between these extremes. This means that the asset manager's task is to pinpoint each client's specific risk comfort level.

It is upon this determination that the selection of particular investment options, such as stocks, bonds, real estate, commodities, mutual funds, and others, depends.

In order to carry out these tasks successfully, asset managers must carry out comprehensive research utilizing both macro and microanalytical resources. This implies the statistical scrutiny of current market conditions, the analysis of corporate financial records, and anything else that could contribute to the primary objective of enhancing the value of the client's assets.

There exists a variety of different types of asset managers, each characterized by the kind of asset they manage and the degree of service they offer, including, but not limited to, registered investment advisors, investment brokers, and financial advisors.

Asset managers may employ different pricing structures. The prevalent model charges a percentage of the managed assets, with the industry average hovering around one percent for portfolios up to $1 million, and decreasing for larger portfolios.

Other asset managers might impose a fee for every trade executed, while certain managers might even earn a commission for selling additional securities to their clients.

For affluent clients, financial institutions may provide additional services, such as check-writing privileges, credit cards, debit cards, margin loans, and brokerage services to account holders.

The advantage of such services to account holders is that all their banking and investment necessities can be fulfilled by a single entity.

9. Austrian Economics

As the principal tenets of neoclassical liberal economics were being consolidated during the late nineteenth century by **William Stanley Jevons (1835–1882)** and **Alfred Marshall (1842–1924)** in England, **Léon Walras (1834–1910)** in France, and others, a distinctive vision of political economy was being developed by a cohesive group of professors living in what was then the Austro-Hungarian Empire.

The labels "Austrian Economics" and "Austrian School" were originally applied to the group by its intellectual opponents across the border in Germany, in order to smear them as provincial and on the fringe of economic thinking. The labels were later proudly adopted by the Austrian professors themselves as their preferred designation.

Concentrated primarily in the capital city of Vienna, the Austrian authors hammered out a theoretical structure that was akin to neoclassical liberalism in espousing free trade and *laissez-faire* principles in general; however, the Austrians went further in several respects.

More specifically, the Austrian vision rested—and still rests to this day—on three great principles:

- The economic value of commodities under conditions of scarcity is determined autonomously by buyers' preferences through the market mechanism (the "subjective theory of value").
- Business cycle crashes are principally due to the misallocation of resources.
- The best way to facilitate economic recovery, and so maximize general prosperity, is to permit failed enterprises to go under ("creative destruction") and resources to be reallocated according to the normal market mechanism, without outside interference.

The Austrian School can be usefully divided into a "first generation" and a "second generation" of three major figures each. Let us look at the first generation in a bit more detail.

The Austrian School's founder is usually taken to be **Carl Menger (1840–1921).** A graduate of the University of Vienna, Menger became a private tutor of the Austrian crown prince, Rudolph. In 1878, he was appointed to a chair in political economy at the University of Vienna by Rudolph's father, Emperor Franz Joseph.

In 1871 Menger brought out his textbook, *Grundsätze der Volkswirtschaftslehre* [Principles of Economics], which is often taken to be the founding document of Austrian economics. He followed this work up with another one in 1883, which attracted even more attention and controversy, *Untersuchungen über die Methode der Socialwissenschaften und der politischen Oekonomie insbesonderen* [Investigations into the Method of the Social Sciences, Especially Political Economy].

In these and other works, Menger's most distinctive contribution to the science of economics was his development of the theory of marginal utility, from which he drew the correct conclusion that the value of an item in an economic exchange is determined primarily by the subjective preference of the buyer.

Jevons and Walras came to a similar conclusion independently and published their work almost simultaneously with Menger in 1871. However, the latter's analysis of the issues involved has traditionally been deemed the most original and insightful of the three.

The next important figure in the history of Austrian Economics, **Eugen von Böhm-Bawerk (1851–1915)**, fell in love with the writings of Carl Menger while a student at the University of Vienna. However, he never actually studied with Menger himself. After completing his studies, he served as a professor at the University of Innsbruck and as a public servant with the Austrian Ministry of Finance. He rose to become the Minister of Finance in 1895.

In 1890 Böhm-Bawerk published his *Geschichte und Kritik der Capitalzinstheorien* [History and Critique of Theories of Interest], which made his reputation. This book eventually became the first volume of a three-part work known as *Capital und Capitalzins* [Capital and Interest].

Böhm-Bawerk's fame outgrew the bounds of the professional academic economic world thanks to a pair of widely read and debated polemical books he published next: first, in 1892, *Positive Theorie des Capitales* [The Positive Theory of Capital], a critique of Marx's theory of capitalist exploitation of labor; and second, in 1896, *Zum Abschluss des Marxschen Systems* [Karl Marx and the Close of His System; literally, Towards the Conclusion of the Marxian System], a more general refutation of socialism.

The third main member of the first generation of Austrian economists was **Friedrich von Wieser (1851–1926).** Böhm-Bawerk was a childhood friend of Wieser's and, like his friend, Wieser fell under the spell of Carl Menger's economic vision while a student at the University of Vienna. Wieser's sister later married Böhm-Bawerk, turning the friends into brothers-in-law.

After graduation, Wieser taught briefly at Charles University in Prague, before moving back to the University of Vienna, where he spent the rest of his career. He published one of his most-influential works, *Der Natürliche Werth* [Natural Value], in 1889. In this book, Wieser pursued a deeper and more-comprehensive analysis of the concept of economic value, which, however, was still in fundamental agreement with Menger's teachings.

While Wieser was very prolific, perhaps his next-most-influential works in the long run were his two late treatises, *Theorie der gesellschaftlichen Wirtschaft* [Social Economics; literally, Theory of Social Economy], published in 1914, and *Das Gesetz der Macht* [The Law of Power], published in 1926. In these books, which were largely sociological in nature, Wieser broke with Austrian orthodoxy, arguing that the system of social (i.e., political) order ought to take moral precedence over the system of economic order, thus justifying departures from the pure *laissez-faire* ideal in order to secure certain advantages for the common good unobtainable through the market mechanism alone.

Wieser was the teacher of the three main figures who made up the Austrian School's third generation: **Ludwig von Mises (1881–1973),Joseph A. Schumpeter (1883–1950)**, and **Friedrich A. Hayek (1899–1992).**

10. Balance Sheet

DEFINITION: A balance sheet is a financial statement that provides essential information regarding a company's assets, liabilities, and shareholder equity.

When combined with other kinds of financial statements, a balance sheet may provide the foundation for an informed analysis of a company's financial condition.

ETYMOLOGY: The first use of the English phrase "balance sheet" dates from 1838.

The word "balance" comes from Middle English via Old French and, ultimately, the Vulgar Latin *bilancia,* which was constructed from the classical Latin prefix "*bi-*" (two) and noun, *lanx, lancis* (plate, flat dish).

The word "sheet" derives from the Middle English *shete* and Old English *sceāta,* which means the lower corner of a sail. *Sceāta,* in turn, is related to Old English *scȳte,* meaning sheet.

USAGE: A balance sheet provides an overview of the state of a company's finances at a moment in time, like a snapshot.

Because a single balance sheet cannot give a sense of temporal trends affecting a company's financial well-being, it is important to compare a company's present balance sheet with ones from earlier months and years.

Various ratios obtainable from a company's balance sheet, such as the debt-to-equity ratio and the acid-test ratio, among others, make it possible for investors to gauge a company's financial health.

Various others financial statements, such as cash flow statements, income statements, statements of changes in equity, and earnings reports, may also help to evaluate a company's financial situation.

A balance sheet is structured around three fundamental accounting quantities, which may be related to one another by means of the following equation:

Assets = Liabilities + Shareholder Equity

This equation holds true because all of a company's assets, that is, its *possessions,* must be paid for either through borrowing (i.e., liabilities, or debt) or through receiving (i.e., investments, or shareholder equity).

The balance between the two sides of the equation indicates the state of a company's financial health.

For example, if a company obtains a loan from a bank for, say, $10,000, this increases *both* its assets *and* its liabilities by that same amount. Thus, the left-hand side of the equation remains equal to the right-hand side.

The same thing is true if a new investor injects, say, $5000 into the company. Both the company's assets and shareholder equity will increase by that same amount.

Profits from operations and investments are assigned to both the company's assets and shareholder equity, thus maintaining the balance.

In short, a company's balance sheet, as its name implies, should always show a balance between assets on one side and the sum of liabilities plus shareholder equity on the other.

If this is not the case, something is wrong somewhere. One must look for the source of the error, which may be due to the assignment of data to the wrong category, inaccuracies in the calculation of inventory, or mistakes relating to exchange rates or straightforward computational errors.

Each of the balance sheet categories is composed of subaccounts that detail a company's financial specifics.

Such subaccounts may differ greatly depending on the industry, such that the same terms may convey different meanings.

However, there are several common elements to each of the major component categories of a balance sheet that all investors should be familiar with.

Let us look at each of these in turn.

Balance Sheet Components

I. Assets

The subaccounts under this category have been listed in descending order of liquidity (meaning the ease with which an asset can be converted into cash).

The subaccounts may be classified into two groups: *current assets,* which can be turned into cash within a year or less, and *non-current* or *long-term* assets, which may take longer than a year to convert to cash.

Current assets are made up of the following subaccounts:

- *Cash and cash equivalents,* being the most liquid asset, include treasury bills and short-term certificates of deposit (CDs), as well as cash itself (currency).
- *Marketable securities* comprise equity and debt securities for which a ready market is likely to be available.
- *Accounts receivable (AR)* means the money owed to a company by its customers. This category is less readily convertible into cash, since it depends on the cooperation of the customers; indeed, some accounts receivable may need to be written off altogether.
- *Inventory* includes any goods that are on hand and ready for sale; such goods ought to be valued at the price originally paid for them or the current market price, whichever is lower.

- *Prepaid expenses* are purchases that have already been paid in full, but not yet received in full, notably contracts for such services as rent, insurance, advertising, and so forth.

Non-current or *long-term* assets are constituted by the following subaccounts:

- *Long-term investments* comprise securities that cannot be converted into cash within the upcoming year.
- *Fixed assets* are made up of land, buildings, heavy equipment and machinery, and other immovable, high-priced assets.
- *Intangible assets* are non-physical assets, such as intellectual property, brands, and goodwill.

II. Liabilities

The term "liabilities" refers to financial obligations that a company owes to other companies or individuals.

The term may refer to a wide variety of kinds of payment obligations, including interest on bonds owed to creditors, bills presented by all sorts of suppliers, employees' salaries, rent, bills for the consumption of electricity, gas, water, waste removal, and other utilities, and so forth.

Liabilities fall into two main categories: *current liabilities,* which are expected to be settled within one year, according to a printed due date, and *long-term liabilities,* which become due after one year from the reporting date.

Current liabilities encompass various accounts, which may include:

- *The current portion of long-term debt:* This represents the portion of a long-term debt that falls due within the next 12 months.
- *Interest payable* refers to the accumulated interest that a company owes; this type of liability is typically associated with surcharges on late remittances and other past-due obligations.
- *Wages payable* involve employees' total compensation, including wages, salaries, and health and other kinds of benefits.
- *Customer prepayments* represent money received from customers before the service or product has been delivered.
- *Dividends payable* are shareholder dividends that have been authorized but not yet remitted.
- *Earned and unearned premiums* are analogous to customer prepayments—monies that a company has received per a contract, but for which the corresponding goods or services have not yet been provided.
- *Accounts payable* are debt obligations arising from invoices generated by normal business operations. Accounts payable—which are among the most common form of liability—are commonly due within 30 to 90 days of receipt of the invoice.

Long-term liabilities encompass various elements, such as:

- *Long-term debt,* which comprises interest and principal payments on bonds issued.
- *Pension fund liability* represents the total amount of the funds a company is legally required to contribute to its employees' retirement accounts.
- *Deferred tax liability* reflects taxes accrued but not due to be paid until the next year. Additionally, this figure ought to take into account such matters as depreciation, as well as any other discrepancies that may occur between a company's tax liability as stated in its financial reports and as currently assessed by the relevant taxing authorities.

III. Shareholder Equity

Shareholder equity, also referred to as *net assets,* represents the funds that belong to the owners or shareholders of a business. This amount is calculated by deducting the company's liabilities (debts owed to non-shareholders) from its total assets.

Retained earnings refers to the net earnings from operations (profit) that a company either reinvests in its operations or uses to repay external debt. Any net earnings remaining after the subtraction of retained earnings may be distributed to shareholders as *dividends.*

Treasury stock refers to shares a company has bought back from its shareholders. Treasury stock may be sold later to generate income when needed, or else held in reserve as a defensive measure against a hostile takeover.

Some companies may issue both *common stock* and *preferred stock,* which will then be listed separately in financial reporting.

Both types of stock are assigned an arbitrary *par value* (*nominal* or *face value*), which is the value of one share. However, this par value will not affect the market value of the shares.

Paid-in capital means the total amount of cash or other assets that a shareholder pays a company to purchase shares of its stock.

Additional paid-in capital (APIC), or *capital surplus,* refers to the amount of paid-in capital left over after the par value of the shares received has been deducted.

Again, these are accounting concepts that are not directly linked to any market price. Moreover, it should be noted that shareholder equity is also not directly linked to a company's *market capitalization.*

Market capitalization is determined by the current stock price, whereas paid-in capital includes the total equity purchased by shareholders at various prices.

Importance of Balance Sheets

Whatever a company's size or field of operation, reading, analyzing, and understanding its balance sheet can be a valuable guide to its financial status.

First, the balance sheet plays a significant role in *assessing risk.* By detailing a company's assets, liabilities, and shareholder equity, the balance sheet reveals whether the company has taken on too much debt, whether it has sufficient cash reserves to meet its current obligations, whether its assets are sufficiently liquid, and so forth.

Second, balance sheets are crucial to *obtaining capital.* Whether applying for a business loan from a bank or seeking equity financing from private investors, companies will be asked to provide their balance sheets for the prospective lender's inspection.

Finally, balance sheets can serve as a tool for *attracting and retaining talent.* Most employees value job security and prefer to work for companies that are financially stable.

Note that publicly traded companies are required by law to disclose their balance sheets. This transparency is especially helpful to prospective employees of a company, as it allows them to inspect its cash reserves, assess its debt management decisions, and accurately evaluate the harmony (or dissonance) between their own expectations and their future employer's state of financial health.

11. Banking

DEFINITION: A bank is an institution which holds money received from depositors in custody and lends money to borrowers.

ETYMOLOGY: The word "bank" in its modern meaning derives from either Middle French *banque* or Old Italian *banca,* both of which originally meant "bench." The word is also connected to the Middle English *benc* and the Old High German *bank,* both also meaning "bench."

USAGE: Banking has roots in Antiquity, specifically in the growth of long-distance trade subsequent to the transition to agriculture. This occurred especially in Mesopotamia and the Indus River Valley civilization around 2000 BC, where local grain merchants began making loans to farmers and long-distance traders.

Some centuries later, in many civilizations from Greece and Rome to India and China, religious temples began to be associated with moneylending. This practice waxes and waned for many centuries.

Banking in a recognizably modern form may be traced to the wealthy Italian city states of the late Middle Ages and Renaissance, notably Venice, Florence, and Genoa, which saw the emergence of merchant banks involved in increasingly wide trading networks with the rest of the world, from the Islamicate (North Africa and the Middle East) to India and China.

One of the best-known of these banks was established by the Medici family in Florence in 1397.

Because Christianity looked askance at lending money at interest and because Jews were not allowed to own real estate in Italy during the Middle Ages, many Jews living in Italy at that time gravitated to banking.

Following the European discovery of the New World by Christopher Columbus in 1492 and the first circumnavigation of the globe led by Ferdinand Magellan, completed in 1522, the need for banks to finance the emerging worldwide trading networks increased exponentially.

At this time, bankers began to raise money by means of debt issues in the form of the sale of stocks.

As the phenomenon of merchant banks spread north of the Alps and throughout the Holy Roman Empire, many new families came to European prominence, notably, the Fugger family, based in Augsburg in Bavaria.

After the formation of the modern nation state, national banks came into being which had a much wider remit than the traditional merchant banks had had. Namely, they were used as a means of helping to control national economies and thus as a tool of governance.

One of the earliest national banks was *Sveriges Riksbank*, founded in Stockholm in 1668.

International banking—which may be defined as multinational banking entities, especially when they lend to sovereign states—came into being during the nineteenth century. The Rothschild family, with roots in Germany, pioneered this new development with its loans to the Bank of England.

As banks have increased in economic and political importance, they have also come under increasingly strict legal control.

At the same time, over the course of the twentieth century, "banking" in a wide sense has greatly expanded the scope of its activities. Today, the financial sector contributes something approaching a quarter of GDP worldwide.

12. Bankruptcy

DEFINITION: Bankruptcy is a legal process by means of which a bankruptcy court determines that an individual or business shall be legally declared incapable of meeting its outstanding debts in a timely manner.

For a bankrupt individual, the process provides relief from creditors and allows a fresh start. Certain categories of the debtor's property are legally protected from liquidation in bankruptcy proceedings.

For bankrupt companies, the bankruptcy process may lead either to reorganization or to cessation of business operations.

For the individual or company's creditors, the bankruptcy process usually provides some payment of outstanding claims, albeit at a discounted rate.

The question of who gets paid how much constitutes the main work of the bankruptcy court and will depend on the competing claims of all creditors, as well as the bankrupt individual or company's financial condition.

The bankruptcy process is usually initiated at the request of the debtor, although sometimes it begins with a petition by one or more of creditors.

ETYMOLOGY: "Bankrupt" enters English during the sixteenth century. It is derived from Middle French *banqueroute,* which is derived from Old Italian *bancarotta,* a construction from *banca* (bank) and *rotta*(broken).

Banca (literally, bench) is of Germanic origin, and is akin to Old English *benc*, with the same meaning.

Rotta is derived from the past participle *ruptus* of the Latin verb *rumpere* (to break).

USAGE: Before the widespread adoption of bankruptcy laws, the failure to repay one's debts was a crime and insolvent debtors were sentenced to debtor's prisons.

The bankruptcy process was introduced into the legal system in England and elsewhere, not only to alleviate the harsh treatment of individual debtors, but also as a perceived benefit to society at large.

The idea was that bankruptcy's social effects would be twofold:

- It would benefit creditors, who received at least partial restitution of what is owed to them; and

- It would allow debtors to continue contributing to the economy (which they could not do from inside prison walls).

In the US today, all bankruptcy cases are processed through the federal court system. Either a federal judge or a "trustee" appointed by the US Trustee Program—operating within the Department of Justice—presides over the court. The trustee, if any, represents the debtor's interests during the bankruptcy proceedings.

If the bankruptcy process proceeds to a successful conclusion—that is, with the agreement of both the debtor and the creditors—the debtor is granted relief from his legal obligation to repay his debts.

In the US, bankruptcy filings are classified according to which of three chapters of the US Bankruptcy Code is applicable.

The majority of filings fall under one of the following three chapters:

- *Chapter 7* involves the liquidation of the debtor's assets (with certain exceptions).
- *Chapter 11* focuses on reorganizations for both companies and individuals.
- *Chapter 13* facilitates debt repayment by means of structured payment plans.

Chapter 7 Bankruptcy

Most individuals who file for bankruptcy do so under Chapter 7, which allows them to be discharged from all unsecured debts, such as credit card balances and medical bills.

Individuals filing under Chapter 7 must liquidate non-exempt personal property to repay as much of their unsecured debt as possible. However, much of an individual debtor's personal property is exempt from this liquidation requirement, including his primary residence, automobile, clothing, household goods, and tools of trade, up to a specific dollar value.

Chapter 11 Bankruptcy

Chapter 11 bankruptcy is commonly utilized by businesses aiming to reorganize and continue their operations.

By filing for bankruptcy under Chapter 11, a company will be able to come up with strategies for enhancing profitability, reducing expenses, and exploring new avenues for generating revenue.

Under Chapter 11, shareholders in possession of preferred stock will receive a high priority with respect to distribution of payments from the debtor's estate, while shareholders possessing common stock will receive the last priority for such distributions.

Chapter 13 Bankruptcy

Individuals who earn too much money to qualify for bankruptcy protection under Chapter 7 bankruptcy have the option of doing so under Chapter 13.

Individuals and companies with stable incomes who file under Chapter 13 will be allowed to negotiate a practicable and structured debt repayment plan, sometimes referred to as a "wage earner's plan."

Chapter 13 repayment plans are typically structured in installments over a period of three to five years.

If the debtor fulfills his obligations to creditors under his repayment plan, the court will permit him to keep all of his property, including non-exempt assets.

Other Bankruptcy Filings

Aside from the commonly known bankruptcy proceedings like Chapters 7, 11, and 13, several other kinds of bankruptcy cases exist, as well:

- *Chapter 9* bankruptcy provides assistance for financially struggling municipalities, including counties, cities, towns, and school districts. Chapter 9 is analogous to Chapter 13, in that under this chapter municipalities avoid asset liquidation and negotiate a repayment plan with creditors.
- *Chapter 10* bankruptcy, which provided for reorganization for companies, was discontinued in 1978 and has in effect been replaced by the Chapter 11 provisions (see above).
- *Chapter 12* provides bankruptcy relief for family farms and fisheries. Under this chapter, they are allowed to maintain their businesses while working out a plan to repay their debts.
- *Chapter 15,* the authorizing law for which was passed in 2005, provides bankruptcy protection for companies with international operations. It is especially designed to deal with assets held abroad and with foreign creditors.

Discharge of Debts under Bankruptcy

When a bankruptcy proceeding is successfully concluded, the debtor's debts specified in the court order are discharged and the debtor is no longer legally bound to pay them. Moreover, the creditors listed in the order are prohibited from trying to collect the debts owed to them.

Not all debts are eligible for discharge via bankruptcy. Non-dischargeable debts include tax claims and other debts owed to the government, child support and alimony payments, liability for personal injury, and any debts not listed by the debtor.

Secured creditors, however, retain the right to enforce valid liens on property owned by the debtor.

Advantages and Disadvantages of Bankruptcy

Bankruptcy offers relief from the legal obligation to repay one's debts. Additionally, it will likely safeguard one's home or business, depending on which chapter one files under.

On the downside, bankruptcy will almost certainly have a negative impact on one's credit rating, thus making it more difficult to obtain bank loans, credit cards, home mortgages, and even to rent an apartment.

A Chapter 7 filing will remain on your credit report for ten years, while a Chapter 13 will be there for seven years.

13. Bear Market

DEFINITION: The phrase "bear market" refers to economic conditions in which the stock market experiences an extended price slump.

To qualify as a bear market, conventionally stocks must decline by 20 percent or more from their recent peak. Such market conditions are also accompanied by widespread pessimism and aversion to further risk-taking on the part of investors.

Bear markets are frequently linked with downturns in a broad market or an index, such as the S&P 500. However, specific securities or commodities can also qualify as being in a bear market if they undergo a decline of 20 percent or more for a considerable period of time, usually spanning at least two months.

Bear markets usually coincide with contractions in the real economy, such as recessions. They stand in opposition to the upward trajectories observed in **bull markets**.

ETYMOLOGY: The phrase "bear market" appears to have originated in the eighteenth century from the practice of frontier bearskin traders, who would require payment from customers for their skins before they had bought the skins from fur trappers.

If prices for skins were generally falling, then the price that traders paid to trappers would be lower than the price they received from customers. In other words, bearskin traders would make a profit in a declining market for bearskins—hence, the association between bears and falling prices.

The association became so well known that a proverb came into being at the time, which spoke of "selling the bearskin before catching the bear."

The English noun "bear" derives, via Middle English *bere,* from Old English *bera.* The latter noun is akin to the Old English adjective *brūn,*meaning "brown."

The English noun "market" derives, via Middle English and Old North French, from the Latin noun *mercātus, mercātūs,* meaning "trade," "traffic," or "business," as well as the place where the trade or business takes place, that is, a "marketplace."

Mercātus, in turn, is linked to the deponent verb *mercor, mercari,*meaning "to traffic in" and "to trade," as well as the noun *merx, mercis,* meaning "goods" or "merchandise."

USAGE: A stock's value most often reflects a company's anticipated future cash flows and profits. When a company's growth expectations are unmet, and its prospects diminish, then stock prices have a tendency to fall.

In such situations psychological factors, such as herd mentality, fear-driven actions, and a collective desire to mitigate potential losses, may result in extended periods of lower asset values.

By convention, a bear market occurs when stocks decline an average of at least 20 percent from their peak. This is an admittedly subjective metric, but it is in line with several other similar measures, such as the notion of "market correction," which is defined as a 10-percent drop in prices.

An even more subjective characterization of a bear market is a phenomenon of mass psychology, namely, the occurrence of a widespread change in the mentality of investors leading them to prioritize caution over risk-taking.

In this type of bear market—which may last for months or even years—investors will tend to avoid more-speculative investments in favor of less-exciting but dependable ones.

Bear markets can arise for many reasons. For example, a bear market may result from an economy that is weakening, slowing, or stagnant.

Potential triggers of a bear market may vary widely from such occurrences as pandemics, wars, and political upheavals to the bursting of market bubbles and major technological shifts, such as the rise of the online economy. Moreover, a bear market may also potentially be caused by government interference in the economy.

All of the foregoing phenomena may lead to unemployment, loss of income, decline in productivity, and reduced profits.

14. Behavioral Economics

DEFINITION: "Behavioral economics" is a subfield of economics which augments the traditional view of human beings as utility-maximizing rational actors with a psychologically more-realistic view of people as motivated by a wide assortment of emotional ("affective") factors in addition to pure reason.

Sub-subfields of behavioral economics include such theoretical perspectives as "bounded rationality" and "prospect theory" (see below).

ETYMOLOGY: The adjective "behavioral," as well as the related noun "behavior" and verb "behave," derive from the Middle English verb *behaven*, meaning "to conduct oneself," "to comport oneself," or "to behave."

The word *behaven* is attested beginning in the fifteenth century.

For the etymology of the word "economics," see the Glossary article "economics."

USAGE: The simplest way to understand behavioral economics is as an attempt to make mainstream economics less ideal (i.e., theoretical), and more realistic (meaning grounded in the empirical study of human nature).

The origins of behavioral economics may be traced to the transition from the old behaviorist ("stimulus-response") orientation, which dominated academic psychology from the 1920s through the 1950s, to the new cognitive science–based approach.

The new cognitive-science approach redirected the energies of psychology as an academic discipline towards the effort to get inside the mind of the human subject as the best way of constructing a theoretical framework for the explanation of human behavior.

One of the first psychologists following the new approach, whose work proved to be foundational for the later development of behavioral economics, was **Herbert A. Simon.**

During the late 1950s and early 1960s, Simon published a series of studies on the concept of "bounded rationality."

Bounded rationality, in a nutshell, is the name for a set of empirical observations of human decision-making. More specifically, it refers to a cluster of the several different ways in which human beings depart from perfect rationality, particularly in relation to behavior under conditions of uncertainty.

It is a well-established fact that human reasoning relies upon several rules of thumb, which under real-world conditions usually result in successful action, but which do not necessarily conform to the formal requirements of probability theory. For this reason, many investigators condemn human beings as fundamentally "irrational."

This is, of course, absurd, seeing that it is human beings who discovered and who recognize the forms laws of logic and probability in the first place.

Rather, it is the idea that early human beings—faced with quickly identifying potential threats to their survival—ought to have stopped to consider their Bayesian priors before acting that is truly irrational, not to say absurd.

Beginning in the 1960s, two Israeli psychologists, **Daniel Kahneman** and **Amos Tversky**, brought a large number of novel psychological considerations to bear on the problem of understanding human behavior, which reached far beyond the limits of bounded rationality.

More specifically, Kahneman and Tversky applied the expanded bounded-rationality theoretical framework to the reformation of the discipline of economics.

Kahneman and Tversky's reformulation of economic theory is sometimes referred to as "prospect theory," because it focused on prospective (future-oriented) decision-making under conditions of uncertainty.

The supplementary factors identified by Kahneman and Tversky to explain economic action include such phenomena as the following, among others:

- loss aversion—the greater negative affect associated with a loss compared to the positive affect associated with a quantitatively equal gain
- confirmation bias—the greater positive affect associated with confirming as opposed to disconfirming evidence
- anchoring effects—the greater positive affect associated with events that conform to a prior expectation
- framing effects—the dependency of the affect associated with a choice upon a framing narrative

Recently, behavioral economics has begun to have an impact on public policy.

Perhaps the best known of such policies is the explicit introduction of the notion of "nudge" into policy deliberations. The concept of "nudge" refers to the intentional use of behavioral economics to shape an economic actor's perceptions.

The nudge policy is particularly associated with **Cass R. Sunstein**, who implemented it while serving as Administrator of the White House Office of Information and Regulatory Affairs during the Obama administration.

15. Blockchain

A blockchain is a ledger of transactions that grows in real time and that is validated at the end of each block (or transaction cycle), so that each existing block as well as the entire chain of blocks to date is validated (in the form of a Merkle tree). Validation takes the form of a hash function applied to blocks individually as well as across blocks, and thus ensures that the ledger formulated as a blockchain has not been tampered with (such as someone attempting fraudulently to modify bookkeeping entries for past transactions).

Blockchain is a central concept of cryptocurrencies. The anonymous Bitcoin founder Satoshi Nakamoto, introduced the concept in his original white paper laying out Bitcoin. Even though the actual term “blockchain” appears nowhere in that whitepaper, the term “block” appears often in it and the terms “ongoing chain” and “record that cannot be changed” appear in the abstract. These all refer to the same idea, namely, a cryptocurrency blockchain, or simply blockchain.

Cryptocurrency blockchains constitute a complete record of all transactions ever conducted in the underlying cryptocurrency. For instance, to see every Bitcoin transaction ever conducted, go to the “explorer” feature at Blockchain.com.

16. Bond

DEFINITION: A "bond" is a type of **negotiable instrument** known as a "tradable financial asset" or "security" (a "financial asset" is a non-tangible asset based on a contractual claim).

A bond is a security which establishes a debt between its seller (the "issuer") and its purchaser (the "holder") with the following conditions:

- The issuer must repay the principal to the holder by a set date (the "maturity date").
- The issuer must also pay interest in predetermined amounts (called "coupons") at fixed intervals.

Thus, a bond is an IOU—that is, a loan—by means of which the bondholder lends money to the bond issuer for a specified period of time.

ETYMOLOGY: "Bond" derives from the Middle English word *band,*meaning "band" or "fetter," which is itself of Old Norse origin. Thus, a bond is an instrument that binds the issuer to repay the bondholder.

USAGE: Bonds are issued by both corporations and governmental entities, whether at the municipal, county, state, or federal level.

Bonds may be issued for the purpose of raising capital to finance long-term investment, special projects, or current expenditure.

Since bonds are essentially securities—that is, tradable financial assets—there are primary and secondary markets devoted to trading them. Seeing that bonds may be traded on the secondary market at prices higher than the principal amount, it is necessary to distinguish a bond's face value from its "valuation."

Both stocks and bonds are securities. The difference between them is that a stock establishes an equity stake in the issuer, whereas a bond establishes a creditor stake in the issuer.

Since secured creditors have legal priority over owners, in the event of bankruptcy an issuer's bonds will be repaid before its stocks.

Another difference between stocks and bonds is that bonds usually have a defined term (the maturity date), whereas stocks normally have no such time limit. However, there is an exception to this rule. Namely, an "irredeemable bond" resembles a stock in lacking a maturity date.

Finally, bonds closely resemble certificates of deposit (CDs) issued by banks. The main difference between the two instruments is that CDs typically have a shorter term.

17. Bubble (Economic)

DEFINITION: An economic bubble occurs when the market price of some good increases rapidly in a way which, in hindsight, turns out to be unsustainable.

ETYMOLOGY: The word "bubble" derives from the Middle English word "*bobel,*" meaning "bubble."

The word, which is first attested in the fourteenth century, is thought to derive by onomatopoeia from the sound made by water flowing over stones in a shallow stream bed.

USAGE: Famous examples of economic bubbles include the Dutch **tulip mania** of the 1660s, the French **Mississippi Company bubble** of 1720, and the British **South Sea Company bubble** of that same year.

Retrospectively, bubbles are obvious. Unfortunately, they are not so easy to discern beforehand.

The question is: What distinguishes an economic bubble from sustainable price increases due to the ordinary play of market forces of supply and demand?

It is sometimes said that bubbles are situations in which an asset's market price "strongly exceed[s] the asset's intrinsic value" (Wikipedia).

But this claim presupposes there is some way to determine an asset's "intrinsic value" apart from its market value.

However, almost all reputable modern economists subscribe to the **subjective theory of value**, which teaches that this makes no sense.

If *all* prices are determined by the subjective preferences of consumers, then there is no such thing as "intrinsic value," at least in the realm of economics.

One might think that the main difference between economic bubbles and normal asset price increases has to do with what psychologists call the "bandwagon effect," that is, the tendency of people to want to "get on board" any promising or fashionable trend.

While there is no doubt that the bandwagon effect drives bubbles, the same might be said for many other successful new products which "take off" and become popular with the public. So, it is not clear how the bandwagon effect can be used to differentiate between bubbles and other breakout products.

One promising idea is to link bubbles to the velocity of the price increases. Another is to survey bubbles against the background of wide economic comment, much of which will typically be warning of a bubble forming.

However, none of these ideas is capable of really separating the wheat from the chaff when it comes to economic bubbles.

Probably the two best protections against becoming caught up by the bandwagon effect surrounding an economic bubble are having long experience with investing, in general, and informing oneself about the details of any investment one makes, in particular.

18. Bull Market

DEFINITION: The phrase "bull market" refers to conditions under which the stock market experiences an extended, across-the-board rise in prices. While the term is predominantly applied to the stock market, it may be extended to other traded assets, including bonds, commodities, real estate, and currencies.

Since normal market trading involves considerable fluctuation in security prices, to qualify as a "bull market" the price rise must be expected to last over many months if not years.

ETYMOLOGY: The origin of the phrase "bull market" is uncertain. The term is attested from the early eighteenth century and appears to have been invented as a complement to the phrase "**bear market.**" The choice of "bull" as the counterpart to "bear" may have been inspired by the twin practices of bull- and bearbaiting. Another theory points to the aggressive, hard-charging behavior of bulls.

The English noun "bull" is attested from the twelfth century. It derives, via Middle English *bule,* from Old English *bula,* which is akin to the Old English verb *blāwan,* meaning "to blow."

The English noun "market" derives, via Middle English and Old North French, from the Latin noun *mercātus, mercātūs,* meaning "traffic," "trade," or "business," as well as the place where the trade or business takes place, i.e., a "marketplace."

Mercātus, in turn, is linked to the deponent verb *mercor, mercari,*meaning "to trade" or "to traffic in," as well as the noun *merx, mercis,* meaning "goods" or "merchandise."

USAGE: Bull markets are marked by optimism, investor confidence, and the anticipation of sustained profits over a considerable time span.

It is not easy to accurately foresee when market trends might shift. This difficulty is partly due to the importance of psychological factors and speculative behavior, which can significantly impact market conditions but are very hard to predict.

There is no universally recognized definition of a bull market. Nevertheless, the most prevalent characterization of a bull market often involves a scenario—symmetrical with a bear market—in which stock prices go up by 20 percent or more from their recent lows.

Popular business news outlets may indulge in the prediction of bull markets; however, given the inherent difficult of forecasting events that depend upon human agency, serious financial analysts tend to limit their discussion of bull markets to hindsight. Only after a bull market has run its course does it become clear that there was one.

Bull markets usually occur during periods of economic recovery or when economic growth is already strong. They often coincide with a reduction in the unemployment rate, a robust gross domestic product (GDP), and/or an upswing in corporate profits.

Under any or all of these conditions, it is natural for investor confidence to grow—which is the principal driver of what, in retrospect, will come to be seen as a bull market.

During a bull market, there is by definition an increase in the demand for stocks, which produces a buoyant state of mind among market participants overall. Moreover, bull markets are generally marked by an uptick in initial public offering (IPO) activity.

Bull market do have several distinctive features even while they are happening. Among these is a surge in trading volume, driven by a greater number of investors who are eager to acquire and retain securities on account of the perceived potential for capital gains.

In addition, in a bull market, the prices of securities often increase due to investors' willingness to pay higher prices in the belief that the value of their stocks will continue to go up.

Furthermore, a bull market is frequently marked by greater market liquidity, owing to heightened demand for securities and a smaller number of sellers. This dynamic facilitates swift and cost-effective buying and selling for investors.

In a bull market scenario, companies that are doing well might choose to enhance shareholder satisfaction by increasing dividend payouts—a particularly appealing prospect for income-oriented investors.

Finally, during a bull market, there tends to be a surge in companies opting to go public and generate funds with an IPO. This avenue presents investors with the opportunity to participate in the progress of young and promising enterprises.

19. Business

DEFINITION: An enterprise engaged in buying and selling with the aim of turning a profit. A business enterprise can provide products (whether real or virtual) or services. Some business enterprises constitute the point of origin for a product or service by respectively either building the product or making the service available in the first place. Other businesses act as intermediaries between such originating businesses and others, taking a cut from the transaction. Businesses may sell their products and services to other businesses (B2B, as in business to business) or end-point customers (B2C, as in business to customers).

In capitalist societies, entrepreneurs create businesses by risking capital (money and other resources) with the aim of recouping their investment and earning a profit. Entrepreneurs may put their own capital at risk or that of others or some combination of the two. When the capital of others is thus put at risk, it can be in the form of a loan from a lender (often a bank). If the business fails, the lender may be able to reclaim some portion of the amount loaned from remaining assets. Alternatively, capital put at risk can take the form of investment where the investor (sometimes called a venture capitalist) puts up capital for an ownership stake in the business. If the business fails, investors typically lose their entire investment.

Businesses can be organized in many ways. The functional structure of a business refers to the way its employees and their work environment is organized to provide the business's products and/or services. The legal structure refers refers to the type of structure it is for legal and accounting purposes (e.g., sole proprietorship, partnership, or corporation).

SYNONYMS: enterprise, company, concern, establishment, firm, venture, trade, organization, pursuit, affair, interest, outfit.

ETYMOLOGY: The term business comes from the old English *bisignes* meaning anxiety, care, concern, or preoccupation. Likewise, the adjectival form *bisig* means anxious, careful, concerned, or preoccupied. From here the term came to mean being occupied and engaged, and therefore diligent and industrious, and hence "busy." The opposite of business is therefore leisure or lack of employment. Business therefore came to denote a person's occupation or work, what they do for a living. By the 18th century, business assumed its present meaning as a commercial enterprise.

It's interesting that the term business originates from the idea of anxiety. To this day we speak of "business concerns," and the word "concern" is a synonym for anxiety. Businesses require diligent care for their success and thus always seem to involve anxiety. Perhaps that's why Aristotle counseled that a life of leisure is preferable to a life of business. Perhaps that's also why Jesus spoke of rich people (presumably business persons) having a hard time getting into heaven, being tied too much to the concerns of this life.

20. Business Cycle

DEFINITION: The "business cycle" is the historically observed tendency of market economies to go through alternating phases of expansion and contraction.

ETYMOLOGY: The word "business" was formed in the fourteenth century from the word "busyness"—the noun form of the adjective "busy"—and meaning a "purposeful activity."

"Busy" derives, via Middle English, from the Old English word *bisig*, meaning "full of activity" or "busy." *Bisig* is connected to the Middle Low German word *besich*, meaning "active," "occupied," "diligent," or "industrious."

The word "cycle" derives, via Middle English and French, from the Late Latin word *cyclus*, meaning a "fixed period of time (especially years)." The word *cyclus* entered Latin from the Greek word *kuklos*, meaning "ring," "circle," or "wheel."

USAGE: The study of the business cycle—that is, the proposal of theories that attempt to explain the business cycle as an empirical phenomenon—forms one of the most important subfields of academic economics.

The first thinkers to identify the business cycle as an important object of study were the English utopian socialist, **Robert Owen**, and, especially, the French economist, **Jean Charles Léonard de Sismondi**, who discussed it in his 1819 *Nouveaux principes d'économie politique* [New Principles of Political Economy].

Broadly speaking, there are two general types of business-cycle theories that have competed with each other for favor over the course of economic history. We may call them the "exogenous" and the "endogenous" classes of theories (with multiple variants of each).

In a nutshell, exogenous business-cycle theories claim that unusual expansions (or "booms") and contractions, also known as "recessions" (or "busts"), are caused by shocks to an economic system emanating from the outside.

A prime example that was frequently discussed during the nineteenth century was warfare. And wars can indeed affect an economy for better or for worse, depending on a multitude of factors.

For example, war may impact a country's economy negatively if it has to redirect valuable resources to its defense or if its agriculture, its industry, and/or its labor force are subjected to physical devastation.

On the other hand, war may impact a country's economy positively if it is not itself a party to the war, but rather sells weapons, food, or other supplies to the warring parties.

From this example, it should be obvious how complex the problem of exogenous shocks to the economy may be.

Even so, the business cycle did not appear to disappear, or even noticeably lessen, during times of peace. Therefore, not all economists were satisfied that exogenous shocks alone could explain the business cycle.

In the later nineteenth and early twentieth century, some economists—especially, **Friedrich A. Hayek** and others associated with the **Austrian school of economics**—developed an endogenous theory of the business cycle.

The basic idea of the Austrian theory was that the business cycle is caused by the misallocation of resources, which in turn is usually caused by perverse (uneconomic) incentives to market actors through government policies relating to subsidy, taxation, and/or regulation.

The misallocation of resources due to government interference in the economy leads business owners to turn in a direction away from the one indicated by market signals. Over the long term, this necessarily results in forgone profits, unsold stock, and business failure.

Now, of course, businesses fail all the time due to misjudgments made by their owners without any help from perverse government incentives. However, such failures are scattered at random throughout the economy.

What makes government interference in the economy particularly insidious is that it causes many business owners to misallocate resources in the same way at the same time, leading to many simultaneous business failures in the same sectors.

Austrian economists say that this type of endogenous shock is the main driver of the business cycle under conditions of government interference in the economy.

Note that government interference counts as "endogenous" if one views the government as internal to the economic system (as one clearly must, since it is an economic actor in its own right).

More recently, economists have attempted to resurrect the exogenous-shock theory of the business cycle under the name, "real business-cycle theory," which argues that the business cycle results from the efficient response of business owners to expected exogenous changes to the economic environment.

21. Capitalism

DEFINITION: In a broad sense, "capitalism" is a social and economic system which permits individuals to participate freely in market exchanges and to accumulate wealth from their economic activity.

Such accumulated wealth may be termed "capital," whence the name of the system.

In this broad sense, "capitalism" is synonymous with "freedom" in relation to the economic dimension of human social interaction.

In a narrower sense, "capitalism" is the specific form that free economic activity took during the Renaissance and Early Modern periods of European history, beginning in Italy, Portugal, and Spain, and then shifting northward to France, the Netherlands, and England.

ETYMOLOGY: The term "capitalism" derives from the word "capital," in its economic sense, meaning "accumulated wealth."

The word "capital," in turn, derives, via either French or Italian, from the Latin adjective *capitālis,* which in turn derives from the noun *caput, capitis,* meaning "head."

Capitālis took on a variety of meanings, from "mortal" and "dangerous" to "first," "chief," or "distinguished."

However, the meanings of *capitālis* of greatest relevance to us here are "relating to the head," a "living thing" (as in a "head of cattle"), a "person," a "person's social status," and, finally, "possessions" or "money."

USAGE: One might suppose that the term "capitalism" is more or less synonymous with any highly stratified socioeconomic system, with a wealthy class at the top and a majority at the bottom living in poverty.

However, that is not correct.

Nearly all human societies have been stratified, with richer and pooper classes, at least since the invention of agriculture and the beginning of the division of labor some 10,000 years ago.

In many of those societies, wealth, prestige, and power did not arise from successful economic activity, but rather from military conquest or the violent imposition of political control.

Obviously, the wealth of raiding societies such as the Visigoths or the Vikings had nothing to do with economic activity in the usual sense.

Similarly, in communist countries wealthy and powerful classes certainly existed, but they were a function of an individual's position within the Communist Party apparatus, not his economic activity.

Therefore, capitalism should be understood as the accumulation of wealth *as a result of successful economic activity*, as opposed to the others means of wealth accumulation just mentioned.

As such, the *phenomenon* of capitalism—in the broad sense mentioned above—is probably coeval with human settled life and civilization. Even in its narrower sense, the phenomenon of capitalism is between five and six hundred years old.

In contrast, the *word* "capitalism" is of relatively recent vintage.

The word from which "capitalism" derives—namely, "capital," in its economic sense —is first attested in English in the early seventeenth century, while the English term "capitalism" itself turns up during the 1850s.

In this article, we will focus on the narrow sense of the term, meaning "capitalism" as a description of the **Industrial Revolution**.

During the course of the eighteenth century, industrialists gradually replaced long-distance traders and other merchants as the primary engine of economic activity, first in England, and then spreading to the European continent, to North America, and, eventually, throughout the world.

Following upon the invention of the steam engine, the agricultural and textile manufacturing sectors were the first to become highly mechanized.

Then, the nineteenth century brought with it an incredible series of brand-new inventions, from the telegraph to the railroad to public sanitation, public gas lighting, and, by century's end, the introduction of electrical power.

All of these startling transformations in the everyday life of tens of millions of individuals were made possible by the accumulation of capital and the growth of a financial infrastructure for investing the accumulated capital in new projects.

In short, capitalism was the engine that drove the modern world.

In more granular economic terms, capitalism can be analyzed as consisting of the following characteristics:

- Capital accumulation: the primary goal of economic activity is earning a profit and accumulating wealth
- Commodity production: most economic activity is aimed at production for market exchange
- Private ownership: of the means of production
- Investment: of capital reserves for the purpose of future production, profit, and wealth accumulation
- Economic efficiency: the use of raw materials and other factors of production is aimed at the optimization of the production process
- Wage labor: is employed on a large scale
- Market prices: determine the allocation of resources

- Freedom: of individuals to act in their own self-interest, both in managing their business and in investing their capital

22. Capitalism, Crony

DEFINITION: "Capitalism" is a set of social and economic institutions that support the exercise of independent economic actors on the free market.

Such arrangements provide for the ability of those independent actors to own property and accumulate wealth without limit.

"Crony capitalism" is a form of capitalism in which some or many large corporations cooperate closely with the state in return for favorable tax and regulatory treatment by the state.

ETYMOLOGY: For the word "capitalism," see the entry on "**capitalism**."

The colloquial word "crony" derives from the ancient Greek adjective*chronios*, meaning "long lasting," which is connected with the noun *chronos*, meaning "time."

The connection is that a "crony" is a friend of long standing. The word is first attested in English in 1665.

USAGE: There are several varieties of crony capitalism, some of which overlap with **state capitalism**.

The main distinction depends upon whether the cooperation of privately owned corporations with the state is voluntary or compulsory.

The classic case of crony capitalism is the voluntary one. In this scenario, the owners and managers of large corporations choose to do the government's bidding because the government makes it worth their while.

In the compulsory case, also known as "corporatism," the state applies strong political pressure on corporations to conform to its wishes, particularly with respect to long-term production goals, planning, targets, and the like.

In the compulsory case, there may still be no direct ownership of the means of production by the state.

Therefore, from a definitional point of view, it remains a case of "crony capitalism."

Perhaps we need to make a further distinction between "crony-capitalism-of-the-carrot" and "crony-capitalism-of-the-stick."

However, even in the latter case, one eventually reaches a point where the line between state management and control of a private company and state ownership of the same company becomes virtually invisible.

From a definitional point of view, as the state begins to take over companies entirely, crony capitalism shades into **state capitalism** (or socialism—see the Glossary entry for "**communism**").

23. Capitalism, State

DEFINITION: "Capitalism" is a social and economic system which permits free market exchanges and the unlimited accumulation of wealth ("capital") by economic actors.

State capitalism is a form of capitalism in which the state owns some, but not all, of the means of production, while still allowing a degree of free market exchange and wealth accumulation by individual economic actors.

The term is sometimes extended to forms of capitalism in which the state does not own, but exerts decisive political control over large corporations. Here, the concept of "state capitalism" shades into that of "**crony capitalism**."

For more on capitalism in general, see the entry "**capitalism**."

ETYMOLOGY: For the etymology of the word "capitalism," see the Glossary entry "**capitalism**."

The word "state" derives, via Middle English and Old French, from the classical Latin past participle, *status*, of the verb *sto, stāre*, meaning "to stand."

USAGE: Few countries in the modern world have, or have ever had, purely capitalist—that is, free market—economies.

Rather—since the collapse of most communist countries—the economies of the majority of countries in the industrially developed world consist of a mixture of privately owned and state-owned enterprises.

Such arrangements are examples of what is often referred to as the "mixed economy."

Sometimes, state capitalism is described as being a form of "socialism."

This is incorrect. Properly speaking, "socialism" aims at the state ownership of all means of production. In this regard, it is no different from "**communism**."

Where socialists may differ from communists is in their tactics for taking power. By and large, socialists are more willing to use the standard processes of democracy to compete against other parties ("bourgeois" parties, in the socialist jargon). But that is a political, not an economic, issue.

In East Asia, state capitalism sometimes takes a special form, shading into "**crony capitalism**," in which corporate conglomerates are run by individual families. Such entities are sometimes known by the Korean term "*chaebol*," though similar arrangements exist in Japan and elsewhere in East Asia.

There is another form of state or crony capitalism known as "corporatism," in which large corporations take orders directly from the state, even though their ownership technically remains in private hands. The German National Socialist state and the Italian Fascist state during the mid-twentieth century were both of this type.

In recent decades, a new form of crony capitalism has arisen—especially, in the US and Western Europe—in which giant corporations work hand-in-glove with particular political parties, whether in control of the government or in opposition, to advance their mutual interests.

In a sense, such arrangements are the opposite of corporatism, in that the corporations may possess greater political power than the state itself.

This is especially true of the immensely powerful, global, information-technology and social media companies, which have come to exercise a near-total control over the public dissemination of information in the Western world.

24. Capitalism, Welfare

DEFINITION: The concept of "capitalism" refers to a set of social and economic institutions which permit independent economic actors to own property, to participate freely in market exchanges, and to accumulate wealth in an unlimited fashion.

The concept of "welfare capitalism" designates a form of capitalism in which the state supports the poor through direct subsidies, as opposed to fiscal or regulatory measures.

ETYMOLOGY: For the etymology of "capitalism," see the Glossary article on "**capitalism**."

The word "welfare" derives from the Middle English phrase *wel faren*, meaning "to fare well."

USAGE: Welfare capitalism is sometimes discussed as though it were a form of "socialism." This is a mistake.

Socialism is a doctrine about the relation between the state and the ownership of property generally, whereas welfare capitalism is a doctrine about the relation between the state and the physical well-being of the poorest members of society.

The confusion may perhaps arise due to the fact that all socialist states are necessarily welfare states. That is, when all property is owned by the state, all individuals must work for the state and receive their compensation from the state.

In contrast, there is no necessary connection between capitalism as a system and the concept of the welfare state.

Some capitalist states—in which, by definition, the means of production are privately owned—may provide for generous support for the poor by means of direct transfer payments and others may not.

Welfare capitalism may also be defined more broadly, in the following way.

In the terminology of the US federal budgetary process, direct transfer payments to the poor are known as "discretionary" spending, meaning that the legal authorization for the spending must be reauthorized by Congress on a regular basis.

In contrast, "non-discretionary" or "mandatory" spending refers to payments that have a permanent status, meaning that legislation would be required to cancel or change the level of this type of spending.

In the US, the two major categories of non-discretionary spending are Medicare (the American healthcare service for the elderly) and Social Security (old-age pension) payments.

In the broad sense, “welfare capitalism” may refer to an economic and political system which provides for both types of transfer payments.

This is of some interest and importance, because the political support for non-discretionary welfare payments is very broad, seeing that nearly the entire population receives such payments.

This fact, in turn, helps provide political support for the discretionary welfare spending on the poor.

25. Capitalism, Woke

DEFINITION: "Capitalism" is more or less synonymous with an economic and political system which permits the marketplace to operate freely and in which individuals are permitted to own property, make profits, and accumulate wealth without limitation (other than that imposed by taxation).

"Woke capitalism" is a form of capitalism in which many or most of the leading companies in the capitalist marketplace subscribe to, and actively promote, the ideology of "wokeness" (see below).

ETYMOLOGY: For the etymology of the term "capitalism," see the Glossary entry entitled "**capitalism**."

Grammatically, the word "woke" is the past participle of the verb "to wake" (which has both transitive and intransitive senses).

The verb "to wake" derives, via the Middle English verb *waken*, from the Old English verb *wacan*, all with the same meaning.

The slang word "woke," which has its roots in African American Vernacular English, originally meant "to wake up" or "to be awake." Over time, it came to mean "to be alert."

In this sense, the word "woke" is attested from at least the 1930s. For instance, it occurs with this meaning at the end of Lead Belly's comments following this performance of his 1938 song, "**Scottsboro Boys**."

Later, the term "woke" came to mean "to be conscious of" and "to be aware of" the particular social phenomena posited by the "woke" ideology (see below).

In this latest iteration of the meaning of the term, the word "woke" began to spread into general usage in the US after about 2010.

USAGE: In its original form, woke ideology began as the claim that American society is essentially and irreparably racist.

This ideology maintained that, despite the seemingly great changes that have occurred over the years—the abolition of slavery with the Civil War, the legal dismantling during the 1960s of the system of *apartheid* reigning in the American South ("**Jim Crow**"), and the rise of a large and prosperous black middle class—nothing fundamental has really changed and that African Americans remain as socially, economically, and politically oppressed in the US in the twenty-first century as they have ever been.

Quite recently, the woke ideology has mutated in such a way that it has come to incorporate many other progressive political causes, notably the promotion of LGBTQ+ and transgender agendas.

It is important to make the following distinction.

The concept of "wokeness" clearly arose out of the social context of the very real oppression of African Americans in the American South, and indeed elsewhere, during the Jim Crow period.

However, the folding of the sex-based ideologies into the woke ideology was an additional action, which had more to do with intellectual trends within the Academy than with the lived experience of African Americans in the US.

At the academic level, woke ideology has three main intellectual sources:

- The so-called "critical theory" of the **Frankfurt School**, beginning in the 1930s
- The "hermeneutics of suspicion," inspired by the mainly French, radical literary theorists such as **Paul de Man** and **Jacques Derrida**
- The neo-Marxist analysis of power found in the writings of the French thinker **Michel Foucault**

All of the above schools of thought were heavily influenced by Marxist thinking, particularly:

1. the idea that the official ideology of a society is a form of "false consciousness" designed to keep the governing "bourgeois" regime in power; and
2. the idea that the primary social reality in any society is its stratification into "classes" and the struggle of the upper classes to maintain power and control over the lower classes

That, in a nutshell, is the nature and origin of the woke ideology.

"Woke capitalism," then, is simply a situation in which many leading companies promote the woke ideology.

On its surface, it may seem strange that woke capitalism exists, given that woke ideology is at bottom a Marxist ideology, which represents a direct threat to the very existence of capitalism.

This seemingly paradoxical state of affairs may be explained by several factors.

First and foremost, there is simply the fact of intellectual fashion. The CEOs of the major corporations mostly received the same education and inhabit the same social world as the academics and the government, legal, and judicial professionals who all promote the woke ideology. For this reason, it would be hard for them to question that ideology.

Another reason may be the perception that corporate managers may have that it is beneficial to their companies to be associated with the popular woke ideology. In short, rightly or wrongly, the idea probably exists that trumpeting woke ideology is good for a company's bottom line.

Finally, there is the fact that woke capitalism is in sync with the progressive principles of one of the American political parties, which is in power as of this writing. This fact provides a strong motivation for corporations to “get on board” with the woke ideology, especially in the context of **crony capitalism** which is ascendant as of this writing (2022).

How does woke capitalism manifest itself?

In addition to the public relations aspect of a company’s commitment to woke ideology, already alluded to, woke capitalism may also take the form of active support of progressive political parties and politicians by means of financial contributions and in-kind contributions consisting of free advertising and other forms of propaganda.

Perhaps more troubling is the active censorship of political opponents by woke information-technology and social media companies.

26. Cash Flow Statement

A *cash flow statement* provides an overview of a company's inflows and outflows of cash during a particular period.

Cash flow statements are usually broken down into three main sections:

- operating activities
- investing activities
- financing activities

Such statements probably provide the best insight into the state of a company's liquidity and solvency.

27. Centralized Bank Digital Currency

DEFINITION: Centralized Bank Digital Currency (CBDC) is a proposed monetary reform according to which a nation's central bank would institute a universal system of digital tracking of all financial transactions occurring under its jurisdiction.

CBDC is intended to replace cash, checks, conventional credit cards, and all other independent media for conducting financial transactions.

USAGE: From a technical point of view, CBDC involves (1) centralizing all financial transactions without exception under the central bank's control and (2) tagging every digital transaction with a unique digital "signature" or tracking number.

In this way, a national bank would potentially be able to obtain complete information about all financial transactions occurring within its jurisdiction. This knowledge, in turn, would give the bank's management—as well as higher government officials—complete control of the financial lives of all the nation's citizens.

The possibility of extraordinary abuse inherent in such a system is obvious. Why, then, would anyone want to put CBDC into effect?

CBDC is being sold to the public (for example, *The Curse of Cash* by **Kenneth Rogoff**) as a way of making the financial industry more efficient and of fighting crime by making money laundering virtually impossible.

On the other hand, it is disquieting to know that, among all the world's countries, it is the People's Republic of China that has led the way in implementing CBDC. As of this writing (the spring of 2022), CBDC has already been rolled out in China on a limited, experimental basis.

What is the special attraction of CBDC for China's leaders?

One can only speculate, but it is hard to believe that the answer does not lie precisely in the additional control over the Chinese people it affords them. After all, from the point of view of the Chinese Communist Party, CBDC is simply a logical extension of the **Social Credit System** of totalitarian political control already in effect in Communist China.

It is sometimes argued that CBDC is unlikely to be adopted in the United States, due both to vested interests in the *status quo* and to the historical significance of the US dollar and the affection in which it is held.

However, the United States, too, is not lacking in government officials and politicians who would like nothing better than to increase their control over the American economy and people.

In short, totalitarian control appears to be a feature of CBDC, not a bug. For this reason, all citizens who value their freedom should be highly skeptical of this technology.

28. Coins and Coinage

DEFINITION: Coins are durable and portable tokens which function as money. They are usually made of an elemental metal, such as gold or silver, or an alloy.

"Coinage" refers to the act of creating (minting) coins by stamping them from sheets of metal by means of a die. The term may also refer to the totality of coins in circulation, whether within a given area at a given time or in full generality.

ETYMOLOGY: The word "coin" derives, via Middle English and Middle French, from the Latin word *cuneus*, meaning "wedge."

The connection between the two concepts is that when the word arose in English in the fourteenth century, coins were stamped by dies that were wedge-shaped.

USAGE: The roots of coinage may be traced back to the mastery of metallurgy by the earliest civilizations. This occurred around 3000 BC in Mesopotamia and around 2500 BC in China.

In Mesopotamia, coins seem to have evolved out of metal ingots used as standard weights. Initially, metal ingots, or bullion, was held primarily as a repository of value. However, there appears to have been a stage in which bullion was used as a means of exchange, as well.

Soon, however, metallic coins were found to be far more convenient as a means of exchange due to their much greater portability.

Gradually, metallic coins came to replace not only bullion, but most earlier forms of money, as well, including cowry shells, natural amber (*electrum*) and other materials, and hand-crafted beads of many varieties.

By around the turn of first millennium BC, metal coins began to appear over a wide geographical area, eventually stretching from the Mediterranean basin to the Pacific.

Moreover, the archaeological discovery of coins in locations far removed from the places where they were minted attests to the early development of international trade routes across the Eurasian land mass.

Coins are most often disc-shaped. Their two sides are called *observe* ("heads") and *reverse* ("tails).

Coins are almost always stamped with a *face value*, which is a number that either represents a weight directly or else stands for a position within a numerical system of convertibility of coins of different weights.

In the latter case, one coin's weight (and hence value—see below) will be deemed the standard unit and other all coins will have either fractional or integral multiple weights (and values) in relation to the standard coin's.

Often, the king or other political authority who sponsored the minting of a coin is represented on it, too, either in words or in a drawing.

However, it should be noted that all coins until very recently were made of *precious metals,* and thus were universally felt to have inherent value.

For this reason, the minting political authority has not traditionally played a decisive role in establishing the value attached to coins. Rather, it is the inherent value of the gold or silver in the coins which played that role.

On the other hand, on some historical occasions and under some political circumstances, some coins might come to be more highly prized than others due to the prestige or the trust adhering to the sponsoring king.

One negative consequence of the historical link between coins and precious metals is that it provided an opening for *debasement* of the coinage, either by criminals or by the minting political authorities themselves.

Coins are debased by reducing the standard weight of the precious metal contained in the coin by mixing it with a *base metal*. In this way, a debased coin contains less precious metal, and hence less inherent value, than is claimed by its face value.

Gradually, over the post–World War II period—in 1965, in the US—the coinage of the developed, industrialized countries has ceased to contain precious metals.

This is to say that today coins are a form of "*fiat* currency" every bit as much as banknotes are.

Fiat currency, of course, is currency with no perceived inherent value, but whose value derives rather entirely from the trust that the populace places in the minting authority.

Thus, a US quarter is worth one-fourth of a $1 bill because the US government says it is, and for no other reason.

It has seemed for going on 60 years now that that is reason enough.

What happens when a political authority that mints *fiat* coins (and prints paper currency) loses the trust of its populace is something that remains to be seen.

29. Collateral

DEFINITION: In the realm of finance, the term "collateral" refers to a valuable asset that a borrower offers as assurance for a loan.

For example, when a prospective homeowner secures a mortgage, the property itself functions as the collateral underpinning the loan. This means that if the homeowner defaults on his monthly payments, then the bank will foreclose on the loan and repossess the home.

Similarly, in the case of a car loan, the automobile being financed assumes the role of collateral.

In the case of a business procuring a bank loan, the firm may offer substantial assets like equipment or real estate as collateral against the loan. In case of default, the lender retains may seize the collateral and sell it to recuperate any losses it has incurred.

Even general personal loans may be "collateralized," meaning it may be backed by some type of asset. For example, secured credit cards require a cash deposit to serve as collateral.

ETYMOLOGY: The English word "collateral" is attested from the fourteenth century.

The noun "collateral" derives, via Middle English and Anglo-French, from the Medieval Latin adjective *collateralis, collaterale,* which, in turn, derives from the classical Latin preposition *cum-*, meaning "with," and the noun *latus, lateris,* meaning "flank" or "side."

USAGE: When a prospective borrower applies for a loan, the bank seeks assurance that the borrower will be able to pay it back. This is the fundamental reason why lenders require borrowers to provide them with a form of protection: namely, collateral.

Collateral serves to diminish a lender's risk by incentivizing the borrower to adhere to his or her financial commitment. In the case of a home loan (known as a "mortgage"), the borrower is motivated to make his monthly payments in a timely fashion by the prospect of losing the home—which serves as collateral for a mortgage—if he defaults.

Loans backed by collateral generally come with significantly reduced interest rates compared to unsecured loans.

A lender's entitlement to a borrower's collateral may be referred to as a "lien," signifying the lender's legal entitlement against the asset for the purpose of settling a debt.

If the borrower defaults and the lender takes possession of the collateral in order to sell it, but the price obtained for the collateral is not sufficient to compensate the lender for its losses, then the lender may initiate legal proceedings against the borrower in order to recover its outstanding losses.

The type of asset accepted as collateral is usually determined by the type of loan in question. For example, in the case of a mortgage, the loan is most often secured by the residence being financed.

Analogously, in the case of an automobile loan, the car being financed usually serves as collateral.

In general, lenders accept as collateral such assets as fully paid-off cars and boats, expensive luxury items such as furs and jewelry, whole-life insurance policies, savings-deposit accounts, and investment accounts. However, in most cases retirement accounts are not acceptable.

Another possibility for borrowing is the secured personal loan. This is a type of loan in which the borrower pledges a valuable possession as collateral. The worth of the pledged item should at least equal the amount of the loan.

When thinking about applying for a secured personal loan, you should choose a financial institution with which you already have a connection, especially if your collateral involves your savings account.

Having an existing relationship with the lender increases the likelihood of your loan application's being approved. It will also improve your chances of obtaining a favorable interest rate.

30. Communism

DEFINITION: The term "communism" refers to a socioeconomic system in which private property is legally limited to personal effects, while everything else—from housing, farms, and shops of all descriptions to factories of all types and sizes—belongs to "society" at large.

In effect, ownership by "society" means ownership by the government, which—in nearly all known historical instances of communist rule—is equivalent to ownership by the Communist Party.

Note: Economically speaking, the term "socialism" is essentially a synonym for "communism," as witnessed by the fact that the old USSR stood for the "Union of Soviet *Socialist* Republics." While it is true that "democratic socialism" may be properly opposed to "revolutionary communism," that is a purely political, not an economic, distinction.

ETYMOLOGY: The term "communism" derives from the concept of property being held "in common."

The word "common" derives, via Middle English and Old French, from the Latin adjective *communis*, meaning "common," "public," "shared," "general," or "universal."

USAGE: The word "communism" entered English, from the French word *communisme*, sometime around 1840. However, the concept and the practice of communism are much older.

The practice of holding a group's property in common may be traced to early Christian communities, as well as to later monastic communities in the Christian and other traditions, many of which still exist today.

Indeed, monastic communities may be more stringently communistic than nation states with communist regimes on the Soviet model. While national communist regimes typically allow some private possession of clothing, household appliances, and similar things, in most monastic groups the possession of private property is even more severely restricted.

The roots of the modern communist movement may be traced to utopian writings, movements, and experimental communities growing out of the wars of religion of the sixteenth century, notably, the German **Radical Pietists** and the English **Diggers** during the seventeenth century, as well as many others during the eighteenth and nineteenth centuries.

Among the main intellectual influences on the modern founder of the international communist movement, **Karl Marx**, we may mention the writings of the troika of French socialist thinkers, **Henri de Saint-Simon**, **Charles Fourier**, and **Pierre-Joseph Proudhon**.

Communism, in its modern sense, may be conveniently dated to 1848, the year of the publication of *The Communist Manifesto,* penned by Marx, together with his wealthy friend and benefactor **Friedrich Engels.**

For Marx's economic thought and writings, see the glossary entry **Karl Marx**.

Revolutionary communism began to take power in countries whose political life had been shattered by World War I.

The most important of these *coups-d'état,* of course, was the takeover of Russia by the **Bolshevik Party** led by **Vladimir Lenin** on November 17, 1917 (October 25 by the Julian calendar—hence, the "October Revolution").

However, communist putsches also occurred in Germany, where a **Bavarian Soviet Republic** was declared in Munich and a separate People's State of Bavaria in Bamberg during the summer of 1919. These statelets reigned for about three months before clashing with each other and being put down by troops loyal to the Weimar Republic.

Similarly, a Hungarian Soviet Republic was established in Budapest the same year under the leadership of **Béla Kun.**

Rotes Wien [Red Vienna] refers to the government formed by the Social Democratic Workers Party of Austria, which controlled the Austrian capital between 1918 and 1934.

However, the USSR was the world's only communist country until the end of World War II, when the Red Army spread Russia's rule to eastern Europe.

In 1949, communist forces led by **Mao Zedong** won the civil war that had been raging in China for years, installing the first communist regime in Asia, the **People's Republic of China.**

During the period of decolonization during the 1950s and 1960s, communist regimes came to power elsewhere in Asia, as well as in Latin America and Africa.

As a theory, communism has great emotional appeal to the young and inexperienced and to others who are naïve about economic matters. However, in practice, communism is hugely inefficient as an economic system and inherently unstable as a political system.

The reason why communism is economically inefficient was made plain by **Ludwig von Mises** and **Friedrich A. Hayek** in the 1930s, during the so-called "Socialist Calculation Debate."

In a nutshell, the reason is that communist economies have no market mechanism for setting prices, and thus provide no reliable price signals regarding the true state of supply and demand in relation to any commodity.

For more discussion, see the glossary article on **Austrian economics.**

The inherent political instability of communist governments arises from their extreme economic inefficiency, but also—perhaps even more so—from their inherent need to employ violence to maintain their political control.

Why is that?

Because the fundamental aims of communism fly in the face of human nature, in at least two broad respects.

First, it asks of people to work as diligently for "society that is, for strangers as they normally would for themselves and their own families.

Second, it proclaims that all people should be "equal" in the material sense, or as nearly so as possible.

In both cases, human nature simply recoils from being asked to perform tasks that violate its own nature: to treat strangers like family and to sever the intimate connection between material reward and skill, diligence, effort, and other personal qualities.

This repugnance elicited by the unnatural and unjust demands placed upon them causes people to revolt against the system which imposes such demands.

Therefore, the only way a communist regime can achieve its ultimate aims is by constantly inducing fear in its population. Whence the constant propaganda, the secret police, and the labor camps that have been the inevitable accoutrements of all communist regimes everywhere. For details, see **Aleksandr Solzhenitsyn**'s magisterial *Gulag Archipelago*.

As a result of these inherent defects, communism could not persist indefinitely.

The first cracks in the edifice of international communism occurred in China around 1979, when Mao's successor, **Deng Xiaoping**, began to push the Chinese Communist Party away from economic communism towards a form of state capitalism. Deng later famously proclaimed: "To get rich is glorious!"

In the fall of 1989, the communist regimes of Eastern Europe all crumbled, culminating in the symbolically charged demolition of the Berlin Wall by the cooperative efforts of the people of East and West Berlin.

The USSR ceased to exist in 1991 and, with a handful of exceptions, most other communist regimes around the world either collapsed outright or mutated into non-communist economic systems.

It must be stressed that some of the formerly communist regimes abandoned communism in the economic sense, while continuing to exert tyrannical political control by the communist party. The People's Republic of China is a prime example of this phenomenon.

31. Comparative Advantage

DEFINITION: "Comparative advantage" refers to an economy's relative level of productivity. More specifically, it refers to the ability to produce some good or service more efficiently—i.e., at a lower cost—than other countries.

The concept of comparative advantage is instrumental for understanding the how international trade can be mutually advantageous for countries that are trading partners.

Basically, if my country produces cotton more efficiently than yours and your country produces sugar more efficiently than mine, then it is obviously good for us both if we trade cotton for sugar and *vice versa.*

ETYMOLOGY: The English word "comparative" is attested from the fifteenth century. It derives from Middle English *comparen,* via Middle French *comparer* and, ultimately, Latin *comparare* (to compare).

"Advantage" derives from the word *avantage,* which is the same in Middle English and Middle French. *Avantage,* in turn, is formed from the French adverb *avant,* meaning "before." Thus, "advantage"basicallymeans "beforeness," that is, priority or superiority.

USAGE: Historically, the concept of comparative advantage is commonly associated with English political economist David Ricardo, who introduced it in his 1817 work, *On the Principles of Political Economy and Taxation.* However, it is probable that Ricardo had learned of the concept from his mentor, James Mill.

Comparative advantage is a cornerstone of modern economic theory. It is a principle that elegantly illustrates the fundamental belief—which underlay the political activism of the nineteenth-century advocates of free trade—that the free market, whether domestic or international, can operate to the mutual benefit of all participants.

To understand the principle of comparative advantage, it is necessary to have a firm grasp of the concept of opportunity cost.

"Opportunity cost" refers to the potential benefits of the actions that one does *not* take. That is, they are benefits that one might have enjoyed but which one forgoes whenever one chooses one course of action over another.

With respect to the economic principle of comparative advantage, to say that one company has a lower opportunity cost than another one means that it gives up fewer potential benefits.

In the context of economics, if not in other realms of life, benefits may be discussed in terms of dollars and cents. For this reason, it will be the company that can produce its trading goods at the lowest cost which will enjoy a comparative advantage over its trading partners with respect to those goods.

The money that the company saves through its more-efficient production may be translated into the terminology of "lower opportunity costs." That is to say, more opportunities may be pursued with the extra money.

Another way of thinking about comparative advantage is as the optimal choice among all possible trade-offs in a given set of circumstances.

That is, in a situation in which two options are being considered, each of which presents a mix of benefits and drawbacks, the one offering the most benefits and the fewest drawbacks may be said to possess the "comparative advantage."

The concept of comparative advantage is familiar from everyday life, though not usually under than name. For example, if one possesses certain skills, one will usually attempt to find work in the field in which those skills provide one with the greatest comparative advantage.

For example, an engineer might choose to work for a private firm rather than for the government.

By parity of reasoning, a group of people with diverse skills creates more opportunities for advantageous trade based on the principle of comparative advantage.

32. Creative Destruction

DEFINITION: The phrase "creative destruction" refers to the failure of inefficient business enterprises under the capitalist system of free-market competition, which then opens up opportunities for entrepreneurs to found new and potentially more-profitable enterprises.

ETYMOLOGY: The adjective "creative" derives, via Middle English and Middle French, from the Latin past participle, *creātus,* of the verb, *creo, creare,* meaning "to make," "to create," or "to produce."

The noun "destruction" derives, via Middle English and Middle French, from the post-classical Latin noun *dēstrūctio, dēstrūctiōnis,* meaning "destruction."

Dēstrūctio, in turn, derives from the past participle, *dēstrūctus,* of the classical Latin verb, *dēstruo, dēstruere,* meaning "to pull down," "to dismantle," "to destroy," or "to ruin."

USAGE: The phrase "creative destruction" was coined by the **Austrian school** economist, **Joseph A. Schumpeter**, in 1942 in his classic study, *Capitalism, Socialism, and Democracy.*

Schumpeter claimed to have been inspired by reading **Karl Marx**, who also discussed the "destructive" aspects of capitalism in his 1867 *magnum opus,* the first volume of *Capital.*

However, Marx's idea was much broader than Schumpeter's.

As a **communist**, Marx believed not just that the capitalist system inevitably results in individual business failures, but that the only way in which capitalism creates wealth and ultimately survives is by destroying existing wealth, whether through the pursuit of war or the intentional and frequent instigation of economic crises.

A few other authors used the phrase before Schumpeter, as well, notably the German sociologist Werner Sombart.

However, it was Schumpeter who focused on the concept of creative destruction as an inherent and significant feature of capitalism and it was through his work that the phrase became generally known.

33. Credit

DEFINITION: The term "credit" has a variety of meanings in the field of business and finance. Nevertheless, two central meanings of the term are clear enough:

First, the term may refer to the ease with which an individual or company is able to borrow money or other valuable assets from a lending institution. A synonym for this sense of the term is "creditworthiness."

In this sense, one commonly speaks of individuals and companies as having "good credit" or "bad credit," as the case may be.

Second, the term may also refer to money that is owed to an individual or company by others. In this sense, it is the opposite of the term "debit"—money that an individual or company owes to others.

In the domain of accounting, this sense of the term indicates a particular type of bookkeeping transaction.

ETYMOLOGY: The English word "credit" is attested from the sixteenth century. It derives from Middle French, Old Italian, and, ultimately, from the Latin neuter past participle, *creditum,* of the verb *credo, credere* ("to trust in," "to rely upon," "to give credence to," "to believe").

The word is also closely related to the Middle English *crede* and Old English *crēda,* both meaning "creed," also from the Latin verb *creo, credere.*

USAGE: Credit in the sense of creditworthiness depends upon an individual or company's state of financial health and reputation for prudent behavior.

Such a financial state of health and reputation for prudence make it likely that any principal amount of money a company or individual may borrow will be repaid in a timely manner, along with interest charges.

That is why creditworthiness makes an individual or company an attractive prospective borrower to lending institutions. It is the primary basis upon which the lender may determine that the borrower will repay his loan in a timely fashion.

Credit in this sense represents an agreement between a lender (the "creditor"!) and a borrower (the debtor). The debtor promises to repay the lender, often with interest, within a given period of time.

Therefore, loosely speaking, "credit" is a short-hand way of referring to the overall practice of lending/borrowing—a human practice that goes back thousands of years.

Different Kinds of Credit

Different kinds of credit exist. Some familiar examples include car loans, home mortgages, personal loans, and lines of credit.

Perhaps the most significant and widespread form of credit in contemporary American society is credit cards, which basically grant consumers the ability to purchase almost any item "on credit," that is, with just a signature, constituting a promise to repay the loan according to the terms of the original credit card agreement.

Credit card transactions are unique in that the card-issuing bank acts as an intermediary between the buyer and the seller of the merchandise purchased. The bank pays the seller in full immediately, while accepting repayment from the buyer—the credit card holder. As with any other type of loan, the bank makes its profit from the interest it charges on the principal amount of the money it lends.

Similarly, the notion of credit extends to situations in which a buyer receives products or services from a seller without having to make an immediate payment.

In such cases, by extending credit to its clients, the seller of a product is acting in the manner of a bank. However, the seller's motivation in such cases is typically not to earn interest, but rather to accommodate the wishes of its valued customers.

Credit Scores

Credit scores serve as a means of categorizing individuals or companies according to the degree of their creditworthiness.

With respect to individuals, such scores are valued not only by banks and other prospective lenders, but also by landlords, insurance companies, and even prospective employers.

With respect to companies, credit-rating agencies (such as Moody's and Standard and Poor's) assign letter-grade scores that reflect the companies' creditworthiness (financial health).

Such scores are closely monitored by bond investors. They also may influence the interest rates that companies need to offer when borrowing money.

Moreover, such scores may even affect the pricing of bonds and other securities issued by governmental entities, based on the creditworthiness of the issuing body.

Credit Instruments

Letter of Credit: A bank-issued document frequently employed in international trade. A letter of credit assures a seller to which it is presented that he will receive full payment for the debt incurred by the holder of the letter (buyer). If the buyer fails to pay his debt to the seller, the bank pays the seller in his stead (and pursues its claim against the buyer by legal means).

Line of Credit: A loan provided by a bank or other financial institution granting the borrower access to a specific amount of credit that can be drawn on as needed, as opposed to receiving the entire sum at once.

Credit Limit: The maximum amount or ceiling of a line of credit that a lender, like a credit card company, is willing to offer to a borrower. The most common example is the dollar limit that the issuing bank puts on the amount that an individual can spend using his credit card.

Revolving Credit: A loan with no fixed end date. A credit card account is the most common example of revolving credit. So long as the account remains in good standing, the borrower can continue to borrow against it, up to whatever credit limit has been established.

As the borrower makes payments, the remaining balance owing declines, thus replenishing the amount available for use. These kinds of loans are often referred to *open-end credit.*

Home mortgages and automobile loans, on the other hand, are examples of *closed-end credit* because they must be paid completely by a date certain.

34. Cryptocurrency

What is a cryptocurrency? A cryptocurrency is more than just an electronic or digital form of money that uses cryptography to secure transactions. For something to be a full-fledged cryptocurrency, it must satisfy the following four conditions. Note that Bitcoin, created in 2008, was the first cryptocurrency to satisfy these conditions.

1. It must be self-contained, not requiring recourse to some other already existing currency;
2. It must allow people to use the cryptocurrency with nothing more than a public and private cryptographic key;
3. It must have a mechanism for controlling the proliferation of the currency; and
4. It must function without a third party being able to deny transactions for reasons extrinsic to the transaction protocol.

The first point about a cryptocurrency being self-contained instantly separates it from the ecash and digital forms of money that predated Bitcoin. Essentially, all the precursors to Bitcoin were payment schemes denominated in a conventional currency (such as U.S. dollars). Payments would be transmitted using cryptographic protocols, perhaps with tokens, but in the end they always had to be unpacked in terms of the conventional currency.

The only exception prior to Bitcoin was Bit Gold, which typically is written uncapitalized as "bit gold." Invented by computer scientist Nick Szabo in 1998, ten years before the release of Bitcoin, bit gold limited the proliferation of its currency by, like Bitcoin, requiring computational puzzles using hash functions to be solved in order for currency to be created.

Bit gold was a proof-of-work system, and it drew inspiration from Hashcash, which had been developed in 1992. Perhaps misnamed, Hashcash was never actually a currency or cash but rather a way of compelling internet users to prove that they had done some computational work in order for an electronic communication (such as an email) to get through to an intended user. Without this proof of work, the communication would be automatically ignored. Hashcash's aim was to control against spam and denial of service attacks by imposing a computational cost on each email or attempt to gain user attention.

In creating bit gold, Szabo repurposed Hashcash's proof-of-work system to deliver a form of digital cash. Bit gold's approach to proof of work using hash functions became a key component of Bitcoin. But bit gold lacked the immutable decentralized ledger of blockchain and depended on one computational puzzle to be solved before the next could be solved, rendering it unwieldy. Bit gold was never implemented, but it proved a fruitful conceptual link in the evolution of cryptocurrency — so much so that its inventor Nick Szabo is to this day regarded as the best candidate for the pseudonymous Bitcoin founder Satoshi Nakamoto (despite Szabo's persistent denials that he is Satoshi).

Compared to bit gold, other precursors to Bitcoin looked a lot less like what we've come to expect and know of cryptocurrencies. Back in the 1980s and 1990s smart cards were often used to handle financial transactions. Once the Web really started to take off in the mid 1990s, many worried that credit card transactions over the Web would be too insecure to rule out massive fraud. This led to proposals such as David Chaum's DigiCash, which offered greater security than giving one's credit card over the Web. DigiCash ended up going bankrupt in 1998, but Chaum did introduce a memorable idea with it, namely, the use of blind signatures to maintain anonymity by rendering payments untraceable.

One of the most successful digital payment schemes was developed the year DigiCash went bust: PayPal. With the rise of the smartphone, conducting financial transactions digitally has become ever easier, as we see with services like Venmo (a PayPal subsidiary) and Zelle (owned by some of our big banks such as Bank of America and Wells Fargo). But in the end, conventional money running through a central source must be used to make these systems work. Conventional money needs be front-loaded or guaranteed via a promissory note to ensure that adequate funds are in place, which can then be securely transferred, perhaps via digital tokens, to complete the transaction.

The visionaries responsible for cryptocurrency as we know it today, however, didn't just want a quick and easy scheme for moving conventional money around electronically. They were cypherpunks, who wanted to use cryptography to ensure privacy, especially in remaining free of government and corporate surveillance. Moreover, they distrusted conventional fiat currency and were looking for an alternative to it, one that was fully decentralized. David Chaum was a key player in this movement, and his idea of blind signatures was designed to ensure anonymity and privacy.

But anonymity in Chaum's DigiCash applied to buyers, not sellers. Blind signatures were used to keep otherwise trusted third parties (such as banks) in the dark about buyers' identities. Blind signatures gave buyers anonymity by getting banks to digitally sign and thereby authorize transfers of money, but because the signatures were blind, transactions involving DigiCash would be untraceable back to the buyer.

DigiCash, in giving banks and established financial institutions the authority to transfer money through blind signatures, centralized its digital currency. In the evolution of cryptocurrencies, however, the move was to eliminate such centralized trusted third parties. Blind digital signatures have therefore assumed a peripheral role in today's blockchain-based cryptocurrencies, though digital signatures as such have remained central. As it is, blind signatures remain of interest to this day in election security (where election workers are able to use blind signatures to authorize voter ballots, thereby ensuring that the election workers don't see who the voters are voting for).

Before 2008, when the pseudonymous Satoshi Nakamoto published his white paper on Bitcoin, all the digital money schemes that had been proposed either fell flat or merely expanded the transactional range of conventional currency (fiat money). But the cypherpunks always aimed higher than merely making conventional fiat currency more digitally tractable. So what finally happened in 2008 that made Bitcoin the revolution in money that it is?

It's not that Satoshi invented anything fundamentally new in cryptography or computer science. Rather, it's that he took items off the shelf and put them together in a novel way to create in Bitcoin a decentralized self-contained cryptocurrency. Satoshi's white paper lays out there all the key elements that Bitcoin, and its many successors, use: digital signatures, hashing, peer-to-peer networks, and blockchain. proof of work/stake, and mining (i.e., controlled ways of generating more of the cryptocurrency. All cryptocurrencies that have succeeded Bitcoin, from Ethereum to Solana, exhibit these elements.

Satoshi Nakamoto, whoever he is, did not invent any fundamentally new concept of computer science or cryptography. Nonetheless, in creatively putting together existing concepts from these fields and thereby creating the first full-fledged cryptocurrency, one that to this day dominates the crypto world (Bitcoin), his influence is enormous.

35. Cryptography's Role Players

In the description of cryptographic protocols, the same roles keep appearing (e.g., sender, receiver, evesdropper). It's convenient to give these roles memorable names, with pride of place going to Alice and Bob. What follows is a list of the names of these cryptographic role players along with an explanation of their roles.

Alice and Bob

Ron Rivest, Adi Shamir, and Leonard Adleman (of RSA fame) immortalized Alice and Bob in their 1978 paper outlining their scheme for public-key cryptography: "A Method for Obtaining Digital Signatures and Public-key Cryptosystems." Alice, the sender, wants to transmit a message securely to Bob, the receiver. The challenge is to determine what Alice and Bob need to make their communications secure, especially against various types of attack against their cryptographic communication system.

Eve

Eve is an eavesdropper who tries to monitor the communications channel between Alice and Bob. Eve is a passive attacker in the sense that she is capable only of listening in on messages being sent, not on changing or disrupting them.

Sybil / Sybil attack

Sybil is an attacker who uses multiple personalities (i.e., invented fake personas) to attack a communications system. Sybil comes from the pseudonym for Shirley Ardell Mason, one of the most famous people to suffer multiple personality disorder (a book and film were made of her case). A Sybil attack attempts to disrupt the network on which Alice and Bob are communicating by creating multiple fake personas and using them to subvert any consensus mechanisms, thereby influencing the network to take actions it would not otherwise take.

36. Debenture

DEFINITION: A debenture is a type of bond or other debt instrument that has no collateral security.

Since debentures are not backed by assets, the reputation of the issuer is the principal factors providing the credibility that makes them attractive to investors.

Debentures are commonly used by both corporations and governments as a way of raising capital or liquid funds.

Much like conventional bonds, debentures may provide regular interest payments known as "coupon payments."

ETYMOLOGY: The English word "debenture" is attested from the fifteenth century. It derives from the Middle English term debenture, which is the third-person plural, present tense, passive voice form of the Latin verb *dēbeo, dēbē*re ("to owe," "to be morally bound to X," "to be due to X"), meaning "they are due."

USAGE: Debentures are legally constituted through a contract called an "indenture." An indenture, in this sense of the term, is a binding agreement between the issuer of the debenture and its holders.

The indenture includes the principal features of a debenture offering, including such determinations as the maturity date of the instrument, the interest payment (coupon) schedule, the method of interest calculation, and other similar specifications.

Governments typically opt for debentures in the form of long-term bonds (those with maturities exceeding 10 years). These government bonds are considered low-risk investments since they are backed by the issuing government itself.

Corporations use debentures essentially as long-term loans. However, unlike secured bonds, debentures rely solely on the financial strength and creditworthiness of the issuing company.

Debentures offer companies several advantages compared to other forms of loans and debt instruments, including lower interest rates and longer repayment periods.

Kinds of Debentures

Registered vs. Bearer: Debentures can be issued in two forms: registered or bearer.

Registered debentures are publicly recorded in the name of the issuer, and any transfer of these securities must proceed via a clearing facility. This process ensures both that the issuer is aware of sales of its debentures and that the issuer is able to make interest payments to the correct holder.

Bearer debentures, on the other hand, are not registered in the name of the issuer. The owner of the bearer debenture, also known as the "bearer," is entitled to interest simply by holding the bond, without the need for any formal registration or notification process.

Redeemable vs. Irredeemable: Redeemable debentures explicitly specify the terms and date on which the bond issuer must fully repay its debt. In contrast, irredeemable (non-redeemable) debentures do not impose any obligation on the issuer to repay the debt by a specific date. For this rerason, irredeemable debentures are also known to as "perpetual debentures."

Convertible vs. Nonconvertible: Convertible debentures are bonds that can convert into equity shares of the issuing corporation after a specified period of time.

Convertible debentures are hybrid financial products, which offer the benefits of both debt and equity.

On the one hand, companies use debentures as fixed-rate loans and pay fixed interest payments. On the other hand, the holders of convertible debenture have the option of either holding the loan until maturity and receiving the interest payments or of converting the loan into equity shares.

However, the flexibility of convertible debentures involves a trade-off, as these securities typically yield a lower interest rate than other fixed-rate investments.

Nonconvertible debentures are debentures that lack the option to be converted into the issuing corporation's equity. To offset this lack of flexibility, nonconvertible debentures offer their holders a higher interest rate than do convertible debentures.

37. Debt (National)

DEFINITION: "National debt" is the overall amount of money owed by a nation state, such as the United States, to its creditors.

Thus, national debt is a type of "government debt," which also comprises debt owed by lower-level governmental entities, such as states, counties, and municipalities.

"National debt" is also sometimes referred to as "public debt" or "sovereign debt."

ETYMOLOGY: The word "debt" derives, via Middle English and Old French, from the Vulgar Latin substantive, *debita* (neuter plural), which is assumed to derive from the classical Latin substantive, *dēbitum* (neuter singular), meaning "a debt."

Dēbitum, in turn, is connected to the past participle, *dēbitus*, of the verb *dēbeo, dēbēre*, meaning "to owe."

The word "nation" derives, via Middle English and Middle French, from the Latin noun, *nātio, nātiōnis*, meaning "birth," "tribe," "race," or "a people."

Nātio is connected to the past participle, *nātus*, of the deponent verb, *nascor, nasci*, meaning "to be born."

USAGE: One might be forgiven for thinking that the national debt was a simple, straightforward subject. Unfortunately, the fact that it is a political football introduces all sorts of complications.

The first thing to say is that the national debt is created by the government's annual budget's consistently running a deficit—which just means that the government spends more money in a year than it takes in.

Each **budget deficit** must be closed by the US government's taking on debt. This may happen in a variety of ways, but the most-principled way is through the sale of government bonds on the open market.

Less-principled ways of closing the budget deficit each year include "borrowing" the money from other government funds (see below), or simply by printing money, backed by nothing—a dire contingency that has lately been resorted to and which is producing runaway inflation as of this writing (June of 2022).

The second thing to say about the US national debt is that it has been growing for a long time and that, over the past few years, it has been growing at an astonishing rate. It now stands at well over $30 trillion, or 130 percent of GDP.

The third thing to say is that not everyone thinks this is a bad thing.

In general, conservative economists and politicians think it's a bad thing, while progressive economists and politicians think that it is either inconsequential or else a good thing.

The fourth thing to say is that partisans point to different figures as representing the "real" size of the national debt.

Those progressives who retain some sensitivity on the subject will try to minimize the amount by redefining the national debt as the "publicly held debt." This is the amount of the debt owed to non-governmental entities, calculated by excluding monies owed to special accounts, such as the Social Security and Medicare trust funds, that is used to pay for general expenditures.

However, this idea is misleading, in that the debt owed to Social Security and Medicare is still a part of the overall debt owed by the US government, and so ought to be accounted a part of the national debt.

At the other pole of economic and political thinking, some conservatives are not content with holding the line against the "publicly held debt" sleight-of-hand. They go on to insist that the "real" national debt ought to include "unfunded liabilities."

"Unfunded liabilities" are implicit promises made by the government to continue non-discretionary spending in the areas of pensions (Social Security) and healthcare (Medicare) at certain levels, even though no taxation mechanism to offset these liabilities has been implemented by Congress.

These conservatives estimate that the magnitude of such unfunded liabilities over the remainder of this century is on the order of $100 trillion.

According to these critics, then, the "real" national debt of the US stands today at something on the order of $130 trillion.

How is it possible that conservatives and progressives have such different views of the national debt?

In a nutshell, progressives are **Keynesians**, who believe that "deficit spending" (which is what creates national debt) is a good thing for the economy, while conservatives subscribe to **Austrian economics** and similar theories, which view deficit spending as the chief engine driving government growth and interference with the free market, which they view as bad for the economy.

Moreover, progressives tend to back **Modern Monetary Theory**, which teaches that printing money will not cause inflation so long as a sovereign nation controls its own currency, whereas conservatives are convinced that, sooner or later, printing money must lead to runaway inflation and debasement of the currency.

As of this writing, it seems safe to say that Modern Monetary Theory has now been tested and found to be false.

38. Deficit (Budget)

DEFINITION: With respect to the federal government, the "budget deficit" is the difference between expenditures and revenues during a given budget cycle in which the former exceed the latter.

If revenues exceed expenditures, then there is said to be a "budget surplus."

ETYMOLOGY: The word "deficit" derives, via the French word *déficit*,from the Latin word *dēficit*, which is the third person singular form of the Latin verb, *dēficio, dēficere*, meaning "to fail" or "to run short."

The word "budget" derives, via Middle English, from the Middle French word *bougette*, the diminutive of the word *bouge*, meaning a "leather bag."

Bougette, in turn,derives from the Late Latin word *bulga, bulgae*, meaning "bag."

Bulga is thought to have entered Latin from Gaulish. It is also akin to the Middle Irish word, *bolg*, and the Middle English word, *bœlg*, both with the same meaning.

USAGE: The concept of the "budget deficit" must be clearly distinguished from that of the "**national debt**." It is the former which creates the latter, bit by bit, over a long period of time.

In the political rhetoric surrounding the budget deficit and the national debt, one must be on one's guard against the claim that the national debt is being "reduced" or "cut," when what is actually happening is that the size of the budget deficit is being reduced.

In order to cut the national debt, one would of course have to run a government budget surplus over a long period of time and apply the extra funds to paying down the debt.

The concept of a budget is quite simple. It is familiar to anyone who has ever run a business—or even a family unit, for that matter.

For individual businesses and families, it is intuitively obvious that consistently running a budget deficit creates a debt that is unsustainable.

In essence, budget deficits—whether familial, commercial, or governmental—can continue to be run only so long as someone can be found to extend credit. However, in the case of families and businesses, a time must inevitably come when one's credit card maxes out or one's bank will no longer increase one's line of credit.

After that, one of three things must happen: the family or business must either (1) find a way to generate more income, or (2) reduce its spending, or (3) declare bankruptcy.

Progressives are fundamentally unconcerned with national budget deficits and the resulting national debt due to their belief in **Keynesian economics** and **Modern Monetary Theory**, which basically say that sovereign nations cannot go bankrupt.

This hypothesis is likely to be tested in the real world, sooner rather than later.

39. Deflation

DEFINITION: Deflation denotes a decrease in the amount of money (nominal price) that must on average be paid for goods. It's not deflation if Walmart puts an item up for sale, thus lowering its nominal price. It is deflation if all stores taken together lower prices on all goods. The opposite of deflation is inflation.

Deflation occurs when the supply of goods and services offered within an extended market system—nowadays, usually a nation state—increases more rapidly than the money supply. In that case, the nominal price of the goods and services will decrease over time until the gap is closed. This means that the purchasing power of each unit of currency increases.

Deflation must not be confused with disinflation, which is a decrease in the rate of increase of nominal prices—that is, a slowing of the rate of inflation.

Deflation, in contrast, signifies an absolute decrease in the value of a nominal price from some reference point as time goes by. To take a concrete example: If deflationary conditions are prevailing within a given market system, then a dozen eggs might cost, say, $2.00 today and $1.50 a month from today.

ETYMOLOGY: "Deflation" is derived from the Latin "*de*," meaning "down," "from," or "out of" + "*flāre*," meaning "to blow."

USAGE: At first, deflation may sound like a good thing, but if it persists, it is a decidedly bad thing.

The reason is that the decrease in the price of goods and services represents a loss to the producer. Therefore, deflation may rapidly lead to recession, business failure, and ultimately economic depression.

For this reason, economists dread deflation far more than they do inflation.

40. Demand

DEFINITION: “Demand,” in the economic sense, is the amount of a given good that consumers are able and willing to purchase on the open market at a given time and place.

ETYMOLOGY: The English noun “demand” derives, via Middle English and Middle French, from the Medieval Latin verb *demando, demandare.*

Demando, in turn, derives from the combination of the classical Latin preposition *de*, meaning “from,” and the verb, *mando, mandare,* meaning “to commit to someone’s charge,” “to order,” or “to command.”

USAGE: Demand for a specific good is a function of the good’s price and its perceived necessity, quality, convenience, and available alternatives, plus the purchaser’s tastes and disposable income, as well as many other factors.

Among the additional factors are such things as fashion and changes in fashion—what **Thorstein Veblen** called “conspicuous consumption” in his classic 1899 study, *The Theory of the Leisure Class.*

Demand is also strongly affected by consumer confidence, which has to do with the expectations of consumers regarding (1) the future price or availability of goods they are contemplating purchasing; (2) their own personal future income and general financial situation, and (3) any expectations they may have about the future performance of the economy, as a whole.

Finally, demand is a function of population growth. Clearly, more people enable more goods to be produced (greater supply). By the same token, more people bring with them their own consumer needs and desires, thus creating greater demand, as well.

There are several more concepts which are specific to the concept of economic demand.

For instance, one may speak of the ”latent demand” in a marketplace, meaning the potential demand for a product that does not yet exist.

The idea behind latent demand is that it is a sort of force which, were a particular good to come into existence, would lead consumers to purchase it right away. It is a kind of demand, which, as it were, neither the supplier nor the consumer himself knew existed until the supply came along to satisfy it.

Another aspect of demand is the extent to which it can be shaped by the active manipulation of perceptions by others. As everyone knows, there is an entire industry which exists to do just this, namely, the advertising industry.

Finally, yet another aspect of demand is its "elasticity," which is the degree to which it is sensitive to price. As one might imagine, this is a very important feature of demand that has long been an object of study by economists.

41. Depreciation

DEFINITION: "Depreciation" is a decrease in the market value of a good over time. It is the opposite of "**appreciation**."

ETYMOLOGY: The noun "depreciation" and the related verb "depreciate" derive from the Late Latin past participle, *depreciatus*, of the verb *depretio, depretiare*, meaning "to depreciate."

The Late Latin term was assembled from the classical Latin preposition *dē*, meaning "down from" or "away from," and noun *pretium, pretii*, meaning "worth," "value," or "price."

USAGE: The word "depreciate" entered the English language during the fifteenth century.

Thus, the term—and the phenomenon—arose in conjunction with the development of long-distance trade routes, which led to the discovery of the New World and to international trade networks.

The Age of Exploration, in turn, was a decisive factor in the explosion of the market economy in Europe that occurred during the late Middle Ages and the Renaissance.

This historical context provides the indispensable background for understanding why the concept and reality of depreciation came into being when and where they did. However, knowing the history alone is not enough to understand depreciation. One must also be familiar with the **subjective theory of value**.

There are several different reasons why goods and commodities may lose their market value with the passage of time.

One reason is that the goods themselves may deteriorate. This is the form of depreciation that most people are familiar with, through the standard tax deductions that rental property owners and others may take on their federal and state income tax forms.

Perishable commodities such as food items deteriorate, as well, which is why many grocery stores offer day-old bread and other old items at a steep discount. This is a somewhat different sense of depreciation.

Another reason why goods may lose their value is that fashions change. Many retail businesses, such as bookstores and clothing stores, may offer last season's stock at a steep discount. This is another type of depreciation.

Yet another familiar form of depreciation is the large loss in the market value that a new car undergoes as soon as it is driven off the lot. Here, there is deterioration as such, or even change in fashion. Rather, the depreciation is due to the preference of people for brand-new cars (and, perhaps, their distrust of used-car dealers).

What all these examples of depreciation have in common is the reluctance of customers to pay the same price in the present that they would have been willing to pay in the past for the same commodity, due to their preference for new, fresh, and/or fashionable goods.

In short, economic value is created by the subjective preferences of consumers, and consumers prefer what is new.

42. Disinflation

DEFINITION: Disinflation is a decrease in the rate of increase of prices, or, in other words, a slowing in the rate of inflation.

ETYMOLOGY: "Disinflation" is derived from the Latin "*dis,*" meaning "separately," "apart," or "in the opposite direction," + "*in,*" meaning "in" or "into," + "*flāre,*" meaning "to blow."

USAGE: Disinflation should not be confused with deflation, which means an absolute decrease in prices over time from some reference point.

43. Diversification

DEFINITION: The term "diversification" refers to a strategy for managing risk that involves forming a mixture of different types of investments within a portfolio.

This diversified portfolio consists of a variety of unique asset types and investment instruments, the purpose of which is to minimize the investor's vulnerability stemming from the risk accruing from any particular kind of asset.

The underlying logic behind diversification is that a portfolio made up of different classes of assets will typically generate greater long-term returns, while reducing the risk associated with any single kind of security.

ETYMOLOGY: The English noun "diversification" is formed from the adjective "diverse," which is attested from the thirteenth century.

"Diverse" derives, via Middle English *divers,* from Old French *divers,* meaning "diverse," which, in turn, derives from the Latin past participle *dīversus* of the verb *dīverto, dīvertere,* meaning "to turn in different directions" or "to differ."

USAGE: Economics research, including mathematical simulations, lends support to the intuitive idea that a properly diversified portfolio—consisting of around 30 different kinds of stocks—provides the optimal balance between cost-effectiveness and risk reduction.

While investing in additional securities always offers some incremental advantage, the effectiveness of the diversification strategy begins to diminish rapidly beyond a certain point.

The goal of diversification is to mitigate the impact of relatively isolated (unsystematic) risk-creating events which may adversely affect a given portfolio. This allows the favorable performance of certain investments to counterbalance the unfavorable performance of others.

However, the advantages of diversification are applicable only when the securities in the portfolio are not too closely correlated. This means they must respond to market forces in different ways, often moving in opposite directions.

Many investment strategies are available for investors who wish to explore options for diversifying their portfolios. These various methods can often be combined to increase a portfolio's diversification still more.

Diversification, as practiced by fund managers and investors, consists in spreading the investments within a portfolio across different asset classes. The managers and investors must also decide on what percentage of the whole portfolio to allocate to each asset class.

Each type of asset class presents distinct sets of risks and opportunities. These classes may encompass:

- *Stocks:* Ownership stakes (shares) in private companies or equity in publicly traded companies
- *Bonds:* Fixed-income debt instruments issued by corporations and governments
- *Real estate:* Property, including land, buildings, natural resources, agriculture, and livestock, as well as water and mineral deposits
- *Exchange-traded funds (ETFs):* Tradable groupings of securities, which track an index, a commodity, or an economic sector
- *Commodities:* Fundamental goods that play a crucial part in the production of other products or services
- *Cash and short-term cash-equivalents (CCE):* Short-term, low-risk investments, such as money-market instruments, Treasury bills, certificates of deposit (CDs), and similar paper

Theory suggests that factors which could have an adverse effect on one asset class may in fact benefit another class.

For example, increasing interest rates may have a negative impact on bond prices. Why? Because the yields on previously purchased bonds—which are already locked in—will be paid out at the old, lower rate, making bonds as a class a less-attractive investment.

On the other hand, increasing interest rates may have a positive impact on other asset classes, such as real estate—which may generate higher income from rents—or commodities—which are also likely to increase in price.

44. Dividend

DEFINITION: The term "dividend" refers to the amount of a company's profits that are distributed to its shareholders from time to time, as opposed to being reinvested in the company.

Distribution intervals may be monthly, quarterly, or annually. The distributions may be received by shareholders in the form of either cash or additional stock.

The board of directors determines the timing and the dollar amount per share of all dividend distributions.

However, dividends must also be approved by the shareholders, voting according to their voting rights (based on the number of shares they own).

Shareholders of dividend-paying companies are entitled to receive a distribution if they purchase their stock before the "ex-dividend date," which is the day before the day of the announcement of the total amount of the next dividend distribution—which naturally results in shares' trading at a lower price.

One can easily calculate one's total dividend distribution simply by multiplying the dollar amount per share times the number of shares that one owns.

However, neither the dollar amount per share nor the total distribution amount is of much use in determining a distribution's relative generosity (or miserliness). This is because a more important factor has been overlooked—that is, the size of the associated share price.

For this reason, a different metric called the "dividend yield" is most often used, instead. It is expressed as a percentage and is calculated as follows:

dividend yield = amount per share ÷ share price

For example, if the dollar amount of the dividend is $2.00 per share and the share price is $50, then the dividend yield is four percent.

ETYMOLOGY: The English word "dividend" is attested from the fifteenth century.It derives from Middle English *divident* and, ultimately, from the gerundive *dividendus* ("ought to be divided") of the Latin verb *dīvido, dīvidere* ("to divide up," "to separate into parts").

USAGE: A dividend is typically derived from the company's net profits. It serves as a reward to shareholders for their investment in a company's equity. As such, it is analogous to interest.

However, even if a company generates fewer or no profits during a given period, it may still elect to make dividend payments to shareholders.

Conversely, if a company continues to generate profits during a given period, it may elect not to make dividend payments and instead to reinvest the profits in the company.

In this way, dividend distributions are disanalogous to interest payments, which are legally required.

In addition to normal, regularly recurring dividends, companies may also issue special dividends from time to time on a one-off, non-recurring basis.

While dividends with the option of being received in cash are the most common, companies may also elect to issue dividends in the form of stock shares alone.

In addition to corporations, various mutual funds and exchange-traded funds may also pay dividends.

Moreover, certain types of companies—notably master limited partnerships (MLPs) and real estate investment trusts (REITs)—are legally required to provide designated distributions to their shareholders.

Various other funds may also distribute regular dividends according to their written investment objectives.

The businesses which most reliably pay dividends are larger, well-established companies with predictable profits.

The following industry sectors are famous for their consistent record of dividend payments:

- Basic materials
- Oil and gas
- Banks and financial institutions
- Healthcare and pharmaceuticals
- Utilities

Startups—particularly in the technology and biotech sectors—may not offer regular dividends.

These companies often retain earnings in order to reinvest in research and development, expand their businesses, and cover operating expenses during the early stages of development.

45. Due Diligence

DEFINITION: The phrase "due diligence" refers to the moral or legal obligation to undertake a comprehensive review—usually involving extensive auditing—of the relevant financial details and other facts relevant to a proposed business purchase, sale, or other transaction.

ETYMOLOGY: The English term "due" is attested from the fourteenth century.It derives from Middle French *deu,* the past participle of the verb *devoir* ("to be obliged to"), which itself ultimately derives from Latin *dēbeo, dēbēre* ("to owe").

The word "diligence" is also attested from the fourteenth century. It derives from identical forms in Middle English and Middle French, and, ultimately, from the Latin noun *dīligentia*; the noun, in turn, derives from the past participle *dīligens, dīligentis* of the verb *dīligo, dīligere* ("to choose," "to prize," "to esteem highly").

USAGE: The phrase "due diligence," as well as the practice it refers to, came into being thanks to the enactment of the US Securities Act of 1933, which required securities brokers to provide full disclosure (transparency) about the financial instruments they were offering.

As a result, failure to disclose material information to potential investors exposed dealers and brokers to criminal prosecution.

In response to this potential legal liability, the financial industry made due diligence a standard "best practice." From there, the practice spread throughout the business world.

The drafters of the 1933 Securities Act acknowledged the possibility that the requirement of full disclosure might subject dealers and brokers to unjust prosecution, if they were unaware of certain material facts at the time of the sale and could not have been reasonably expected to know about.

To address this concern, the act incorporated the following legal defense: As long as dealers and brokers diligently investigate the companies whose equities they are selling and openly share the findings, they will not be held legally liable for any information that remains undisclosed.

Specialized equity research analysts, individual investors, broker-dealers, fund managers, and companies that are considering acquiring other companies all perform due diligence.

Due diligence conducted on the part of individual investors is voluntary. However, broker-dealers are legally bound to perform due diligence on securities before selling them.

Kinds of Due Diligence

Commercial due diligence: This type of due diligence involves assessing a company's competitive position, market share, and growth potential. It usually includes such things as an evaluation of the company's supply chains, both incoming from vendors and outgoing to customers, thorough analyses of the market and sales pipelines, and research and development activities. Finally, this form of due diligence may include a thorough examination of the company's overall operations, covering the composition and activities of the management, human resources, and information technology teams, among other things.

Legal due diligence: The purpose of this kind of due diligence is to ensure that a company is in full compliance with all legal and regulatory requirements. This thorough examination covers various aspects of a company's legal involvement, including ongoing or potential legal disputes, the safety of intellectual property rights, and confirmation that the company was correctly incorporated. In essence, the process ensures that all legal matters are appropriately addressed within the company.

Financial due diligence: This form of due diligence involves a comprehensive review of a company's financial statements and records with a view to identifying any anomalies and ensuring the company's financial integrity and stability.

Tax due diligence: This type of due diligence examines the company's tax liabilities, potential outstanding, as well as its opportunities for minimizing its future tax obligations.

Hard versus Soft Due Diligence

Hard due diligence: The primary focus of this sort of due diligence is on analyzing the numerical data presented in financial statements, such as the balance sheet and income statement. It involves conducting fundamental analysis, including utilizing financial ratios, in order to obtain insight into a company's present financial health and to make responsible future earnings projections. While this type of due diligence may help to identify potential issues or accounting discrepancies, it is worth noting that it is primarily driven by objective mathematical and legal considerations. That said, it is essential to be cautious of overly optimistic interpretations from enthusiastic salespeople, as they may attempt to present a positive picture of the company's financial situation that is unwarranted on the basis of hard due diligence alone.

Soft due diligence: This form of due diligence takes a more qualitative approach. Business success is influenced by various factors that cannot be entirely quantified, including effective leadership, employee relationships, and corporate culture. For this reason, soft due diligence focuses more on human factors like the caliber of the company's management and personnel, and the loyalty of its customer base. Unfortunately, a significant number of mergers and acquisitions—more than 70 percent—end up failing, often due to ignoring the all-important human element in the due diligence process.

46. Economics

DEFINITION: Economics is the scholarly study of the human activity of producing and exchanging goods, whether material or intellectual.

ETYMOLOGY: The word "economics" derives from the Greek words *oikos*, meaning "household" or "home," and *logos*, meaning (in this context) "reason" or "rational thought."

This etymology also explains a common spelling of the word found in older books: "œconomics."

USAGE: Both the word "economics" and the discipline itself trace their origin back to the ancient Greeks.

Specifically, there are two surviving texts entitled *Economics*(*Oikonomika*), **one** by the author Xenophon and the **other** long attributed to the philosopher **Aristotle**, but now thought to have been written by his pupil, **Theophrastus**.

These texts mainly deal with matters involving household and agricultural estate management. However, in places they do touch upon more foundational issues that we would recognize today as properly belonging to the science of political economy, or economics.

Some economic content may also be found in the Scholastic authors of the High Middle Ages, such as **Thomas Aquinas**.

Nevertheless, it is closer to the mark to say that philosophical reflection upon problems that are recognizably *economic* when viewed from a modern perspective really begins during the Renaissance, especially during the sixteenth-century efflorescence of civilization in Spain known as the **Siglo de Oro**.

With respect to philosophy more specifically, the Spanish Golden Age may also be viewed as part of a wider renewal of the Scholastic style of philosophy, which became known as the **Second Scholastic**.

This philosophical renaissance was still centered in Spain, although it was present to a lesser extent in Italy, France, and elsewhere. Because many of the Spanish authors who were active at this time and who wrote on economics either studied or taught at the University of Salamanca, they are often grouped together in the history of economic thought as forming the **Salamanca School**.

The Salamanca School authors were the first thinkers in history to devote sustained and systematic attention to the analysis of such phenomena as money, inflation, interest rates, taxation, markets, and international trade.

On the whole, the results of the Salamanca School authors were in line with the ideas advanced by the founders of the "classical" school of economic thought, including **Adam Smith**, **David Hume**, **Thomas Malthus**, and **David Ricardo** in England, and **Anne-Robert-Jacques Turgot** and **Jean-Baptiste Say** in France, among others, some two centuries later.

The classical school made many important discoveries, but above all it advanced two theses:

- According to the doctrine of comparative advantage, first proposed by Ricardo, there is a natural division of labor among nations just as there is among the individuals within a nation; for this reason, free trade is to the advantage of all nations; and
- According to Adam Smith's concept of the "invisible hand" and the French *physiocrate* (liberal) idea of *laissez-faire*, the economy works more efficiently and productively when the marketplace is left alone than it does under any form of centralized control.

Classical economics is also known as "economic liberalism," because it was analogous to the political liberalism which became ascendant in England at about the same time. Both forms of liberalism aimed to constrain the power of the king to control his subjects' lives, whether political or economic.

Thus, we can see that political and economic freedom have gone hand in hand for more than two centuries.

The science of economics that developed during the late nineteenth century made many new discoveries, notably, the insight that the value of a thing is determined by the subjective demand for it in the marketplace and not by the amount of labor that went into its production.

This key idea, known as the "subjective theory of value, was advanced by the Austrian **Carl Menger**, the Frenchman **Léon Walras**, and the Englishman **William Stanley Jevons** at roughly the same time, in the 1860s.

In other work by Jevons—as well as his successor at Cambridge University, **Alfred Marshall**, and others—many of the ideas of the classical economic consensus were given a more rigorous mathematical form.

At this point, idealized mathematical models begin to replace verbal descriptions of economic reality as the primary substance of the academic discipline of political economy.

Perhaps the summit of this new direction was the "general equilibrium theory" first advanced by Walras in the 1870s.

These new formal methods, together with the subjective theory of value, were then combined with the classical theory to form a new synthesis usually referred to as "neoclassical economics."

During the late nineteenth and early twentieth centuries, the main competitor to the classical and neoclassical schools was the economics of **Karl Marx**. However, Marx's economic analyses—as opposed to his political agitation—were not taken seriously by the academic economics discipline and thus had limited influence on the field.

Up until the stock market crash of 1929 and the Great Depression, neoclassical economics reigned supreme. However, the crisis of the early 1930s resulted in serious soul-searching among academic economists.

In 1936, the neoclassical consensus was shattered by the groundbreaking book of **John Maynard Keynes**, *The General Theory of Employment, Interest, and Money*.

In a nutshell, **Keynesian economics** renounced one of the two basic theses of the classical and neoclassical schools, namely, that markets work more efficiently and productively on their own than they do under centralized government control.

Through a combination of mathematical sophistication and literary flair, Keynes convinced many readers of his *magnum opus* that the fundamental notion of *laissez-faire* was erroneous, and that the government must inject money directly into the economy to support selected industries, in order to achieve maximum productivity and full employment.

It took time, but by the end of World War II, Keynes's ideas had permeated the halls of power in nearly all the Western industrialized democracies.

At first, economic growth worldwide under the Keynesian regime was startling, leading to some 30 years of steadily increasingly prosperity between 1945 and 1975—what the French call "*les trente glorieuses*."

However, things then began to break down. The combination of high inflation and low or negative growth ("stagflation") that appeared during the second half of the 1970s eventually led to a partial repudiation of Keynesianism and a course correction back towards the neoclassical consensus.

This phase of economic history has come to be known as the reign of "**neoliberalism.**"

For a while, the new neoliberal (really, more of a Keynesian-lite) consensus was quite successful, both in the developed and also in the developing world. With the spread of free-market policies and the rule of law to the world's poorest countries, notably, China, the prospect to an end to human economic misery appeared to many to be within sight.

Then, as though at the beat of a metronome, 1929 happened all over again.

In 2009, an asset-price bubble in the housing industry burst, resulting in a worldwide chain of bank failures and sending political shockwaves around the world.

The 2009 financial crisis, together with the insolvency of several of the European Union's smaller states over the next few years, marked a remarkable turning point in the history of economics.

Today, in 2022, we find ourselves in an unprecedented situation:

Not only is neoliberalism dead and buried; not only has Keynes been resurrected; but Marx himself has been heard stirring in his grave.

47. Entrepreneurship

DEFINITION: Entrepreneurship is the undertaking of business ventures, especially new kinds of ventures or traditional ventures that operate in novel ways.

ETYMOLOGY: The English word "entrepreneur" is a direct borrowing from French, which occurred sometime during the nineteenth century, most likely from the writings of **Jean-Baptiste Say**.

The French noun "*entrepreneur*," originally meaning "supplier," contractor," or "businessman," the adjective "*entreprenant*," meaning "enterprising," and the verb "*entreprendre*," meaning "to undertake," all derive from the French preposition *entre*, meaning "between," and the verb "*prendre*," meaning "to take."

The French word "*entre*," in turn, derives from the Latin preposition "*inter*," meaning "between," while the French "*prendre*" derives from the Latin verb "*prehendo*," meaning "to lay hold of," "to seize," or "to grasp."

USAGE: Jean-Baptiste Say greatly admired **Adam Smith**'s 1776 classic, *The Wealth of Nations*.

However, Say mentioned that one of the things he found disappointing about the book was its neglect of the creative role of the individual in coming up with new ideas and risking his capital through the act of founding a new enterprise.

In this way, the French word "*entrepreneur*" was explicitly given its modern meaning.

The word itself, with its new economic connotation of a creator of business firms—or *enterprises*—was soon adopted by English-speaking economic thinkers, as well.

One might suppose that once the French term was adopted into English, the idea it stands for would become a subject of conscious economic reflection and analysis. However, this did not in fact occur for some time.

One of the first important studies of entrepreneurship was **Frank H. Knight**'s *Risk, Uncertainty, and Profit*, published in 1921.

Knight made several important distinctions relevant to enterprises, notably, that between risk and uncertainty.

Risk, on Knight's telling, refers to processes whose outcomes are known to be structured according to some probability distribution, while uncertainty signifies processes about whose outcomes nothing at all can be predicted.

Knight pointed out that the profit that entrepreneurs realize from creating a successful enterprise may be viewed as just compensation for his willingness to assume responsibility for risk and uncertainty.

Another very important economic thinker who investigated the role of entrepreneurship in political economy was **Joseph A. Schumpeter**. Schumpeter is best known for his concept of "creative destruction," presented in his 1942 book *Capitalism, Socialism, and Democracy*.

Schumpeter pointed out that capitalism involves a perpetual change in the mix of businesses present in a market over time, as new, more-successful firms replace older, less-successful firms, which may have once been profitable, but are no longer under the new market conditions. He dubbed this process of constant turnover "creative destruction."

Lastly, we may mention the **Austrian economist Israel M. Kirzner**, whose book *Competition and Entrepreneurship* was published in 1973.

In this book, as well as many other writings, Kirzner criticized mainstream economic theory for being preoccupied with mathematical models that assume perfect competition. He pointed out that this practice neglects the important role of the entrepreneur in economic life.

It is interesting to note that Kirzner's efforts to integrate the phenomenon of entrepreneurship into modern, neoclassical economic theory has been more successful than most other doctrines advanced by proponents of Austrian economics.

48. Equity

DEFINITION: The term “equity” refers to the total amount of money that would be distributed to a given shareholder if he were to liquidate all his shares.

The term may also be used in a collective sense, in which case it is also known as “shareholder equity” (in the case of publicly traded companies) or “owners’ equity” (in the case of privately held companies).

In the collective sense, equity refers to the total amount of money that would be distributed to all shareholders as a group if all the company’s assets were liquidated and the value of all its outstanding shares paid out.

ETYMOLOGY: The English term “equity” is attested from the fourteenth century. It derives from Middle English *equite*, Middle French *équité*, and, ultimately, from the Latin noun *aequitas,aequitatis*, meaning “evenness,” “impartiality,” “fairness,” “justice.” The noun, in turn, is derived from the Latin adjective *aequus*, meaning “even” or “equal.”

USAGE: When a company is acquired, its equity in the collective or “shareholder equity” sense is determined by deducting any liabilities from the total value of the sale (assets).

shareholder equity = total assets – liabilities

Moreover, shareholder equity can serve as the “book value” of a company. It can even be used, on occasion, as payment-in-kind.

Listed on a company’s **balance sheet**, equity is a vital piece of information often used by analysts to evaluate a company’s financial health.

The “assets-minus-liabilities” shareholder equity formula makes it possible to make an objective assessment of a company’s finances by considering precise figures representing its assets and liabilities.

Shareholder equity is readily understood by investors and analysts. It may function as the capital raised by a company that is then used to support operations, acquire assets, and invest in new projects.

Companies may raise capital by means of either debt (loans or bonds) or equity (selling stocks). Investors frequently prefer the latter, seeing that owning stock shares offers a greater chance of participation in a company’s growth and profits.

Possessing company stock also provides shareholders with the opportunity for receiving dividends and earning capital gains. Moreover, equity ownership (in the individual sense) grants shareholders the right to vote on corporate matters, including in elections of boards of directors. In these ways, equity ownership stimulates shareholders' continuing interest in the company.

Shareholder equity in the collective sense can be either positive or negative. Having positive equity indicates that a company's assets are greater than its liabilities. Having negative equity means that the company's liabilities are greater than its assets.

The appearance of negative equity on a company's balance sheet, which persists over some time, may indicate that the company is insolvent.

Companies with negative shareholder equity are often perceived to be risky investments. However, by itself shareholder equity is not a conclusive metric of a firm's financial well-being. Rather, equity must be combined with other factors to portray accurately a company's overall financial health.

Components of Shareholder Equity

Retained earnings: Retained earnings make up a portion of shareholder equity, which represents any net earnings that are not distributed as dividends. Thus, companies' retained earnings are similar to individuals' savings, inasmuch as they accumulate over time, forming a fund set aside for future use. Retained earnings increase as the company reinvests a portion of its income.

Over time, the accumulated retained earnings might surpass the equity capital contributed by stockholders. For companies with a long operational history, retained earnings often become the largest component of stockholders' equity.

Treasury shares: The phrase "treasury shares," also known as "treasury stock" (nothing to do with US Treasury bills), refers to the company's own stock that has been repurchased from existing shareholders.

Companies may decide to repurchase shares when it is difficult for them to make optimal use of all available equity capital. These repurchased shares are called treasury shares, whose dollar value is recorded in a separate treasury stock account. If there is a need to raise capital in the future, companies may reissue treasury shares to stockholders.

Other Kinds of Equity

The notion of equity is also applicable in contexts beyond the evaluation of companies' balance sheets.

In a broad sense, equity is simply the proportion of ownership of an individual or company in any asset considered as a fraction of the total amount of debt associated with that asset.

Among several different kinds of equity, we may mention the following:

- In the context of margin trading, the term "equity" refers to the value of securities in a margin account minus the amount borrowed from the brokerage.

- In the context of real estate, "equity" signifies the difference between the property's current fair market value and the amount the homeowner still owes the bank, i.e., the outstanding mortgage amount.
- In the context of a company's bankruptcy and liquidation, equity is the amount remaining after all its creditors have been repaid. This is often called "risk capital," "liable capital," or "ownership equity."

Public vs. Private Equity

If a company's stock is publicly traded, determining the market value of its shareholder equity is straightforward, obtainable by finding the company's share price and market capitalization.

For private companies—that is, ones whose stock is not publicly traded—the market mechanism is absent. For this reason, alternative valuation methods must be used to estimate their value.

Privately held companies may attract investors by directly selling shares through private placements. These private equity investors may include accredited individuals and institutions such as pension funds, insurance companies, and university endowments.

Private equity plays a role at various stages of a company's existence. Generally speaking, a start-up company without revenue or earnings will not be able to secure loans, so it often relies on capital from friends, family, or individuals known as "angel investors."

Later on, venture capitalists become involved when the company has developed its product or service and is prepared to bring it to market. At this stage, private equity is frequently offered to funds and investors specializing in direct investments in private companies or engaging in leveraged buyouts (LBOs) of public companies.

49. Escrow

DEFINITION: The term "escrow" refers to an arrangement, often prescribed by law, in which one or both parties to a transaction entrust assets to a third party, who holds them on their behalf until the transaction is successfully completed.

Escrow funds will be deposited by the third-party agent into an escrow account. The agent will then manage the account, releasing specified quantities of the assets (often, but not exclusively, in the form of cash), either upon satisfaction of certain contractual stipulations or upon receiving appropriate instructions from the parties involved.

ETYMOLOGY: The English noun "escrow" is attested from the late sixteenth century. It derives from Middle French *escroue* and Old French *escroe*, meaning "parchment scroll."

The related English verb "to escrow," meaning "to place in escrow," dates from only 1949.

USAGE: Escrow is mainly used in situations where there is uncertainty about the fulfillment of the respective obligations of the parties to the transaction.

Escrow is especially useful in certain types of transactions, such as those involving banking, real estate, mergers and acquisitions, legal matters, the Internet, and intellectual property, among others.

Why is this?

To understand the usefulness of escrow, imagine a company engaged in the trade of some luxury item, such as antiques. A customer places an order with the company for delivery of, say, a Ming vase.

Since fine porcelain is fragile, there is a degree of uncertainty surrounding this transaction. The customer wants to make sure it receives its vase in good condition before it coughs up the money. The company, in contrast, wants to make sure it gets paid for the vase in a timely manner.

Using an escrow agent can satisfy both of these needs at the same time. But it is the uncertainty, or risk, inherent to the transaction that is the real driver of the need for escrow in the first place.

First, the customer places the funds with the escrow agent. Next, the company ships the vase. Third, upon hearing from the customer that the vase has arrived in good condition, the escrow agent releases the funds to the company.

If a dispute should arise, the escrow agent would continue to hold the funds until the dispute is resolved.

In this way, escrow turns an inherently uncertain or risky transaction into one which is comfortable for both parties.

Real Estate Escrow

Real estate is the field of commerce in which escrow accounts are most often used. Two different basic types of escrow account are in common use in this field.

***Before closing*:** By depositing a specified amount of money (usually one or two percent of the purchase price of the home) with a bank or real estate agent, the prospective buyer can demonstrate to the seller his good faith intention to make the purchase, pending the satisfaction of some requirement, such as the house's passing an inspection or the performance of **due diligence**. In other words, the escrow payment is used by the prospective buyer to give the seller an incentive to wait—essentially, to hold his place in line—for a short time. If the buyer nonetheless decides to walk away from the deal, he may forfeit the escrow money unless he can show a sufficient cause for doing so.

***At and after closing*:** Escrow accounts are also commonly created during the closing process for the purpose of receiving periodic payments towards required annual expenditures related to ownership of the property, notably homeowners' insurance premiums and real estate taxes. Such escrow account payments are commonly structured as a dedicated portion of the monthly mortgage payment, above and beyond the amount shown on the actual mortgage's schedule of payments. The extra amount is arrived at by dividing the total insurance premium and/or real estate tax liability by twelve, in the case of monthly mortgage payments. All of this may be represented by the following formula:

total monthly mortgage payment = scheduled mortgage payment + escrow payment

This type of escrow account will naturally continue to exist throughout the life the mortgage.

Insurance and tax escrow accounts are usually required by the bank or other lender that is being repaid by means of the monthly mortgage payments. The purpose of such accounts is to put the payment of insurance premiums and tax liabilities under the direct control of the bank itself. In this way, the bank protects the integrity of its principal security for its loan: the borrower's property.

Escrow can also be associated with an escrow account established during mortgage closing. In this case, the escrow account is designated to cover future payments for homeowners' insurance and property taxes.

An escrow account for the payment of insurance premiums and tax liabilities is advantageous for the borrower, as well, seeing that he need not worry about saving up to make those payments when they become due. His savings are made for him automatically though the escrow portion of his monthly mortgage payments.

In addition to real estate, escrow is used in several other fields, notably, in the issuance of stock shares to shareholders under certain circumstances and in the online sale of high-valued items.

50. Exchange Rate

DEFINITION: The phrase “exchange rate” refers to the rate at which one national currency can be traded for another.

The exchange rate influences international trade and therefore the flow of money across national boundaries.

Exchange rates are influenced both by the value of the domestic currency and by the value of the foreign currency.

As an example, as of September 6, 2023 (the date of this writing), the exchange rate between the € (euro) and the $US (US dollar) stood at 1/1.07, meaning that one euro would purchase about $1.07.

Expressed the other way around, the exchange rate between the $US and the € stood at 1/.93, meaning that one dollar would purchase about 93 euro cents.

ETYMOLOGY: The English phrase “exchange rate,” or “rate of exchange,” is attested from the early eighteenth century.

The English noun “exchange” derives, via Middle English *exchaunge,*from Middle French *eschange,* which is connected to the verb *eschangier,* meaning “to exchange.” The latter verb derives from Vulgar Latin *excambiare,* also meaning “to exchange.”

The English noun “rate” is attested from the fifteenth century. It derives, via Middle English and Middle French, from the Medieval Latin adjective *rata,* which itself derives from the phrase *pro rata*(*parte*), meaning “according to a fixed proportion.”

The latter phrase, in turn, derives from classical Latin. The modifier *rata* is the past participle of the deponent verb *reor, rēri,* meaning “to reckon.” For further details, see the Etymology for the Glossary entry, “**pro rata**.”

USAGE: The value of a nation’s currency at any given point in time depends upon various economic factors. Among these are the gross domestic product (GDP), interest rates, and the unemployment rate of the countries whose currencies are to be exchanged.

These rates, often referred to as “market exchange rates,” are established within the global financial market, where banks and other financial entities engage in continuous currency trading influenced by the variables just mentioned.

Frequent fluctuations in exchange rates may result, ranging from minor adjustments on a daily, or even hourly, basis, to substantial changes over longer time periods.

In financial contexts, exchange rates are often discussed using three-letter abbreviations that represent the respective national currencies. For example, “USD” stands for the US dollar, and “EUR” signifies the euro.

When expressing the exchange rate between the US dollar and the euro, it is represented as EUR/USD.

Exchange rates can assume one of two primary forms: free-floating or fixed.

A *free-floating exchange rate* fluctuates on the foreign exchange market in response to market dynamics.

A *fixed exchange rate* is linked to the value of another currency.

For example, the Hong Kong dollar maintains a fixed exchange rate pegged to the US dollar, being allowed to fluctuate only within a narrow, specified range (7.75 to 7.85). Consequently, the value of the Hong Kong dollar will remain confined within this narrow window of price variation in relation to the value of the US dollar.

Exchange rates are characterized by two key values: the “spot rate,” also known as the “cash value,” and the “forward rate.”

The spot rate represents the current market value of a currency.

In contrast, the forward rate of a currency refers to its value on a parallel market, where a currency’s price is determined by traders’ anticipation of the likelihood of the future rise or fall of the currency’s value in relation to its spot rate (its general market value).

51. Externality

DEFINITION: In economics, an "externality" is an economic consequence of some economic activity, which affects an economic actor that was not involved in the activity.

Theoretically, an externality may be either beneficial (positive) or harmful (negative) to the economic actor in question. However, as a practical matter, harmful externalities are of most interest to economists.

Therefore, an externality may be thought of as an "indirect" or "external" cost to an economic activity.

ETYMOLOGY: The English adjective "external" derives from the Latin near-synonymous adjectives, *exter*, meaning "outward," "foreign," or "strange," and *externus*, meaning "outside" or "external."

The noun "externality," which is derived from the adjective "external," is first attested during the seventeenth century. However, its current meaning within the context of economics is relatively recent, dating from the late nineteenth century.

USAGE: The classic example of a harmful (or "negative") externality is air pollution.

If one economic actor—say, a factory—emits pollutants into the atmosphere from its smokestack, then it may create a harm, which constitutes a cost that must eventually be borne by another economic actor.

In this example, the other economic actors which must bear the cost of the externality may be either the citizens who must breathe the polluted air or possibly a government entity charged with compensating for the pollution in some manner.

As already mentioned, the concept of externality may be traced to the nineteenth century. The eminent British economist **Alfred Marshall** mentioned the concept in passing in his writings.

However, it was a British economist of the following generation, **A.C. Pigou**, who first made externality a subject for focused theoretical analysis during the 1920s.

Pigou also clearly distinguished between "positive" and "negative" externalities.

During the second half of the twentieth century, up until today, the notion of externality has continued to increase in prominence in academic economics.

52. Factors of Production

DEFINITION: The phrase "factors of production" refers to the various elements required to produce a good or service. Typical examples of factors of production include capital, labor, land, and entrepreneurship.

Individuals in a society who own or otherwise wield authority over the factors of production are often able to amass the most wealth in that society.

In the capitalist style of economic organization, it is usually those who own or invest in important companies who control the factors of production.

In contrast, in the socialist style of economic organization, it is the government which exercises majority (or exclusive) control over the factors of production.

ETYMOLOGY: The phrase "factors of production"is attested from the early nineteenth century, notably in the work of the English economist **David Ricardo**. The concept itself, however, probably extends back to Antiquity.

The English noun "factor" is attested from the fifteenth century. It derives from Middle English *factor,* meaning "agent" or "representative," which derives from Middle French *facteur,* with the same meaning. The latter word derives from Medieval Latin *factor,*meaning "doer," which, in turn, comes from the past participle *factus* of the classical Latin verb *facio, facere,* meaning "to do" or "to make."

The English preposition "of" derives from the identical Middle English form, meaning "off" or "of," which, in turn, derives from the identical form in Old English. The latter is akin to Old High German *aba,*meaning "off" or "away."

The English noun "production" is attested from the fifteenth century. It is made from the related noun "product," which itself derives, via Middle English, from Medieval Latin *productum*, meaning "product." The latter word derives from the past participle *prōductus* of the classical Latin verb *prōduco, prōducere,* meaning "to bring forward" or "to produce."

USAGE: The theory of factors of production in contemporary economics may be traced back to classical, nineteenth century political economy. Today's ideas integrate previous economic perspectives, including older conceptions of land or labor as the primary factors of production, into a unified conceptual framework.

One of the landmark achievements of so-called “neoclassical” theory was the realization of the crucial role that capital—in the form of savings, investment, and entrepreneurship—plays in modern industrialized economies.

During the twentieth century—and continuing until today—capital and labor came to be seen as the most important inputs for generating goods, services, and income. The manufacturing sector’s performance, for instance, can be assessed using specific indices, including the ISM manufacturing index.

The term “capital” may seem to denote primarily the concept of money—think of the iconic figure of the capitalist with his round belly and top hat on the Monopoly board game.

However, in the present context, the concept of “capital” must be understood to include more than just money in the bank, since money by itself does not directly bring about the production of goods or services.

Rather, in this context, “capital” is understood to comprise the things that money pays for. It is a factor of production on account of the types of productive activity it makes possible, such as the acquisition of land and equipment or the remuneration of labor.

For these reasons, according to contemporary mainstream economic thought, capital holds the central role in determining value, which is what makes it a principal factor of production.

Nevertheless, capital is not the only factor of production. Other factors, such as land, entrepreneurship, and labor also play a significant role in the creation of vale. Hence, they too count as factors of production.

53. Federal Funds Rate

DEFINITION: The "federal funds rate" is the **interest** rate at which banks and credit unions ("depository institutions") lend "reserve balances" to other depository institutions overnight on an uncollateralized basis.

"Reserve balances" are funds belonging to depository institutions which are held by the US Federal Reserve System ("the Fed") to meet those institutions' reserve requirements—whence the name commonly used for this special interest rate.

ETYMOLOGY: The word "federal" derives from the Latin noun, *foedus, foederis*, meaning "league," which in turn derives from the verb, *fīdere*, meaning "to trust."

The word "funds" derives from the Latin noun, *fundus*, meaning "bottom" and, by extension, "ground," "soil," "farm," "estate," "property," or "capital."

For the etymology of the word "rate," see the article **prime rate**.

USAGE: The basic purpose of the federal funds rate is to establish a uniform interest rate for the overnight lending of reserve-balance funds among depository institutions nationwide.

Why do such loans need to be made in the first place?

The reason is the following.

Depository institutions are legally required to maintain an account with the Fed in a minimum amount that is calculated depending on the institution's size. These are the institutions' "reserve balances."

The amount of an institution's reserve balance may fluctuate daily as the institution make deposits into and withdrawals from its account.

A depository institution with a surplus in its reserve balance account—that is, when the balance in its account is greater than required by law—is said to have "federal reserve credit."

Federal reserve credit can be converted into federal reserve notes. Additionally, a depository institution with a federal reserve credit may lend its federal reserve credit to other depository institutions, which wish to maintain a larger reserve balance, typically for the purpose of overnight processing.

There are actually two federal rates, called the "effective" rate and the "target" rate.

The effective federal funds rate is set by the market and is published by the Federal Reserve Bank of New York every business day. Specifically, the effective rate is the median interest rate for all overnight federal funds transactions.

The federal funds target rate, in contrast, is set by the members of the Federal Open Market Committee, which meets for this purpose roughly eight times a year. Special meetings of the Committee outside of the normal schedule may also be held from time to time, as necessary.

By buying or selling government-backed securities ("Treasury bills"), the Federal Reserve strives to bend the effective rate towards the target rate. This is the Fed's chief means of influencing the money supply of the US.

The federal funds rate also functions as a significant reference point, or "benchmark," used by financial markets in setting the interest rates offered by depository institutions and so, indirectly, the prime rate.

The relation between the federal funds rate and the prime rate is discussed further in the article, **prime rate**.

54. Fiat Money

DEFINITION: The phrase "fiat money" refers to currency that cannot be exchanged for a given amount of a physical commodity like gold or silver, but rather whose value is guaranteed by nothing more than the trust that people place in the issuing government.

That is to say, fiat money lacks any of the intrinsic value that commodity-based money enjoys.

Today, most modern paper currencies—such as the US dollar, the euro, the Russian ruble, the Chinese yuan, and other prominent global currencies—are fiat currencies.

ETYMOLOGY: The English term "fiat" in the financial sense is attested from the early seventeenth century. It derives from the Latin verb *fīo,fieri,* meaning "to become," "to happen," or "to be done." (*Fīo, fiere* is used as the passive voice of the verb *facio, facere,* which means "to make" or "to do.")

The word *fiat* is the third person singular, present subjunctive form of *fīo, fieri*; thus, it means "let it be done," "let it happen," or simply "let it be."

The idea is that, say, a one-dollar note counts as *currency* because the US government, in effect, says "let it be so."

The most famous occurrence of the term comes from the Latin Vulgate version of the Old Testament, where it is written (Gen 1:3):

dixitque Deus fiat lux et facta est lux

[and God said let there be light and there was light]

Perhaps this celebrated text lay in the back of the mind of the Englishman, whoever he was, who first used "fiat" in its present financial sense: i.e., with the Crown standing in the place of God.

USAGE: Prior to the adoption of fiat money, governments used to mint coins from precious metals like gold or silver, which were commodities with a certain inherent value that fluctuated according to supply and demand.

When they began to issue paper money for its greater convenience, governments stipulated that the notes were redeemable for a specific amount of gold or silver. In this way, the value of a government's currency rose and fell along with the price of gold or silver, as the case might be.

In contrast, fiat money cannot be automatically converted into a particular amount of any physical commodity.

Fiat money can, of course, to be used to *pay for* gold and silver, but that is a completely different matter. The point is that a currency note is not r*edeemable* for a particular fixed amount of any commodity metal.

Since it lacks such backing, the physical piece of paper that a one-dollar note is printed upon has a specific monetary value (namely, $1.00) only because of US government has decreed that the piece of paper should *count as* a one-unit note of the national currency, which is *called* the "dollar."

If this seems a little like pulling a rabbit out of a hat—creating something out of nothing—in a sense, it is.

The magic trick works so long as people will accept dollar bills in payment for the goods and services they sell. And they will only do that as long as they have a certain level of trust in the fundamental political and financial stability of the US government (or whatever government has issued the currency they are being asked to accept).

Thus, fiat money is always at risk of losing its value. This can happen is several ways.

The most common way is through **inflation**, which basically occurs when governments print more currency notes than the country's economy requires to function well. When there are "too many dollars chasing too few goods," in the standard maxim, the law of supply and demand requires that the value of the dollars (measured by the amount of stuff it will buy) must decrease. This principle usually manifests itself in increased prices.

If the government persists in the folly of simply "printing money" (without issuing any offsetting debt), eventually, inflation will become **hyperinflation**, in effect destroying that government's credibility and, with it, its fiat money.

None of this would happen if the government's currency were backed by gold or silver, because in that case the requirement of convertibility would place an absolute limit on the government's profligacy—simply continuing to run the printing presses would be illegal.

But printing too many currency notes is not the only threat to fiat money. Trust in government may also dissipate as a result of political instability and strife.

In such cases, the decline in faith in the government will translate into a suspicion of the government's fiat money, which will once again manifest as a decline in that money's decline in value—i.e., in inflation.

55. Fiduciary

DEFINITION: A fiduciary is an individual or entity charged with the responsibility for representing and working on behalf of another person (the "client").

Fiduciaries prioritize the interests of their clients above their own. Being a fiduciary involves both the moral and the legal obligation to act in the client's best interests.

The standard which the proper discharge of this legal obligation must meet—dating back to 1830—is often referred to as the "prudent person standard of care."

The failure of an individual or entity to live up to its fiduciary obligations is a form of professional malpractice called "fiduciary negligence."

In some cases, a fiduciary may be called upon to assume responsibility for the overall welfare of another individual. An example of a fiduciary with such a broad responsibility would be the legal guardian of an underaged individual.

However, in most cases, being a fiduciary involves the responsibility for handling a client's *financial* affairs.

ETYMOLOGY: Both the adjectival and the nominal uses of the English word "fiduciary" are attested from the seventeenth century.

The English word derives from the Latin adjective *fīdūciārius,* meaning "committed" or "given in trust," which in turn derives from the noun *fīdūcia* ("confidence," "reliance," "trust") and the verb *fīdo, fīdere* ("to trust," "to confide in").

USAGE: The prudent-person rule mandates that a fiduciary entity must prioritize the interests of its clients above all else. This means that extreme vigilance must be exercised against the creation of any possible conflicts of interest between the fiduciary and the client.

In many instances, the fiduciary entity is only allowed to profit from the relationship with its client to the extent that was explicitly agreed upon at the commencement of the relationship.

Many different kinds of financial and business professionals bear fiduciary responsibility towards their clients in the ordinary exercise of their duties. Among these relationships, we may mention the following:

- Lawyers and clients
- Executors and legatees

- Guardians and wards
- Trustees and beneficiaries
- Insurance companies/agents and policyholders
- Financial advisors (money managers, accountants) and their clients
- Investment corporations and investors
- Corporate board members and shareholders
- Stock promoters and subscribers

Special Fiduciary Responsibilities of Corporate Board Members

Duty of Care: The duty of care involves the way in which corporate board members reach decisions that influence the future of the business. The duty basically prescribes an obligation to thoroughly investigate all potential options and assess their potential impact on the company. As such, it is similar to the concept of **due diligence**.

Duty to Act in Good Faith: Even after conducting a thorough investigation of available options, the board bears the responsibility of selecting the option that it genuinely believes will most effectively serve the interests of the business and its shareholders. This is the duty to act in good faith, which is conceptually a step beyond "due diligence." One might call it "due action."

Duty of Loyalty: The duty of loyalty prescribes that the board must prioritize the company and its investors above all its other financial and other interests. Board members are obliged to avoid any personal or professional engagements that could compromise their allegiance to their company's best interests.

If a board member violates his fiduciary duties of care, good faith action, and loyalty, he may be held legally accountable by the company or its shareholders in a court of law.

56. Fungible

DEFINITION: Something is *fungible* if it can be replaced with something equivalent so that when the replacement is made, you are neither better nor worse off than before. Fungible therefore refers to things that can be interchanged without gain or loss. If you and I swap one-dollar bills, neither of us is better or worse off. If we swap equal amounts of bitcoins or some other cryptocurrency, we're likewise no better or worse off (save for transaction fees). So too, if we swap the same number of fungible tokens (such as gambling tokens, whether these be physically stored behind a counter or digitally stored on a blockchain), we're likewise no better or worse off.

ETYMOLOGY: *Fungible* entered the English language in the 1600s from the Latin. In classical Latin, its root appears as a verb that takes the passive form, so if you try to look it up in the standard *Lewis & Short Latin Dictionary*, you won't find it as *fungo* but rather as *fungor*. According to *Lewis & Short*, the word has two main meanings:

1. to busy one's self with or be engaged in something; to perform, execute, administer, discharge, observe, do;
2. to perform, discharge, contribute, pay any thing due from one.

Already here we see actions performed in legal and financial contexts. When fungible entered English in the 17th century, it came in through the Medieval Latin adjective *fungibilis*, where it assumed the meanings of *useful* and *interchangeable* (interchangeable things, after all, tend to be useful). This usage came especially to the fore in idiomatic phrases such as *fungi vice* (the "vice" here refers not to corruption but to the Latin *vicis*, meaning to alternate or reciprocate, as in the phrase *vice versa*) and *fungi pro* (as in to take the place of).

Fungible has thus come to refer to anything (especially goods and services) that can be readily replaced with or exchanged for things that are not merely similar but essentially equivalent.

USAGE: Strictly speaking, fungible does not admit matters of degree. If something is fungible, it should be replaceable with no additional benefit or deficit, period. In other words, the swap should be clean with no remainder. Cash denominated in bills or coins have traditionally played such a role, but so have other commodities as well. Thus gold and oil are fungible commodities.

Nonetheless, it seems that the usage of fungible can be extended to admit degrees. For instance, the more indispensable someone is, the less fungible they are. Thus some might argue that Steve Jobs was for Apple less fungible than Bill Gates for Microsoft.

57. Glass Ceiling

DEFINITION: The "glass ceiling" is a metaphor used by progressive economists, sociologists, politicians, and others to explain the fact that the higher up a corporate hierarchy one looks, the fewer the number of women one finds.

USAGE: While there are many more female CEOs and other high-level corporate officers today (2022) than there were in the past, it still remains the case that men far outnumber women at the top of the corporate pyramid.

The question is, Why?

The concept of the glass ceiling was invented to explain this empirical fact.

Progressives believe the answer to this question is the lingering presence of male chauvinism, patriarchal attitudes, and "good-old-boy" networks.

On this theory, then, female employees with similar educational backgrounds and experience to their male peers fail to be promoted in proportion to their numbers in an organizational structure for the simple reason that misogyny, or anti-woman prejudice, still exists.

However, it is not necessarily part of this analysis that this form of prejudice is conscious (though it may be). Rather, the claim is that the capitalist system within which commercial institutions are embedded is systematically structured by patriarchy, conceived of as a set of practices.

In summary, the concept of the glass ceiling maintains that the lack of women in corner suites may be explained by systematic anti-woman prejudice. In the twentieth-first century, this type of prejudice is no longer out in the open—whence the metaphor of a ceiling that is invisible to the naked eye—but it is nonetheless very real, indeed effectively impenetrable.

In other words, women in the contemporary business world are allowed to rise so high in the corporate hierarchy, but no higher.

Conservative critics point to alternative explanations of the empirical facts.

Among these explanations are the greater proportion of women, in comparison with men, who:

- give up their career to raise their family
- refuse to put in the regular 80-hour weeks their male peers do
- are less aggressive than men and less comfortable pushing themselves forward

58. Globalization

DEFINITION: The term "globalization" refers to the flow of trade of all kinds—economic goods and services, jobs, financial products, information, technology, and cultural images, ideas, and practices—far beyond national borders, eventually extending to the entire world.

In economic terms, "globalization" describes the growing interdependence of nations around the globe that is resulting from the afore-mentioned kinds of trade.

ETYMOLOGY: The verb "globalization" was coined about 1960 by the Harvard economist Theodore Levitt. However, the related verb "to globalize" is attested from some 15 year earlier.

Both "to globalize" and "globalization" derive, of course, from the English noun "globe," which is attested from the fifteenth century.

"Globe" derives, via Middle English, from Middle French *globe,* with the same meaning, which, in turn, derives from Latin *globus, globi,*meaning "ball," "sphere," or "globe."

USAGE: Globalization provides international corporations with a robust competitive edge, enabling them to reduce operational expenses by a variety of different means, including outsourcing production overseas, skirting tariffs to procure cheaper raw materials, and gaining entrée to large new markets composed of millions of previously inaccessible consumers.

Globalization comprises many different aspects, including legal, political, social, and cultural dimensions:

- In the realm of *law,* globalization has brought about changes in the enactment and enforcement of international legal norms
- With respect to *politics,* globalization has focused attention on the role of intergovernmental organizations, such as the World Trade Organization (WTO) and the United Nations (UN)
- In regard to *society,* globalization has fostered increased migration and other forms of interaction among diverse populations hailing originally from many different countries

- On the level of *culture*, globalization has contributed to the proliferation of ideas, values, and artistic expression across political and ethnic boundaries and spheres of influence. Moreover, globalization represents, for better or worse, the emergence of an increasingly unified global culture.

Some will contemplate these trends with satisfaction, others with alarm. But both sides in the "culture wars" will be obliged to acknowledge that these effects of globalization are real, they are consequential, and they are likely to endure.

In a sense, globalization is not a recent phenomenon. In Antiquity, traders embarked on long journeys to obtain scarce and valuable goods, which they would then sell when they returned home.

The Industrial Revolution of the eighteenth and nineteenth centuries introduced vast improvements in transportation and communications, which facilitated international trade.

Globalization in the modern sense began to take off in earnest during the 1990s, notably, with the signing of the North American Free Trade Agreement (NAFTA) in 1993. One notable outcome of NAFTA was that American auto manufacturers began to shift many of their production facilities to Mexico, to save money on labor costs. This trend has greatly expanded over the intervening 30 years.

Globalization fosters new employment opportunities and economic expansion through the international movement of goods, capital, and labor. However, it also has at least two major drawbacks.

For one thing, while each factory that moves abroad to take advantage of low-cost labor brings with it real economic opportunities to the foreign community that welcomes it, those opportunities are not evenly distributed among the various nations of the world.

The same thing is true for particular sectors in specific nations. For example, the textile industry in the United States or corn farming in Mexico, have experienced significant disruption or even complete collapse due to the heightened competition flowing from NAFTA.

For another thing, every factory that relocates abroad leaves behind it in its former country a community that is economically devastated.

In addition to globalization's obvious practical advantages, the public discussion surrounding the phenomenon includes no small amount of idealistic rhetoric. Yet, the establishment of a global free market has primarily favored major corporations headquartered in Western countries.

Thus, globalization's effects present a complex picture for workers, small businesses, and communities worldwide, spanning developed and emerging nations alike.

Pros and Cons of Globalization

Pros

- An enlarged market for goods and services
- Lower consumer prices

- Outsourcing, which may benefit both domestic firms and foreign labor
- A rising standard of living in the foreign country

Cons

- Many developing countries may be left out
- Homogenization of cultures and consumer products around the world
- Concentration of wealth
- Devastation of communities in the international company's original home country

59. Goodwill

DEFINITION: As the term is used in the context of business and economics, "goodwill" is an *intangible* asset of a company.

More specifically, goodwill is a type of value consisting of such nonphysical but economically significant things as a company's name, brand, customer base, and reputation for the excellence of its products, customer service, employee relations, and proprietary technology, among others.

Goodwill may also be given a more exact, technical definition, suitable for use in mathematical calculations.

Namely, within the context of the acquisition of one company by another one, goodwill may be defined as the economic value obtained by the acquiring company, defined as the excess portion of the purchase price over the value of the acquired assets less the liabilities assumed during the acquisition.

Thus, the concept of goodwill explains why such a value (price) in excess of the acquired net assets exists at all. That is, obtaining goodwill is the reason why one company may pay a premium to acquire another.

ETYMOLOGY: The English word "goodwill" is attested from the eleventh century. However, its use in the economic sense discussed here is of much more recent vintage.

The term is of course made up of the two component words, "good" and "will."

The word "good" derives, via Middle English, from the Old English word *gōd* ("good"), which is akin to the Old High German *guot,* also meaning "good."

The word "will" derives, via Middle English, from the Old English word *willa,* meaning, in the relevant sense, "disposition" or "inclination."

USAGE: While goodwill exists independently of any particular economic transaction, it is commonly most commercially relevant during the process of acquisition.

The goodwill possessed by the acquired company is revealed, as it were, by the purchase price, or, more specifically, by the portion of the purchase price that is in excess of the net market value of the assets, as already explained.

In this way, the rather abstract notion of goodwill may be ascribed a precise economic value.

When the acquiring company pays less than the acquired company's book value, it is said to obtain negative goodwill, meaning that the purchase was made at a discounted price.

On the acquiring company's **balance sheet**, goodwill is documented as an intangible asset, categorized under the long-term assets account.

Goodwill is classified as an intangible (or non-current) asset because it lacks physical form, unlike tangible assets like equipment and buildings.

According to generally accepted accounting principles (GAAP) and International Financial Reporting Standards (IFRS), companies must assess the value of goodwill in their financial statements at least annually, acknowledging any impairments to their goodwill relative to the past.

Calculating goodwill is relatively straightforward in theory but can be difficult in practice.

To calculate goodwill using a simple formula, one should deduct the fair market value of the acquired company's net assets from the purchase price, to wit:

$$Goodwill = P - (A - L)$$

where:
P = Purchase price of the acquired company
A = Fair market value of assets
L = Fair market value of liabilities

While this formula makes the calculation of goodwill appear very simple, difficulties may arise because goodwill may involve estimating future cash flows and other uncertain or unknown quantities.

While these problems may not be very serious in most cases, they may become significant for certain purposes—for instance, when accountants need to compare the reported assets or net income of an acquired company to those of a company that has never been acquired.

60. Greater Fool Theory

DEFINITION: The expression "greater fool theory" is used to explain the market success of a good (often a corporate share or other form of investment) that ought not to be economically successful, given the underlying fundamentals.

In a nutshell, the greater fool theory hypothesizes the following:

> Though it was foolish of *X* to buy a given good in the first place, the price is still going up because there are even *greater fools* than X present in the market who are prepared to buy it at an even higher price.

USAGE: The expression "greater fool theory" was made famous in 2022 by **Bill Gates**, when he appealed to it to explain what he considered to be the irrational market success of **non-fungible tokens** (NFTs).

To invoke the greater fool theory is, in effect, to predict that the good in question is undergoing a **bubble**, which must burst, sooner or later.

Unfortunately, it is not possible to distinguish between bubbles (bad investments) and price increases driven by ordinary market forces of supply and demand (good investments) before the fact.

Therefore, the greater fool theory is simply the expression of a commentator's opinion until it becomes apparent that the price increase really did represent a bubble—which can only be determined in hindsight, after the bubble has burst.

In this *ex post facto* situation, the greater fool theory may have some limited utility in explaining how the bubble was possible. However, even in this situation the theory must be considered together with other theories, such as the "bandwagon effect."

For further discussion, see the Glossary article on **Ponzi schemes**.

61. Gross National Product (GNP)

DEFINITION: The phrase "gross national product" (GNP) refers to the total value of all the products and services produced by a particular country over a specified period of time.

To calculate a country's GNP, one first calculates the estimated sum of all the country's personal consumption and governmental expenditures, private domestic investment, net exports, and income earned by residents from foreign investments.

(Note that "net exports" refers to the value of a country's exports of goods and services less the value of its imports.)

Next, one subtracts from this number the income earned by foreign residents. This number is the GNP.

ETYMOLOGY: The phrase "gross national product" was introduced in 1949.

In its economic sense, the English word "gross" means the economic value of something, such as the price of a good or service, or an income, that does not take account of the costs involved in generating the said good, service, or income. The figure obtained by subtracting such costs from the original value is called the "net" amount. In the sense of the contrary of "net," "gross" is attested from the late sixteenth century.

The English adjective "gross" itself derives, via Middle English, from Middle French *gros* and, ultimately, Latin *grossus,* meaning "obvious," "big," or "bulky."

The English adjective "national" is attested from around 1600. The associated noun "nation" is derived from Middle English *nacioun,*Middle French *nation,* and, ultimately, Latin *nātio, nātionis* ("birth," "race," "nation"), which in turn is derived from the past participle *nātus* of the deponent verb *nascor, nasci,* meaning "to be born."

The English noun "product" is attested from the fifteenth century. In the general sense (as opposed to the mathematical sense), it derives directly from the past participle *prōductum* of the Latin verb *prōdūco, prōdūcere,* meaning "to bring forward," "to advance," "to promote," or "to produce."

USAGE: The concept of the GNP is closely connected to another crucial economic measure known as the "gross domestic product" (GDP), which considers all output produced within a country's borders, regardless of the ownership of the means of production.

GNP differs from the GDP by adding residents' investment income from overseas investments and deducting foreign residents' investment income earned within the country.

The GNP metric aims to quantify the overall monetary value of the output produced by a country's residents. For this reason, it begins with the value of the GDP—that is, all the output produced within the country's borders.

Then, it adds the value of any output generated outside the country's borders by individuals residing inside its borders and subtracts any output generated inside the country's borders by individuals residing outside its borders. The resulting figure is the country's GNP.

It is important to note that, to prevent double counting, the calculation of the GNP excludes the value of intermediate goods and services, because their value is already included in the calculation of final goods and services.

Until 1991, the US relied upon the GNP as its primary indicator of economic activity. After that date, it used the GDP figure.

Why did it make this switch? For two main reasons:

First, the GDP metric dovetails better with other US economic data relevant to policymakers, such as indices of (un)employment and industrial production. For these purposes, the GDP concept is a superior indicator because it measures all productive activities within the US, apart from the place of residence of the economic actors.

Second, the shift from the GNP metric to the GDP was made to facilitate international comparisons, since at the time most other countries employed the GDP concept.

62. Headhunter

DEFINTION: "Headhunter" is a colloquial term for a human-resource or other business management professional who specializes in recruiting highly qualified candidates for executive and other senior-level positions (such as, for example, president, vice-president, chief executive officer, or chief financial officer) in the public, private, and not-for-profit sectors.

ETYMOLOGY: The term "headhunter" is a humorous allusion to the practice of certain indigenous tribal societies of taking their slain enemies' heads as trophies of war.

USAGE: Headhunters may work for a larger organization, such as an executive search firm or other consulting firm, or else they may work as an independent consultant.

Filling the role of a headhunter may involve the exercise of a variety of skills, notably researching the availability of executives presently working for competitor organizations —a polite way of saying "industrial espionage."

Once a headhunter has identified a list of highly qualified candidates who appear to fulfill the client's requirements, the headhunter himself or the executive search firm that employs him may act as a go-between, contacting the candidates to gauge their interest in leaving their current position to move to a new employer.

Headhunters may also conduct initial interviews in order to screen the candidates to eliminate all but a small number of the best ones. Once a small pool of the best candidates has been identified, their names may be passed on to the customer.

Occasionally, the headhunter or his company may enter into direct negotiations with candidates relating to such things as compensation and benefits.

Once negotiations have been successfully concluded and both parties—the employer and the candidate—have signed off on an agreement, the headhunter may then prepare the employment contract.

The headhunter model of specialized executive search has been extremely popular—to the point where it has begun to expand into other economic sectors and to be applied to less-senior positions.

63. Hedge Fund

DEFINITION: The phrase "hedge fund" refers to a kind of investment fund whose chief characteristic is that investors in the fund accept a higher-than-average level of risk to their principal in exchange for the possibility of obtaining a greater-than-average return.

Legally, a hedge fund takes the form of a limited partnership of private investors who pool their investments and hire skilled professionals to manage the fund on their behalf.

ETYMOLOGY: The phrase "hedge fund" was coined in 1967.

The English noun "hedge," meaning a boundary, fence, or barrier consisting of shrubs, bushes, or low trees, derives from Middle English *hegge* and Old English *hecg.*

The English noun "fund," which is attested from the late seventeenth century, is derived from the Latin noun *fundus,* meaning "bottom," "bottom land," or simply "piece of property."

The phrase "hedge fund" is counterintuitive, seeing that "to hedge" means to limit one's risk, whereas hedge funds are riskier than other types of investments. How can we account for this anomaly?

Ther answer is that when hedge funds were first introduced, in the late 1960s, they were primarily used to "**short**" the market, hence acting at that time as a genuine "hedge" against market declines.

Over the past 50 years, the nature of the risk associated with hedge funds has changed dramatically, but their name has remained the same.

USAGE: Hedge fund managers employ diverse strategies, such as leveraging or trading unconventional assets, constructing complex portfolios, dealing in derivatives such as options and futures, and shorting the market, to name a few, with a view to achieving returns that exceed the market average.

Since hedge funds bear a relatively high risk, certain restrictions are often imposed on prospective investors. For instance, there is often a high minimum investment requirement for participating in a hedge fund or even a minimum net worth requirement that must be met.

Affluent investors are, of course, primarily attracted to hedge funds by the prospect of increasing their capital gains. However, another allure of the best-known and most prestigious hedge funds lies in a kind of mystique cultivated by their managers. From a sociological perspective, the high-rolling world of hedge funds may be said to function much like an exclusive club.

Individual investors in hedge funds must typically be "accredited investors," meaning that they satisfy a minimum income requirement.

In addition, many hedge funds are composed of institutional investors, notably, insurance companies and pension funds.

Hedge fund investments are considered "illiquid," since investors are often required to commit their funds for a minimum period of one year, known as the "lock-up period."

Even after the lock-in period has expired, withdrawals may be limited to specific intervals, such as quarterly or semi-annually.

Hedge fund managers focus on specific investments and portfolios of securities with the potential for highly profitable returns.

Different hedge fund managers may pursue different types of strategies. The following are four different kinds of hedge funds that one might commonly encounter:

- ***Global macro hedge funds:*** Actively managing investments with the goal of taking advantage of significant market movements triggered by economic or political events around the world.
- ***Equity hedge funds:*** Either global or country-specific investing in profitable stocks, which also seeks to counteract market downturns by shorting overvalued stocks or stock indices.
- ***Relative value hedge funds:*** Attempts to profit from temporary price or spread inefficiencies in related securities.
- ***Activist hedge funds:*** Investing in businesses and taking other actions that enhance the stock price. This may involve making demands for cost-cutting measures, asset restructuring, or changes in the board of directors.

64. Horizontal Integration

DEFINITION: The phrase "horizontal integration" refers to the acquisition of a company within the same industry in the same country.

In other words, in the case of horizontal integration—as opposed to **vertical integration**—the acquiring company and the company acquired are both in the same line of business.

ETYMOLOGY: The phrase "vertical integration" was probably coined around the turn of the twentieth century. The practice was made famous by the consolidation of the petroleum production industry by **John D. Rockefeller, Sr.**

The English adjective "horizontal" is attested from the mid-sixteenth century. It is formed from the noun "horizon," which derives, via Middle English *orizon,* from Late Latin *horizon,* which, in turn, derives from the Greek past participle *horizōn, horizontos,* meaning "boundary," of the verb *horizō, horizein,* meaning "to divide." The latter verb is formed from the noun *horos, horou,* meaning "boundary," "limit," or "border."

The English noun "integration" is attested from the early seventeenth century. It is formed from the verb "to Integrate," which is derived from the Latin past participle *integrates* of the verb *integro, integrare,*meaning "to make whole."

USAGE: Horizontal integration is a competitive strategy whose primary purpose is to create economies of scale.

Consolidation makes it possible for a company composed of two formerly independent businesses to generate greater revenues than the two companies could have generated by operating independently.

Horizontal integration enhances a company's market influence over both suppliers and distributors, which stimulates product differentiation and market expansion, or entry into new markets.

On the other hand, horizontal integration may hurt consumers, particularly if the consolidation results in reduced competition. For this reason, regulators subject horizontal mergers to intense scrutiny to determine if they infringe antitrust laws.

The principal motivation for horizontal mergers is company-owners' desire to reduce the competition they face. This may derive from existing competitors, from competition from potential newcomers to the market, or from competition from businesses offering alternative or substitute products.

For the most part, horizontal integration takes one of three fundamental forms: acquisition, merger, or internal expansion.

Acquisition

An acquisition occurs when one company assumes full control over another company's operations. While the two companies combine to create a new entity, the acquiring company maintains dominance.

In most cases, the acquiring company keeps its own executives, staff, and operational structure, while the acquired company's executives and staff are often laid off, and its assets placed under the control of the acquiring company's management.

Companies frequently embark upon acquisitions with a particular purpose in mind. For example, when Microsoft acquired Activision Blizzard in January of 2022, it had a precise goal in mind, namely, that of bolstering its position in the video game industry.

Merger

In a merger, two distinct and more-or-less equal companies come together to form a new, unified organization. Either a new brand name may be created or the brand of one of the pre-existing companies may be used for the new, combined entity. Usually, operations and personnel are retained from both entities and integrated together.

Moreover, both companies' product lines are often similar and equally competitive within a particular market. Thus, in a merger, both companies are basically seeking to expand their market share.

For these reasons, most mergers involve firms that are able to integrate their similar operations in a relatively smooth fashion.

Internal Expansion

Companies may also engage in horizontal integration by shifting its focus, redirecting its resources, and reallocating internal capital expenditures toward a new goal.

For example, a candy manufacturer might decide to diversify into the production of bottled drinks, or a grocery store might choose to broaden its services to include a café or a buffet.

In these and similar instances, a company maintains its existing mode of operations. However, instead of investing its capital to acquire or merge with an external company, it opts to reallocate those resources internally for such things as staff retraining, equipment purchase, and capital investments designed to support the new line of business.

65. Housing Bubble

DEFINITION: A "housing bubble," also known as a "real estate bubble," occurs when the housing stock of a region or country undergoes a rapid and ultimately unsustainable increase in prices.

Housing bubbles are one form of a more general phenomenon: asset price bubbles. They are price bubbles in a market in which the asset being traded is housing stock and real estate. Like other kinds of asset price bubbles, housing bubbles may occur for a variety of reasons.

Bubbles in the housing market often begin with a surge in demand. The supply of housing stock, by its very nature, cannot be increased very quickly to meet this increased demand; hence, prices will inevitably rise.

If the housing market were functioning properly, this would not be a problem. The rise in prices would stimulate investment in the construction of new housing, and as new homes are built, over time prices would fall back towards the preexisting level, without collapsing through the floor.

Housing bubbles, then, are due primarily to forces that distort this normal functioning of the market.

ETYMOLOGY: The use of the term "bubble" in the economic sense is first attested from the early eighteenth century, more specifically in connection with the British South Sea Bubble of 1720. It is uncertain when the concept was first applied to the real estate market.

The English abstract noun "housing" is attested from the fourteenth century. It derives, of course, from the concrete noun "house," which in turn derives from Middle English *hous* and Old English *hūs*, both meaning "house." The Old English form is identical to the same word in Old High German.

The English noun "bubble" is attested from the fourteenth century. It derives from Middle English *bobel.*

USAGE: Housing bubbles may arise for many reasons, but generally speaking they occur mainly due to either government interference in the operation of the free market or else the "irrational exuberance" (in the famous words of longtime Federal Reserve Chairman **Alan Greenspan**) of investors, who get caught up in the outsized and apparently never-ending profits to be made by speculating in the housing market.

Real estate speculators may even be well aware that they are involved in a potentially dangerous bubble. But it appears to be a feature of human nature to believe that we ourselves can safely navigate the risks we know lead other people to ruin.

And, besides, the thought of getting out while the getting is good, which means forgoing an unknowable quantity of easy profits, is unendurable for many speculators. Leaving easy money on the table appears to require a nearly inhuman degree of self-discipline.

Sooner or later, though, the bubble must burst. And by the time prices start to crash, it may be too late to unload one's holdings, leading to financial catastrophe.

The other major factor which often helps to generate housing bubbles is government interference in the marketplace.

For example, the US government contributed to the 2008 real estate crash and subsequent cascading financial crisis by pressuring the management of the public-private mortgage lenders, Fannie Mae and Freddie Mac, as well as purely private lenders, to drastically loosen the criteria for qualifying for a home mortgage.

This policy not only fueled a massive spending spree, driving up home prices, it also led to a tsunami of defaults on those easy-to-get loans by individuals who lacked the financial wherewithal to service the debt they had taken on.

Defaults on home mortgages were followed in short order by waves of foreclosures.

Moreover, these foreclosures left many banks and other lending institutions—including some of the largest and most prestigious in the country—holding large numbers of worthless loans on their books.

This was so, in part, because the properties that the banks acquired through foreclosure were themselves worthless, since the real estate market had collapsed.

All of this led to a second tsunami of bank failures and, ultimately, to the politically unpopular expedient of government "bailouts" of companies deemed "too big to fail."

The social consequences of a housing bubble may be far-reaching, affecting individuals belonging to diverse socioeconomic classes, reaching across many different regions, cities, and neighborhoods, and undermining the broader economy of a society.

Housing bubbles can compel people to explore various means of meeting their monthly mortgage payments or of paying off their mortgages entirely. Unfortunately, many end up dipping into their retirement accounts or other savings to stay afloat financially.

As a result, housing bubbles have been a major factor behind the significant decrease in the amount of money set aside in savings by the average American household over the past several decades.

With the passage of time, this trend will end up causing significant financial hardships for many. For this reason, if for no other, housing bubbles ought to be a topic of general concern.

66. Hyperinflation

DEFINITION: Hyperinflation is a very high and/or rapidly increasing rate of inflation.

ETYMOLOGY: “Hyperinflation” is derived from the Greek “*huper,*” meaning “over,” “beyond,” or “exceeding,” + the Latin “*flāre,*” meaning “to blow.”

USAGE: While there is no formal quantitative definition of “hyperinflation” that applies to all times and places, the phenomenon is a lot like pornography—one knows it when one sees it. It is basically inflation that is running out of control.

Under what conditions does hyperinflation occur?

While ordinary inflation has been observed historically in a great variety of times and places, hyperinflation is basically a phenomenon of the twentieth and twenty-first centuries.

Why is that?

One reason is that modern economies have become detached from any commodity store of value, such as silver or gold. Such untethered currencies are known as “*fiat*” currencies, because their value wholly resides in governmental stipulation and the trust placed in those governments by their citizens.

Fiat currencies permit modern governments to evade the financial discipline imposed by the gold standard. While all governments have a natural desire to spend money they do not have, only governments with *fiat* currencies can readily do so without immediately causing the devaluation of their currency.

While *fiat* currencies are a necessary condition for hyperinflation, they are not a necessary one. More often, they merely lead to garden-variety inflation—which eventually causes populations to rebel and governments to return to financial discipline.

For hyperinflation to occur, another factor is required. That factor is social and political chaos.

All of the principal cases of hyperinflation have taken place in countries either devastated by warfare or under the control of an unpopular authoritarian regime.

In such cases, governments may become unwilling or unable to stop the printing presses and return to financial responsibility without unleashing what they perceive to be even worse consequences—their own political demise.

A look at a few of the best-known historical cases will illustrate this point.

Weimar Germany: Between 1920 and 1923, in the aftermath of World War I, Germany experienced what is probably the most-famous case of hyperinflation in history. At its peak, November 1923, the monthly inflation rate reached nearly 30-thousand percent. The highest denomination of the currency released by the government during this episode was the 100-trillion-Mark note. Note that "billionen" in German means "trillion" in English.

Hungary: Though the case of Weimar Germany is more famous, the highest-recorded case of hyperinflation occurred in Hungary in 1945–1946, in the aftermath of World War II. In that case, the peak monthly inflation rate, in July 1946, reached an astounding 42-quadrillion (42×10^{15}) percent. The highest-denominated currency was the 100-quintillion (10×10^{20})-pengő note. This is the highest denomination of banknote ever issued, worth 10^{20} or 100 quintillion Hungarian pengő.

Zimbabwe: During 2004–2008, Zimbabwe experienced crushing hyperinflation, basically due to the authoritarian character of the government of **Robert Mugabe.** The peak monthly inflation rate, which occurred in November 2008, was approximately 80 billion percent. The highest denomination of the currency was the 100-trillion-Zimbabwean-dollar note.

Venezuela: The most recent well-known instance of hyperinflation occurred in Venezuela between 2016 and 2018. The statistics for this case are difficult to verify because of international political factors (the government of socialist autocrat **Nicolás Maduro** is backed by China). But we may safely say that at its peak, in April 2018, the monthly inflation rate reached at least 234 percent. The highest-denominated currency was the 500-million-Venezuelan-bolívar banknote.

67. Income Statement

DEFINITION: An *income statement* (also known as a *profit and loss statement*) summarizes the revenues, costs, and expenses incurred by a company during the course of its ordinary operations over a given period of time.

As the name implies, an income statement shows the total net profit or loss a company has incurred over the time period in question.

As such, it is perhaps the single most valuable type of financial statement.

68. Indemnity

DEFINITION: The term "indemnity" refers to an extensive type of insurance coverage designed to protect against certain types of damages. In a business context, "indemnity" is primarily associated with financial losses, while in a legal context, it mainly pertains to liability.

Indemnity is a contract (called a "policy") involving two parties, where one party (the "insurer") commits to cover potential damages incurred by the other party ("the policyholder" or "the insured"). In return, the policyholder commits to pay premiums to the insurer according to a fixed schedule.

In an indemnity arrangement, the insurer essentially guarantees to fully compensate the policyholder—ensuring that the individual or business is made whole—in case the latter incurs damages covered by the policy.

ETYMOLOGY: The term "indemnity" is attested from the fifteenth century.

The English noun "Indemnity," and the related verb "indemnify," are constructed from the Latin adjective *indemnis,* meaning "undamaged," "unhurt," or "uninjured." *Indemnis* is composed of the preposition *in-*, here a privative prefix, and the noun *damnum,*meaning "loss," "damage," "injury, or "harm."

USAGE: Most insurance policies include an indemnity clause, but the type and amount of coverage it provides may, depending upon the type of policy and its terms.

In any indemnity agreement, there is a defined period of indemnity during which the payment is effective. Likewise, numerous policies incorporate a letter of indemnity, ensuring compliance with the contract terms by both parties, failing which an indemnity obligation goes into effect.

Indemnity clauses are found especially in policies involving both individuals and businesses, such as contracts for obtaining car insurance. However, such policies may also be extended to other circumstances, encompassing, for example, relationships between businesses and governments, or even among the governments of several countries.

Occasionally, local governments, businesses, or entire industries find themselves shouldering a portion of the financial burden of significant public concerns, such as natural disasters or disease outbreaks. In such cases, the federal government may provide "indemnity" (or "indemnification") to such financially stressed entities, not on the strength of a legal contract, but under the moral pressure of public opinion.

For example, during the devastating bird flu epidemic that ravaged the US poultry industry in 2014 and 2015, the Department of Agriculture paid out $200 million to indemnify farmers who had to cull their flocks to halt the virus's transmission.

69. Index Fund

DEFINITION: An index fund is an investment fund whose portfolio is designed to rise and fall with the stock market as a whole.

Whether taking the form of a mutual fund or an exchange-traded fund (ETF), an index fund attempts so far as possible to mirror the composition of a specific financial market index, such as the Standard & Poor's 500 Index (S&P 500).

The primary objective of an index fund is to offer its investors broad exposure to the overall market, while requiring minimal intervention and thus operating expense.

By design, index funds always closely follow their benchmark index, regardless of current market conditions.

Index funds represent a form of passive investing, as opposed to the active investing pursued by portfolio managers that is characteristic of ordinary mutual funds.

ETYMOLOGY: The intellectual origins of the concept of an index fundextend to around 1960, when University of Chicago graduate students Edward Renshaw and Paul Feldstein published a paper exploring the idea in depth.[1] However, the concept was first put into practice and promoted by **John C. Bogle** beginning around 1975.

The English noun "index" is attested from the sixteenth century. It derives from the Latin noun *index, indicis,* meaning "informer" or "indicator." The noun, in turn, is derived from the verb *indico, indicare,*"to make known," "to show," "to indicate."

The English noun "fund" is attested from the seventeenth century. It derives from the Latin noun *fundus*, meaning "bottom" and, by extension, "bottom land," "ground," "soil," "estate," or, simply, "piece of property."

USAGE: Index funds are generally held to be excellent assets for retirement accounts, including individual retirement accounts (IRAs) and 401(k) accounts.

Many highly regarded experts, including Warren Buffett, endorse index funds as a safe and solid basis for saving following retirement.

For the average retired investor lacking special financial expertise, it makes sense to take advantage of the convenience of purchasing all the companies in the S&P 500 through an index fund, as opposed to selecting individual stocks.

---

[1] Edward F. Renshaw and Paul J. Feldstein, "The Case for an Unmanaged Investment Company," *Financial Analysis Journal*, 1960, **16**: 43–46.

Buffett points out that for such investors, index funds represent a low-cost way of obtaining the security that comes with diversification.

Almost every financial market boasts an index—and with it, an index fund.

In the United States, the S&P 500 is the most popular index, which is why the index funds that track it are also the most popular.

Nonetheless, there are numerous other widely followed indexes, notably, the following:

- *Wilshire 5000 Total Market Index:* the largest US equities index
- *MSCI EAFE Index:* made up of foreign stocks from Europe, Australasia, and the Far East
- *Bloomberg US Aggregate Bond Index:* comprehensively tracks the total bond market
- *Nasdaq Composite Index:* consists of 3,000 stocks listed on the Nasdaq exchange
- *Dow Jones Industrial Average (DJIA):* comprises 30 large-cap companies

For instance, an index fund that tracks the DJIA would invest in exactly the same 30 large, publicly owned companies that constitute that index.

Index fund portfolios experience significant changes only when their benchmark indexes undergo significant movements, whether up or down.

In the case of a weighted index, fund managers may rebalance the proportions of different securities from time to time to match changes in the corresponding weights in the index serving as the standard or benchmark. (Weighting is a method of equalizing the impact of individual holdings within a portfolio.)

One significant advantage of index funds is a lower management expense ratio. Generally speaking, a mutual fund's expense ratio—encompassing various operating costs such as advisor and manager fees, transaction costs, taxes, and accounting fees—is far lower in the case of index funds.

Since index fund managers seek to replicate the performance of a benchmark index, they do not need to employ research analysts and other professionals involved in the stock-selection process. For this reason, index fund managers are involved in fewer trades, resulting in lower transaction fees and commissions.

In contrast, actively managed funds must maintain larger staffs and conduct more frequent transactions, all of which leads to higher operational costs.

70. Industrial Revolution

DEFINITION: The "Industrial Revolution" was the transformation in human productive capacity—beginning in the eighteenth century, initially in England, then spreading to Europe and North America—thanks to the invention of many new types of manufacturing machinery.

As a result of the Industrial Revolution, the general prosperity of Western populations increased exponentially.

ETYMOLOGY: The adjective "industrial," and the related noun "industry," derive, via Middle English and Middle French, from the classical Latin noun *industria, industriae,* meaning "diligence."

The word "revolution" derives, via Middle English, Middle French, and Late Latin, from the classical Latin verb *revolvo, revolvere,* meaning "to roll backwards," "to unroll," "to come around again," or "to return."

USAGE: The Industrial Revolution was based on technological innovation, notably, the development of various types of steam engines over the course of the eighteenth century.

The earliest steam engines were used to pump water out of mines. However, they were rapidly put to a wide variety of other uses, above all, the automation of the spinning of yarn and the weaving of cloth.

By the early nineteenth century, steam had been harnessed to power ocean-going ships and locomotives. By century's end, the first internal combustion engines using petroleum-based fuels were being developed.

It is sometimes theorized as the so-called "first industrial revolution," based on steam power, in contrast to the "second industrial revolution," based on electrical power generation, and the "third industrial revolution," based on computer and information technology.

However, it is perhaps more useful to think of the Industrial Revolution against the background of the longer arc of human history as a whole.

From this point of view, the first great revolution in human life occurred around 8000 BC, with the invention of agriculture and the settled way of life.

Despite the development of many singular inventions during the millennia which followed—including the widespread use of simple machines such as wedges, levers, pulleys, and screws; horse harnesses; sailing ships; the harnessing of wind- and water-power with mills; and many more—in its essentials the economic foundation of human life changed very little until the eighteenth century.

From this perspective, the Industrial Revolution appears to be a much more singular phenomenon, now nearly 300 years old and still gathering steam (no pun intended). The point can perhaps be made most vividly through statistics.

For the 400-year period from roughly 1300 until 1700—for which economic data are reasonably reliable—the curve of a graph showing per capita GDP in England would be relatively flat. There was little or no growth in average wealth during that time.

Then, around 1700, the curve begins a gentle upward climb, such that over the next 200 years, by 1900, the figure for per capita GDP doubled.

Finally, over the course of the twentieth century, the upward slope of the curve became much steeper, such that by roughly the year 2000, the per capita GDP had undergone a *fivefold* increase.

In other words, the average inhabitant of a modern industrialized country such as the UK or the US was *ten times* richer in the year 2000 than his counterpart just 300 years earlier.

In fact, for the most part, even the relatively poorest members of a modern industrialized society live a life of material abundance that would have been unimaginable to the most affluent Englishmen prior to the Industrial Revolution.

In the past several decades, we might add, the curve representing change in per capital GDP over time has become nearly vertical.

In short, the Industrial Revolution created the world we all inhabit, and the pace of the continuous enrichment we all owe to it goes on accelerating, with no end in sight (yet).

71. Inflation

DEFINITION: Inflation denotes an increase in the amount of money (nominal price) that must on average be paid for goods. It's not inflation if Walmart raises the cost of some particular item, thereby increasing its nominal price. It is inflation if all stores taken together increase prices on all goods. The opposite of inflation is deflation.

Inflation occurs when the money supply increases more rapidly than the supply of goods and services offered within an extended market system—nowadays, usually a nation state. In that case, the nominal price of available goods and services will increase ("inflate") over time until the gap is closed. This means that the purchasing power of each unit of currency decreases.

Inflation and deflation therefore occur when a disequilibrium exists within an extended market system between the aggregate supply of goods and services and the aggregate money supply available to purchase those goods and services.

Note that an increase in nominal prices implies a decrease in the purchasing power of each unit of currency. In other words, when prices go up, your money does not go as far and thus holds less real value.

ETYMOLOGY: "Inflation" is derived from the Latin "*in*," meaning "in" or "into," + "*flāre,*" meaning "to blow."

USAGE: Inflation may appear to be a relatively simple phenomenon. However, the causes of inflation can take different forms and may be quite complex.

In any extended market system, prices are always fluctuating, depending on various factors affecting supply and demand in a random way. When such factors are no longer random, but begin to act in concert in the manner described above, then inflation will likely result.

Throughout recorded history, inflation has been noticed and its causes discussed. One of the forms in which inflation was most often encountered before the modern period was through adulteration of the coinage.

That is, the value of the coins in circulation in ancient and medieval societies was tied to specified weights of some precious metal (usually gold or silver). In that case, adding some other metal (i.e., creating an alloy) during the minting process was tantamount to spreading a given weight of precious metal over more coins.

This, of course, reduced the amount of the precious metal—which, remember, was considered to be the real store of value—in each coin. Eventually, this practice caused prices to rise and the purchasing power of each debased coin to fall.

Another premodern historical example of inflation occurred in Spain during the sixteenth century, as silver and gold began to pour into the country from the newly conquered “Indies” (Central and South America). The Spanish Scholastic thinkers Juan de Mariana and Martín de Azpilcueta (see the article on the Salamanca School) gave the correct explanation for this phenomenon.

Under the circumstances of a growing economy, prices will increase over time unless the money supply keeps pace with that growth in productive output. In modern industrial democracies, it is the central bank’s job to add to the money supply (“print money”) to achieve the goal of maintaining a rough equilibrium between the natural growth in the productive output of the economy and the money supply.

Even so, inflation may occur. When it does, it may be for either (or both) of two distinct reasons.

First, external factors in the cost of production or the transportation of goods may lead producers to increase their prices. This is known as “cost-push” inflation.

Second, if central governments print too much money, usually to meet obligations incurred for political reasons, then there will be “too much currency chasing too few goods and services,” causing the price of the latter to increase until the gap between the supply and the demand is closed. This is called “demand-pull” inflation.

Inflation has been called the “unfairest tax” because rising prices for essential commodities naturally hit the poorest segment of the population the hardest.

72. Insider Trading

DEFINITION: The phrase "insider trading" refers to the practice of buying or selling corporate stocks, or other publicly traded securities, based on private information about the economic status of the corporation in question or pending government legislation or regulation.

"Private information," in this context, means information obtained by virtue of one's own position within a corporation or the government, or else through one's connections with friendly parties who have such positions.

ETYMOLOGY: The word "insider" derives from the Old English preposition *in*, meaning "in," and the Old English noun *sīde*, meaning "side." *Sīde* is also related to the Old High German word *sīde*, with the same meaning.

The nominal form "insider" is attested beginning in 1848.

The word "trading" derives, via Middle English, from the Middle Low German word *trata*, meaning "track" or "course."

The English word "trade" in its modern meaning of "having dealings" or "exchanging goods" is attested from the sixteenth century.

USAGE: The reason why insider trading is considered to be a bad thing is that it is based on an asymmetry of information between one of the economic actors in a marketplace and all the others.

Although some academic economists feel that insider trading ought to be allowed, most ordinary people feel that the practice provides the economic actor in possession of the privately obtained information with an unfair advantage.

That is the basic reason why various sanctions against insider trading have been enacted by different countries at different times over the past half century or so.

It is important to stress that it is not a question of the information's having been *obtained* illegally.

Rather, the point is that anyone who comes into the possession of such information in the ordinary course of his affairs thereby assumes a moral—and, in most jurisdictions today, legal—obligation *not to act* upon it.

When an economic actor ignores this obligation, then in theory he should be subject to the sanctions provided for by law.

However, insider trading is hard to prove, which makes prosecution of the crime difficult and evasion of the legal sanctions easy.

For this reason, the practice continues to thrive. Indeed, thanks to modern communications systems, insider trading flourishes today perhaps more than ever before.

73. Interest

DEFINITION: The term “interest” signifies a payment by a borrower to a lender (or investor or depositor) that is above the principal amount of the original loan.

From the point of view of the lender, interest is profit earned by providing the borrower with the use of the principal amount of money for a fixed period of time.

ETYMOLOGY: The term “interest” derives, via Middle English, Anglo-French, and Medieval Latin, from the Latin verb *intersum, interesse*,meaning “to be between,” “to concern,” or “to be important.”

Thus, in modern parlance, the economic/financial use of the word “interest” is borrowed from the everyday sense in which the “interest” that individuals have in a thing is the concern they have for it, or its importance to them.

Here are some examples of the common-language use:

Q: “What are you main interests?” A: “Victorian novels, classical music.”

Q: “Did you go to the demonstration?” A: “No, I felt it was not in my interest to be seen there.”

USAGE: The concept of “interest” is distinct from several superficially similar concepts.

For example, interest must be distinguished from fees, which are payments for services rendered that have nothing to do with borrowing or lending money.

Interest is also distinct from dividends. Like interest, dividends are paid by corporations to their shareholders. However, dividend payments are not made on the basis of a specific rate agreed upon in advance, but rather as a share of a corporation’s profits.

Thus, a corporation’s dividend payments depend upon its economic performance. Namely, dividends are paid when the company’s revenues exceed its total costs.

Interest payments, in contrast, are typically payable independently of a company’s economic performance.

It is worth quickly reviewing the history of interest.

Christianity and Islam, at certain periods of their history, forbade making a profit on moneylending.

That is, while Christians and Muslims could freely lend money, they could not accept in return any monetary payment above the principal amount lent.

It was for this reason that Jews filled the economic void created by these prohibitions against lending money at interest, which is to say, on a commercial basis.

For this same reason, during the late Middle Ages and the Renaissance, Jewish families organized the first modern-style **banks**in northern Italy, which played an essential role in fueling the growth of capitalism and, eventually, the economic take-off of Western Europe as a whole.

This history highlights the primary economic importance of interest—which is the stimulation of **entrepreneurship** and the financing of new business ventures.

Interest is considered one of the main factors that influence the economic activity of a society. Thus, it is unsurprising that a great many further distinctions and analytical concepts relating to interest have been made by modern economic science.

Here, we will just mention two: **yield** and the **prime rate**.

74. Invisible Hand

DEFINITION: The metaphor of the "invisible hand" represents the totality of the myriad mostly unrecognized and even unknowable economic, technological, environmental, political, and other causal influences affecting the collective behavior of a free market economy.

The invisible hand operates through the individual's pursuit of his own self-interest in circumstances in which he has the freedom to produce and consume as he pleases.

This continual interaction among the countless individual forces affecting market supply and demand is what creates the natural movement of prices and the flow of trade.

Many modern economists believe that the operation of the invisible hand—that is, of the economy under free market conditions with minimal government interference—results in optimal economic performance and in the long run is in the best interest of rich and poor alike.

ETYMOLOGY: The metaphor of the "invisible hand" was introducedin 1776 by the Scottish Enlightenment philosopher Adam Smith in his book, *The Wealth of Nations.*

The English adjective "invisible" is attested from the fourteenth century. The word in identical form derives from Middle English and Middle French, and, ultimately, from the Latin roots *in-*, meaning "non-" or "un-," and *visibilis,* meaning "visible," from in turn derives from the past participle *vīsum*, "seen," from the verb *video, vidēre,* "to see."

The word "hand" derives from Old English via Middle English. The word is akin to Old High German *hant.*

USAGE: Although the phrase "invisible hand" was introduced by Adam Smith in 1776, the basic idea may be traced back to (at least) two preceding works: (1) *Essai sur la Nature du Commerce en Général* [Essay on the Nature of Commerce in General] by the French businessman and banker, Richard Cantillon, composed around 1730 and published after his death in 1755; and (2) earlier still, *The Fable of the Bees* by the Dutch physician, poet, and author, Bernard Mandeville, published in 1714.

The latter book by Mandeville is particularly remarkable for the way in which the author likens the operation of human society to what we would now call the "self-organization" of a beehive.

The concept of the invisible hand is the intellectual foundation of the free-market or *laissez-faire* philosophy of political economy, especially as embodied by the **Austrian school of economics**.

In essence, Austrian economists, libertarians, and "neo-liberals" (those who hard back to the classic, nineteenth-century view) maintain that equilibrium conditions under conditions of the free market will naturally produce the best results for the overall economy, and thus for the common good.

According to this theory, any intervention in the economy on the part of the government will distort this theoretically optimal equilibrium, producing sub-optimal results.

Social and political purposes may dictate that we make a trade-off between optimal economic productivity and some other good (for example, armament production during wartime).

But we must do so with our eyes open and not delude ourselves that we are not forgoing significant economic benefits in pursuing our other goals through government intervention.

The metaphor of the invisible hand encapsulates two essential concepts.

First, every voluntary exchange within a free market generates valuable signals about the supply and demand of goods and services within that free market. In this way, voluntary trades produce far-reaching and generally advantageous consequences.

Second, these benefits outweigh those of a heavily regulated, planned, or "command" economy.

The signals about supply and demand generated by voluntary exchange within a free market become manifested through the price system. Prices generated in such a spontaneous way, then, naturally guide competing consumers, producers, and distributors in fulfilling the wants and needs of their customers as efficiently as possible, all the while pursuing their own individual interests.

In contrast, government bureaucrats far removed from market conditions are faced with an impossible task when it comes to setting prices efficiently for all the innumerable goods that constitute a given market.

This is the basic reason why socialist and communist societies experience chronic shortages of all categories of commodities, including even the most basic necessities of life. It is simply beyond human capability for one or a small number of individuals to gather the information that would be necessary to determine all those prices efficiently in the absence of the invisible hand (the "market mechanism").

Smith's *Wealth of Nations* was published during an early phase of the Industrial Revolution, the very year that the thirteen North American colonies declared their independence from the British crown.

Smith's analysis of political economy, including his striking metaphor of the invisible hand, became one of the primary reasons for the adoption of a free trade policy and a generally free market economic system by the fledgling democracy that would become known as the United States.

As a result, from the very beginning US business and government leaders developed a broad consensus that the less the government intervenes in the economy, the more efficiently it operates and the more productive it is.

Historically, even when the US government has seen fit to intervene in the economy to achieve some specific political purpose, it has often done so by adopting rules that incorporate the invisible hand of the market to the greatest extent possible.

75. Job Market

DEFINITION: The concept of the "job market," also known as the "labor market," is an abstraction corresponding to the totality of interactions between employees and employers in a given national or regional space.

In other words, the job market is a "virtual" market (not a physical location) in which employers seek employees possessing certain experience and abilities, and potential employees search for employers who can provide them with jobs meeting their financial and other requirements.

The idea of the job market helps to reveal the dynamic nature of the interaction and competition among various productive and labor forces.

Technically, these forces are symmetrical: that is, from the employers' point of view, employees constitute the supply necessary to meet their demand for labor, while from the employees' point of view, employers represent the supply necessary to meet their demand for a source of income.

However, in practice, the phrase "job market" tends to be used mainly from the employers' point of view, in which employers provides the demand for labor and employees provide the supply of labor.

ETYMOLOGY: The origin of the phrase "job market" Is uncertain, but most likely the term was introduced in the early twentieth century.

The economic sense of the word "job," meaning a defined "task" or "piece of work," derives from the late seventeenth century word "job," meaning "lump." This explains the curious expression "job of work."

The English noun "market" derives, via Middle English and Old North French, from the Latin noun *mercātus, mercātūs,* meaning "business," "traffic," or "trade," as well as the place where the business or trade takes place, i.e., a "marketplace."

Mercātus, in turn, is connected to the deponent verb *mercor, mercari,*meaning "to traffic in" or "to trade," as well as the noun *merx, mercis,*meaning "goods" or "merchandise."

USAGE: The job market's fluctuations are caused by changes in the balance between labor demand and the available workforce supply.

Moreover, specific industry requirements—such as the need for particular educational backgrounds or skill sets—and essential job functions play a crucial role in shaping the job market. As a vital component of any economy, the job market is thus intricately connected to the demand for goods and services.

The job market shares a direct correlation with the unemployment rate. This rate represents the percentage of individuals in the labor force who are currently unemployed but actively searching for employment.

When the unemployment rate is higher, it indicates an increased supply within the overall labor market. A larger labor supply (pool of applicants) gives employers the advantage of being more selective or, potentially, of offering lower wages.

Conversely, a decline in the unemployment rate compels employers to compete more vigorously for available workers, often leading to an increase in wages.

Wages influenced by the job market provide significant information for economic analysts and policymakers, guiding decisions based on the state of the overall economy.

In times of economic hardship, unemployment tends to increase as employers lay off employees to save money, thus reducing the number of overall job opportunities and making it more difficult for job seekers to find work.

High unemployment rates can prolong economic stagnation, which is defined as little or no economic growth. It can also be a contributing causal factor leading to social unrest and political turmoil.

76. Junk Bond

DEFINITION: "Junk bond" is a colloquial term for a high-**yield**, high-risk type of tradable financial instrument, or security, known as a "**bond**."

A junk bond is more formerly referred to as a "speculative-grade" bond or a "non-investment-grade" bond.

ETYMOLOGY: The word "junk" derives from the Middle English word*jonke,* meaning scraps of used cordage that are recycled to make a variety of objects, including swabs, mats, and oakum.

For the etymology of the word "**bond**," see the linked article.

USAGE: The determination of the level of yield and risk of different securities is made by one or more of the principal credit-rating agencies, notably, Moody's, Standard & Poor's, and Fitch.

Thus, a given bond offered for sale on the open market is a "junk bond" if one of those agencies says it is.

The purpose of labeling high-risk bonds as "junk bonds"—and, indeed, the purpose of the very existence of credit-rating agencies—is supposed to be the protection consumers who are considering purchasing high-yield bonds.

Therefore, it is important to keep in mind that the labeling of bonds is only as reliable as the agencies themselves.

The nature of the risk associated with high-yield bonds is by and large the risk of default. Default occurs when a bond issuer is unable to make scheduled interest and principal payments to bond owners.

In plain speech, the risk is that of losing one's entire investment.

The attraction, of course, is that of making a large profit quickly from a junk bond's high yield.

Historically, the default rate on junk bonds has averaged about five percent. However, that number may increase during a recession or other period of economic instability.

The largest purchasers of junk bonds are institutional investors, such as insurance companies, banks, pension funds, and mutual funds.

For the most part, individual investors own junk bonds as a portion of their mutual fund portfolios.

77. Just-in-Time

DEFINITION: The phrase "just-in-time" refers to an approach to the management of supply chains which minimizes the time that supplies need to be held in inventory waiting to be used or delivered.

More specifically, "just-in-time" means synchronizing the delivery of raw materials or intermediate products received from suppliers with production schedules, or else the delivery of finished products from wholesalers with customer delivery schedules, as the case may be.

The idea is that supplies should arrive "just in time" to be used or delivered, minimizing the need to store them on site.

ETYMOLOGY: The concept of "just-in-time" is usually held to have been invented by the Toyota company in Japan in the 1970s.

The English adverb "just" derives, via Middle English, from the Middle French adjective *juste* and the Latin adjective *iustus,* meaning "just," "equitable," or "fair," which, in turn, is derived from the noun *iūs, iūris,* meaning "right" or "law."

The English preposition "in" derives from identical forms in Middle English and Old English; the latter is akin to identical forms in Old High German and in Latin.

The English noun "time" derives, via Middle English, from the Old English word *tīma,* with the same meaning. It is akin to Old Norse *tīmi,* also with the same meaning.

USAGE: The just-in-time inventory system—sometimes abbreviated as "JIT"—serves to reduce inventory levels while enhancing operational efficiency.

Since JIT production systems procure materials and components only as required for production, they reduce the need for holding large amounts of inventory, thus minimizing or even eliminating the need for on-site storage of supplies, thus minimizing the expenses associated with inventory storage.

Additionally, JIT reduces the danger of manufacturers' being stuck with surplus inventory if orders are canceled.

A prime illustration of the JIT inventory system is evident in the case of automobile manufacturing—the very industry which first developed the concept.

Auto manufacturers typically maintains minimal inventory levels, thus relying heavily on their supply chains to provide parts they require on a need-based schedule.

Consequently, an auto manufacturer typically places orders for essential vehicle components only after receiving order from their customers.

For JIT manufacturing to be implemented successfully, a number of requirements must be fulfilled: notably, dependable suppliers, consistent production, flawless functioning of plant machinery, and exceptional craftsmanship.

78. Keynesian Economics

DEFINITION: Keynesian economics, or "Keynesianism," advocates the partially centralized control of the economy. More specifically, it maintains that governments ought to spend as much money as necessary to "stimulate" the economy until full employment is achieved, without worrying about any possible negative effects stemming from commodity-price inflation or government indebtedness.

ETYMOLOGY: Keynesian economics derives from the work of the British economist **John Maynard Keynes** (1883–1946), in particular the ideas presented in his 1936 classic, *The General Theory of Employment, Interest, and Money.*

USAGE: Apart from a partial rollback during the 1980s and 1990s under the influence of "**neoliberal**" ideas, Keynesianism has been the dominant school of economic thought in developed countries around the world since World War II.

In fact, Keynes's name was already being invoked during the late 1930s by government officials in Europe and the US charged with combatting the Great Depression. In this sense, one might say that the "New Deal" program of **President Franklin D. Roosevelt** was a form of Keynesian economics *avant la lettre.*

Keynesianism has sometimes been characterized by its critics as a form of "socialism." However, this is not technically correct. Socialism is usually defined as involving government ownership of the principal means of production.

While this has never been a feature of Keynesianism as such, it is true that the government control of the economy that Keynesian economics does recommend—also known as *dirigisme*—has been historically associated with the implementation of limited socialist measures.

Specifically, in the immediate aftermath of World War II a form of near-socialism arose in a number of Western countries—perhaps most notably in the United Kingdom—which combined Keynesian *dirigisme* with the nationalization of certain major industries, such as coal mining, gas, electrical power, and steel production, banking, telecommunications, railroads, aviation, and healthcare.

The resulting combination of Keynesian *dirigisme* and limited state ownership of the means of production came to be known as the "mixed economy."

Between the 1950s and the late 1970s, the mixed-economy model of semi-socialist Keynesianism spread to many countries throughout the developing world, especially those politically aligned with the communist countries.

However, in the developed capitalist countries, the model ran into strong political opposition, which restricted its further proliferation. Even in the UK itself, after 1980 state ownership fell from favor and many nationalized industries were sold off.

Then, with the collapse of the USSR in 1991, it seemed as though socialism, whether in full-strength or diluted form, had been relegated to the trash heap of history. Moreover, by this time Keynesian *dirigisme* had itself been beating a retreat for two decades under the assault of neoliberalism, as already mentioned. Or, so it seemed to most observers.

However, a closer examination of the period after about 1980—when Keynesian *dirigisme* became decoupled from socialism and free-market ideas seemed ascendant—reveals that Keynesian economics never really went away. It is more accurate to say that the developed capitalist countries' supposed conversion to *laissez-faire* was more in the nature of a dialing down than a full-throated renunciation of Keynesianism.

In any case, since the worldwide asset-price bubble and stock market crash of 2008, as well as the sovereign-debt crisis of Greece and other European Union member states a few years later, it has become clear that the neoliberal experiment with moderating the *dirigiste* Keynesian consensus was little more than a passing phase.

From today's perspective, it appears that the underlying reality all along was the universal triumph of the Keynesian vision.

Looking back at the 85+ years since the publication of Keynes's *General Theory,* it would be more accurate to say, not only that, "We are all Keynesians now," but also, "At heart, we always have been."

79. Key Performance Indicator

DEFINITION: The phrase "key performance indicator" refers to a group of metrics which may be used to gauge the success and ongoing progress of the company.

These indicators encompass evaluations of a company's strategy, its financial status, and its operational achievements, among other things, particularly in relation to its competitors and other businesses in the same industry.

ETYMOLOGY: The origins of the use of key indicators to evaluate performance may be traced back at least to 1494, the year of publication of the *Summa de arithmetica, geometrica, proportioni et proportionalita* [Summary of arithmetic, geometry, proportions and proportionality] by the Italian Franciscan friar and mathematician, Luca Pacioli.

Some would trace the idea back still farther, to around the fourth century AD, when a Chinese dynasty is reported to have instituted a rating system for evaluating the performance of members of the imperial family!

The origin of the English phrase itself is uncertain, but it probably dates to the 1970s, give or take a few years.

The English word "key" derives, via Middle English, from Old English *cǣg*, "key," akin to Middle Low German *keige*, "spear."

The English noun "performance" is attested from the fifteenth century. It derives from the verb "to perform," which itself derives from Middle English *performen*, which, in turn, derives from Anglo-French *performer* and Old French *perfournir*. The latter form is constructed from the Latin preposition *per-*, meaning "through" or "throughout," and the French verb *fournir*, meaning "to complete" or "to equip."

The English word "indicator" is attested from the seventeenth century. It derives from the verb "indicate," which, in turn, derives from the Latin past participle *indicatus* of the verb *indico, indicare*, "to make known," "to show," "to indicate."

USAGE: Key performance indicators—often referred to by the acronym "KPI"—are sometimes also referred to as "key success indicators."

KPIs exhibit diversity across companies and industries, contingent upon performance benchmarks.

For instance, a technology-sector company that aspires to swift expansion might prioritize year-over-year revenue growth as its principal performance gauge. (Year-over-year revenue growth is the annual percentage increase in revenue.)

By way of contrast, a retail enterprise might assign greater significance to same-store sales as the best metric for assessing its growth. (Same-store sales figure measure the amount of sales growth that is attributable to new store openings.)

The collection, storage, refinement, and consolidation of data is central to the successful implementation of KPIs. This data, which may pertain to any department within the organization, can encompass either financial or nonfinancial information.

The purpose of KPIs is to facilitate the provision of concise results to management so it may undertake better-informed strategic deliberations.

The majority of KPIs belong to one of four distinct categories, each possessing its unique user base, attributes, and timeframe.

1. ***Strategic KPIs*** offer a glimpse into a company's performance at a broad level, albeit without delving deeply into specifics. Strategic KPIs are primarily employed by executives, with illustrative examples, such as overall company revenue, profit margin, and return-on-investment.
2. ***Operational KPIs*** focus on a more compressed time span. These indicators gauge the company's performance on a month-to-month, or even day-to-day, basis. They scrutinize various processes, segments, or geographic regions. Operational KPIs are especially useful to managerial personnel, serving to address queries stemming from the analysis of strategic KPIs.
3. ***Functional KPIs*** home in on specific departments or functions within an organization. For instance, the finance department might monitor on a monthly basis newly registered vendors in their accounting system, while the marketing team might assess the click-through rate of their email campaign. The primary worth of functional KPIs lies in catering to a specific user groups.
4. ***Leading/lagging KPIs*** characterize the essence of the analyzed data, indicating whether it relates to forthcoming events or to events that have already happened. For example, take two distinct KPIs: the tally of overtime hours clocked and the profit margin associated with a flagship product. The number of overtime hours worked might act as a leading indicator if the company discerns a decline in manufacturing quality on the horizon, while profit margins by definition stem from operational outcomes and therefore qualify as a lagging indicator.

80. Knowledge Economy

DEFINITION: The phrase "knowledge economy" refers to the consumption and production of intellectual capital insofar as these activities take an economic form.

Often, the phrase is employed more narrowly to refer to efforts to develop scientific breakthroughs and practical research for economic benefit.

A substantial portion of the business goals pursued within most advanced economies today is involved with the knowledge economy.

Within this framework, a large proportion of value may be attributed to intangible resources, such as the intellectual attainments and know-how of the workforce.

ETYMOLOGY: The term "knowledge economy" was coined by the Austrian-born American economist Fritz Machlup in his 1962 book, *The Production and Distribution of Knowledge in the United States,* and later popularized by the German-born American economist and author, **Peter Drucker**.

The English noun "knowledge" derives from Middle English *knowlege,* which derives from the Middle English verb *knowen.* The latter verb, in turn, derives from Old English *cnāwan,* "to know," which is akin to Old High German *bichnaān,* "to recognize," and Latin *nosco, noscere,* "to come to know."

The English social-science technical term "economics" was invented in the late eighteenth century. The related noun "economy" derives from Middle French *yconomie,* which, in turn, derives from Medieval Latin *œconomia,* and, ultimately, from Greek *oikonomia,* "household management," which is compounded from the Greek words *oikos,*"house," and *nomos,* "law."

USAGE: The chief economic activities of developing nations tend to be agriculture and low-tech manufacturing.

Highly developed nations, in contrast, allocate a greater portion of their activities to high-tech manufacturing and services. Among the latter are typically such knowledge-centric pursuits as research and development, consulting, and technical assistance.

The knowledge economy refers to the realm where scientific and engineering breakthroughs are created and traded.

From a legal point of view, this valuable information may be transformed into commercial products through patents and other intellectual property safeguards.

The scientists and research laboratories who develop these products are also integral components of the knowledge economy.

Globalization is in the process of transforming the global economy in a knowledge-centric direction, incorporating optimal approaches from diverse national economies.

Additionally, these knowledge-oriented transformations are shaping an interconnected globe in which human skills and proprietary trade insights from all nations are viewed as valuable economic assets.

On the other hand, it remains crucial to emphasize that, according to the generally accepted accounting principles (GAAP), companies are generally *not* permitted to list knowledge-centric assets on their balance sheets.

The concept of the knowledge economy revolves around the idea that education and knowledge—often referred to as "human capital"—represent valuable assets and marketable commodities. These commodities, when sold and traded internationally, can generate profits for businesses, individuals, and the overall economy.

The knowledge economy places significant emphasis on intellectual abilities, instead of relying on natural resources or other tangible inputs.

Advances in the knowledge economy in technical and scientific domains are driven by products and services rooted in intellectual prowess. This fact motivates public and private investment in the upstream sources of this intellectual prowess. Such advances also foster innovation downstream throughout the broader economy.

The World Bank characterizes knowledge economies by the following four fundamental pillars:

1. Institutional frameworks that incentivize the use of knowledge in entrepreneurship
2. Presence of an excellent education system and an efficient workforce
3. Accessibility to advanced information and communication technology (ICT) infrastructure
4. A dynamic innovation environment embracing private enterprises, academia, and civil society

Academic establishments, companies that engage in research and development (R&D), programmers who create innovative software, and healthcare professionals who utilize digital information to enhance treatments are all important players within the knowledge economy.

These knowledge-economy participants may transfer the results of their research to individuals in conventional sectors.

For instance, farmers may benefit from software applications and digital tools that assist with crop management, medical practitioners may advance the boundaries of therapy with procedures like robot-assisted surgery, and educational institutions may offer digital resources and online courses to students, to name only a few of the myriad spin-offs from knowledge-centric economic activity.

81. Labor

DEFINITION: In a broad sense, labor is the physical effort expended by human beings to transform the material world for some human purpose.

In a narrower economic sense, labor is a commodity offered by a supplier ("employee") to someone demanding the labor ("employer") in exchange for some form of compensation, nowadays, usually monetary.

The compensation exchanged for labor is commonly referred to as a "wage."

ETYMOLOGY: The word "labor" derives, via Middle English and Middle French, from the Latin noun *labor, laboris*, meaning "work," "labor," "toil," or "effort," and the Latin verb *labōro*, meaning "to work," "to toil," or "to labor."

USAGE: Labor has been intensively studied by economists. It is useful to discuss the economics of labor in three separate contexts: as a factor of production, as the basis of economic value, and (in the form of manual labor) as an economic class whose welfare is affected by interactions with various non-economic social, political, and legal institutions.

First, then, is the idea that labor is one among several primary factors of production, other prominent factors including land and capital. As such, labor is often conceived of as constituting a market all its own.

However, labor markets are constrained in various ways. For one thing, most jobs in the modern world require a greater or lesser amount of prior education or training.

Thus, the "labor market" as a whole is in fact fragmented into a multitude of smaller markets for doctors, lawyers, bankers, physicists, chemists, biologists, engineers, airline pilots, air traffic controllers, crane operators, and a plethora of other careers that require extensive training.

Moreover, each of these generic markets is subdivided into several more specific markets, in some cases, many more of them.

For example, in the field of engineering alone, there are separate markets for civil engineers, mechanical engineers, electrical engineers, aerospace engineers, petroleum engineers, computer engineers, nuclear engineers, biomedical engineers, and many more.

Moreover, labor markets may be constrained by geography, in several different ways. One way has to do with national boundaries. Thus, a well-qualified physician from India may wind up driving a taxi in the US because his qualifications are not recognized in the American market for physicians.

Another way in which the labor market may be constrained geographically has to do with changes in economic production in a given locality. For example, if a large manufacturing plant closes its doors, the local market for manual labor will be drastically affected.

When this occurs, two main possibilities arise: either manual laborers may sever their roots to their local community and move away in search of better market conditions, or else governments may intervene in the economy in such a way that manufacturers wish to return, thus restoring the local labor market to the *status quo ante.*

Either way, it is clear that labor markets are constrained in a distinctive way by geography.

The second context in which labor has been studied is the theory of economic value.

Beginning with the founders of political theory in the eighteenth century, notably, **Adam Smith**, it was thought that the price of a consumer good was determined by the cost of its production, especially the amount of labor that went into making it. This became known as the "**labor theory of value**."

The labor theory of value was espoused by nearly all economists through the middle of the nineteenth century and became the centerpiece of the political economy of **Karl Marx**.

However, it was disputed by three distinguished economists during the 1860s and the 1870s, namely, the Austrian **Carl Menger**, the Englishman **William Stanley Jevons**, and the Frenchman **Léon Walras**.

These three economic thinkers, working independently of one another, put in place the foundations of what we now know as the "**subjective theory of value**."

The subjective theory of value simply states that the chief determinant of the value of a consumer good is the preference that potential buyers have for it in comparison with other goods.

A little thought is sufficient to show that this is so. No matter how much labor has gone into the production of something, if no one wants to buy it, its market value is effectively nil.

The third context in which economists have studied labor—especially, manual labor, but increasingly, white collar labor, as well—has to do with the way it forms an economic class whose welfare is affected by interactions with various social, political, and legal institutions.

For example, among the social institutions studied by labor economists are labor unions. There are also political and legal aspects to the operation of labor unions.

For example, in some jurisdictions, laws have been passed by local or state governments requiring either "closed" or "open" or shops. This means that union membership is either required or not required of all laborers working in a given unionized factory.

Similarly, legal institutions may be more lenient or more restrictive with respect to the rules governing the picketing of factory premises during strikes.

Beyond unions, there have been many political crusades over the past century and a half or so, resulting in many legal reforms, which have improved working conditions, especially for manual laborers.

Such achievements as the 40-hour work week, paid holidays and vacations, pensions, minimum age requirements, and safe working conditions have all resulted from political pressure exerted by public figures and political parties to improve the welfare of the laboring class.

Another legal institution that continues to be heatedly debated to this day is the minimum wage.

It may appear self-evident that passing laws raising the minimum wage improves the welfare of laborers. And it is true that they benefit those workers fortunate enough to be able to find entry-level work doing manual labor.

However, most economists believe that minimum wage laws reduce the total number of entry-level jobs available. Critics of minimum wage laws claim that more laborers are harmed than are helped by such laws.

Similarly, laws favoring closed union shops and lenient picketing rules may seem like a good thing from the point of view of a laborer lucky enough to have a job in a union factory.

However, overall, such laws act as an artificial restraint on trade, often making such jobs exceedingly hard to obtain.

Labor economists investigate the pros and cons of these and other controversial proposals to advance the welfare of the laboring class.

82. Labor Theory of Value

DEFINITION: The idea that the source of the economic value of a thing is the amount of labor that went into its production.

USAGE: In a general way, the labor theory of value was the original understanding of the source of economic value among the founders of classical economic theory, including **Adam Smith** and **David Ricardo.**

However, ever since the clear articulation of the subjective theory of value, developed independently in the 1860s and 1870s by **William Stanley Jevons**, **Carl Menger**, and **Léon Walras**, the labor theory of value has been most closely associated with the name of **Karl Marx.**

In his economic writings, especially *Capital* (1867), Marx defends the labor theory of value at great length. In many ways, it constitutes the linchpin of his entire theory of political economy.

The truth of this claim may best be seen by means of the following chain of reasoning:

Marx's labor theory of value forms the foundation of his concept of "surplus value," which is basically the notion of "profit" reinterpreted as rightfully belonging to the worker, rather than the owner.

The idea of surplus theory, in turn, is the basis for the claim that the system of capitalist production unjustly "exploits" the working class.

Finally, the idea of unjust exploitation legitimates the call for violent communist revolution and dictatorship of the proletariat.

The labor theory of value contains fatal conceptual flaws. A moment's thought is sufficient to reveal that there is no necessary link between the labor necessary to produce a commodity and its economic value.

Otherwise, the uninspired but industrious artist starving in his garret would be able to command a good price for the unwanted canvases he produces with so much toil.

83. Laffer Curve

DEFINITION: The Laffer curve is a mathematical function linking economic output to federal tax revenue.

The Laffer curve purports to show that, within certain limits, a decrease in the tax-rate that businesses pay will result in economic growth that will generate enough additional tax revenues to provide positive net income to the federal government.

ETYMOLOGY: There is some dispute involving the actual origin of the Laffer curve. However, the popularization of the concept and its name dates from 1974, when the American economist **Arthur Laffer**—who was working as a consultant with the US Department of the Treasury at the time—sketched the curve on a napkin in order to help explain the idea to some of his colleagues.

USAGE: The Laffer curve was an important element in the successful selling of the concept of **supply-side economics** to the administration of **President Ronald Reagan.**

However, the predictions made by the Laffer curve were not borne out by the real-world consequences of the policies implemented by the Reagan administration, whose eight-year tenure in office resulted in a $100 billion increase to the deficit.

For this and other reasons, the Laffer curve has not been well received by the academic economics establishment, to put it mildly. The Harvard economist **Greg Mankiw** has summarized the consensus on the Laffer curve in the following terms:

> The Laffer curve is undeniable as a matter of economic theory. There is certainly some level of taxation at which cutting tax rates would be win-win. But few economists believe that tax rates in the United States have reached such heights in recent years; to the contrary, they are likely below the revenue-maximizing level.

84. Laissez-Faire

DEFINITION: The phrase *"laissez-faire"* is shorthand for a type of economic theory which advocates minimal government involvement in the economy.

The phrase, which may be loosely translated as "let it be" or "leave it alone," presumes that it is the free activity of individuals which leads to the optimal performance of an economy, and not government supervision or regulation.

The concept of *laissez-faire* lies at the heart of free-market capitalism in all its forms.

ETYMOLOGY: The French phrase *"laissez-faire"* [literally, "let do"] was popularized in the 1750s by **Vincent de Gournay**, a French public official and leader of the **Physiocrat** school of economic thought.

Gournay is said to have taken the phrase from a 1751 discussion between French Controller-General of Finance, **Jean-Baptiste Colbert**, and a delegation of businessmen. Colbert is supposed to have asked: "How can the government help you?" The leader of the businessmen's delegation is supposed to have answered: *"Laissez-nous faire"* ["Leave us alone"].

The French word *"laissez"* is the second-person plural, imperative mood of the verb *laisser*, meaning "to let," "to allow," or "to leave [alone]." Thus, *laissez* means, roughly, "let it be!" or "leave it alone!"

The verb *"laisser"* derives, via Middle French, from Old French *lesser,*meaning "to let" or "to allow," which, in turn, derives from the Latin verb *laxō, laxare*, meaning "to unfasten," "to relax," or "to release." The Latin word is also akin to Old High German *lāzan*, meaning "to let," "to let go," or "to leave."

The French verb *"faire"* is in the infinitive form and means "to make" or "to do." It derives, via Middle French, from Old French *faire*, which derives (presumably) from the Vulgar Latin infinitive **fare* (the asterisk indicates the form is not actually attested), which is an elision of the infinitive form of the classical Latin verb *facio, facēre,*meaning "to make" or "to do."

USAGE: *Laissez-faire* economics presupposes the belief that a competitive free market embodies an inherent natural order which always leads to optimal results for an economy, considered overall.

Laissez-faire may be thought of as the logical complement to the invisible hand: it is essentially a prescription to rulers saying, in effect, "Leave the invisible hand alone to do its work."

Proponents of *laissez-faire* economics contend that government intervention is not only unnecessary to achieve optimal economic performance, it is actually counterproductive, seeing that any intervention on the part of the government is bound to cause a deviation from the optimal equilibrium achieved by the invisible hand, resulting in a less-than-best-possible outcome.

According to the theory behind the concept of *laissez-faire,* such a sub-optimal outcome will be the inevitable result of any and all efforts on the part of the government to shape or steer the economy in some desired direction, by means of, for example, such popular measures as subsidies to failing industries, minimum wage laws, corporate taxes, and tariffs, duties, and other trade barriers.

From a *laissez-faire* perspective, such government interference is tantamount to rewarding economic failure and punishing success. In other words, government interference in the economy creates an inversion of the normal incentive structure.

As such, it is a sure-fire recipe for economic stagnation, social malaise, and political resentment, as the government makes the people unfulfillable promises of a radiant economic future which raise unrealistic expectations that are bound to be dashed.

The laissez-faire perspective is basically the same as that of nineteenth-century classical liberal political economy and, later, that of **Austrian economists**, libertarians, and neo-liberals.

All of these schools of thought view the role of the state as that of providing a bare minimum of essential services, which basically boil down to the following three governmental functions, which are the only ones viewed by strong *laissez-faire* advocates as legitimate:

- A military function of safeguarding the country's national security
- A police function of enforcing the rule of law, especially with respect to the safety of citizens' lives and property
- A public service function of providing for public goods—such as a postal service, roads and bridges, and other infrastructure—which might not attract private investment, yet which most citizens would view as being for the benefit of all

Much of the content of the political discourse of a modern developed nation consists of debate about what the proper limits of such "public goods" ought to be, with "conservatives" essentially arguing that as few things as possible ought to count as "public goods" and "liberals" arguing that a great many things (or essentially anything at all) ought to count as "public goods."

85. Life Insurance

DEFINITION: "Insurance," by definition, is an agreement or contract between a provider ("insurer") and a purchaser ("policy owner"), in which the insurer promises to indemnify the policy owner, partially or wholly, in case some good or property belonging to the policy owner is accidentally harmed or destroyed.

An insurance contract is referred to as a "policy." The policy specifies the parties to the contract, the property indemnified, the amount of the indemnification, and the precise conditions that must be fulfilled in order for indemnification to occur.

"Life insurance" is a type of insurance in which the "good" indemnified is the life of the policy owner.

By its nature, life insurance necessarily involves a third party, called the "beneficiary," who is appointed by the policy owner to receive the indemnification upon the latter's death.

ETYMOLOGY: The word "life" derives from the Middle English word*lif*, and the Old English word *līf*, both meaning "life." The Old English noun *līf* is connected to the verb *libban*, meaning "to live," which in turn is related to the Old High German verb *leben*, with the same meaning.

The word "insurance" derives from the Middle English verb *insuren*, meaning "to insure," which is probably an alternative form of the verb *assuren*, meaning "to assure." *Assuren*, in turn, derives, via the Middle French verb *assurer*, from the Medieval Latin verb *assecurare*. The word *assecurare* is composed of the classical Latin preposition *ad*, meaning "towards," "at," "on," or "according to," and the adjective,*sēcūrus*, meaning "free from care," "safe," or "secure."

USAGE: Life insurance shares some of its technical terms with other forms of insurance.

We have already mentioned the terms "policy" and "beneficiary." Another such term is "premium," which is a payment made according to the terms of an insurance policy by the policy owner to the insurer that is made in a pre-established amount according to a pre-established schedule.

A term that is unique to life insurance is "underwriting," which is the process by which an insurer determines whether a policy on a certain person's life shall be issued, and if so, at what price and under what conditions.

The main conditions that the prospective policy owner is usually required to satisfy are minimal conditions pertaining to the state of his health. A person meeting such conditions is said to be "insurable."

Life insurance policies are offered on the market in a variety of forms, but the following distinction is fundamental:

- ***Protection policies:*** Also known as "term life," this is the simplest form of life insurance and the one most similar to other forms of insurance, such as fire insurance. Term life policies are in force for a set period of time and specify dollar amounts for the monthly premium and the benefit amount payable to the beneficiary in the event of the policy owner's death. Term life policies do not accumulate any cash value.
- ***Investment policies:*** The best-known variant of this form of life insurance is "whole life." Like term life policies, whole life policies also specify dollar amounts for the monthly premium and the benefit amount payable to the beneficiary in the event of the policy owner's death. However, they are in force for the life of the policy owner, however long that may be. In addition, whole life policies accumulate a cash "endowment" amount that may be distributed to the policy owner during his lifetime.

Benefit payments from either form of life insurance policy may be taken by the beneficiary either as a lump sum or as an annuity—which is paid in regular installments for either a specified period or for the life of the beneficiary.

There are several other types of life insurance policies, but they are basically variants on these two themes.

86. Limited Government

DEFINITION: The phrase "limited government" refers to a form of government whose scope for action is legally circumscribed by a constitution which accords it specified and enumerated or otherwise specified powers.

Nations with limited governments possess fewer regulations governing the actions of individuals and businesses.

Unlimited governments have no legal constraints preventing them from treating individuals and businesses in any way they like. Such governments may vary from interventionist to authoritarian to totalitarian.

In practice, the governments of most countries exhibit some mixture of limited and unlimited characteristics.

Even developed Western countries, such as the US, whose governments are nominally constrained by a constitution, have had a tendency to drift towards interventionism and authoritarianism over time, with the constitution eventually becoming mostly a dead letter.

ETYMOLOGY: The phrase "limited government" is apparently first attested in the writings of King James VI of Scotland (later James I of England) in the late sixteenth century.

The English adjective "limited" derives from the verb "to limit," which is, of course, closely connected to the noun "limit." The latter, in turn, derives, via Middle English, from Middle French *limite,* a "limit," and, ultimately, from Latin *līmes, līmitis,* a "cross path" or "boundary-line."

The English noun "government" derives from Middle English *governement,* which is connected to the Middle French verb *governer,* and ultimately derives from the Latin noun *gubernātor,gubernātoris,* meaning "*helmsman*"or "*governor.*" The latter is akin to the Greek *kubernētēs, kubernētou,* also meaning "helmsman."

USAGE: The idea of limited government (as opposed to the phrase) can be traced back to philosophical discussions of the seventeenth century.

The idea is particularly associated with nineteenth-century discipline of political economy ("classical liberalism")—most of whose architects advocated ***laissez-faire*** and free trade—as well as more-recent schools of thought, such as **Austrian economics**, libertarianism, and neo-liberalism.

In simplest terms, a limited government focuses on maintaining the rule of law, safeguarding citizens and their property, while imposing only the taxes necessary to fund the services connected to this primary objective.

In other words, within a classical, limited-government framework, the ruling body might impose taxes on its citizens for the provision of police or national defense. However, it would not attempt to directly influence the economy, nor would it involve itself in citizens' personal conduct or convictions.

An alternative viewpoint defines a limited government as one that confines its activities exclusively to the explicit powers bestowed upon it by a founding constitution.

In the case of the US, this type of constitutional government calls for rival political institutions—specifically, the legislative and judicial branches—to help constrain the potentially dangerous power of the executive branch through a system of separation and balance of power among the three branches of government.

To be sure, this works only so long as the constitution continues to exercise authority over the minds of public servants and citizens alike.

The nineteenth-century classical liberal tradition was a part of the general reaction against European absolute monarchies, in favor of what came to be known as "constitutional monarchies."

The latter form of government typically involved legal protections for individual rights, including freedom of speech, of assembly, of the press, and so forth.

The rise of classical liberal political economy may usefully be viewed as the extension of individual rights from the political context to economics.

More specifically, classical economic liberalism arose within the English common-law tradition, which embodied personal freedoms—equivalent to limitations on the king's power—and extended back for centuries to the Magna Carta in 1215.

The US Constitution (1787) and Bill of Rights (1791) were largely based on this English common-law tradition of personal freedom. The American Founding Fathers were mindful of the need to place limitations on executive power, which is the reason why they placed the separation of power among the three branches of government at the heart of the US constitution.

Thus, the notion of limited government has centuries-long roots in the Anglo-American political tradition.

87. Lobbyist

DEFINITION: The term "lobbyist" refers to someone who attempts to influence politicians and government officials to pass legislation favorable to the private ("special") interests whom the lobbyist represents.

ETYMOLOGY: The noun "lobbyist," and the associated verb "to lobby," stem from the word "lobby," meaning "anteroom."

The connection between the place and the function is that representatives of private interests frequently conversed with politicians in the antechamber to the main parliamentary chambers.

The word "lobby" derives from the Medieval Latin word *lobium*, meaning a "gallery." *Lobium* is also related to the Old High German word *louba*, meaning "porch."

The origin of the word "lobbyist" can be traced to the 1830s.

USAGE: Lobbyists may work directly for the companies they represent or they may work for independent firms that specialize in offering lobbying services to companies across a spectrum of economic sectors and issues.

In the American context, many independent lobbying groups are based in Washington, DC, as might be expected. Washington-based lobbying firms tend to cluster together on K Street, which is why the phrase "K Street" is sometimes used to refer to the lobbying industry collectively.

In modern liberal democracies, lobbyists are ubiquitous, but they are also controversial.

On the one hand, it might be argued that in a democracy government officials ought to be responsive to the concerns of their constituents.

On the other hand, the monetary and other blandishments and the none-too-subtle political pressure brought to bear on government officials by lobbyists sometimes cross the line into improper—or downright illegal—bribery and intimidation.

Another concern is that lobbyists magnify the already-disproportionate influence that very large and wealthy corporations exert on the political process.

Finally, the constant churn of individuals flowing between Capitol Hill and K Street is yet another unseemly aspect of the lobbying phenomenon.

All these concerns about the outsized influence of lobbyists on the workings of democracy have generated a host of regulations—mostly, to little avail.

The influence of lobbyists upon the American political system remains undiminished today.

88. Margin

DEFINITION: The term "margin," when used in the realm of finance, refers to the collateral that investors must place with their broker or exchange.

The purpose of this collateral is to mitigate the potential credit risk to the broker or exchange that might be created by an investor's actions.

Investors can create credit risk for brokers and exchanges when they borrow financial instruments for the purpose of short selling, when they borrow funds from the broker to acquire financial instruments, or when they deal in derivative contracts.

Margin-buying takes place under the following circumstances. First, an investor borrows money from his broker for the purpose of purchasing an asset. Second, the broker counts the collateral that the investor has already deposited with him as collateral for the new loan. This second step is what makes the loan "on margin."

ETYMOLOGY: The term "margin," when used in the financial context, is short for "margin of safety." It was introduced to the financial literature in 1934 by Benjamin Graham and David L. Dodd in the first edition of their classic textbook, *Security Analysis.*

The English word "margin" is attested from the fourteenth century. It derives from Middle English and, ultimately, from the Latin noun *margo, marginis,* meaning "edge" or "border."

USAGE: The concept of "margin" relates to the level of ownership that investors maintain within their brokerage account.

The concept of "buying on margin" means using funds borrowed from a broker to acquire securities.

Thus, buying on margin presupposes owning a margin account, which is distinct from a regular brokerage account.

A "margin account" denotes a brokerage arrangement in which the broker extends a loan to the investor, enabling the latter to acquire a greater volume of securities than the investor's regular brokerage account balance would allow.

The term "margin" may be used in a variety of different contexts, apart from finance.

For instance, margin may be said to represent the difference between the selling price of a product or service and its production cost.

Another way of looking at margin is as a representation of the proportion of a company's profit in relation to its revenue.

Finally, the concept of margin may also be used to describe the segment of interest rate within an adjustable-rate mortgage (ARM) that is added to the adjustment-index rate.

Using margin for acquiring securities is akin to leveraging the existing cash or securities within an account as a guarantee for a loan. Such a loan is secured by collateral and involves a recurring interest rate obligation.

By employing borrowed funds, the investor would be able to increase his potential for both gains and losses.

The margin investing strategy may prove beneficial when the investor believes he can generate a superior rate of return on the investment compared to the interest expense of the loan.

For example, take a scenario in which your margin account calls for an initial margin investment of 60%. If you intend to buy securities valued at $10,000, your margin requirement would amount to $6,000. This amount would then entitle you to raise the remaining $4,000 through a loan from the broker.

This maneuver would make financial sense for the investor on the assumption that the $10,000 borrowed can be used to generate a return on investment that is greater than the amount needed to service the loan.

Of course, if such returns are not realized, the investor is liable to lose the funds in his margin account, which will usually constitute a greater loss than the loss of the security for a regular bank loan—which will normally have a lower security requirement—would represent.

It is important to note that the Securities and Exchange Commission (SEC) has emphasized that margin accounts are inherently risky and may not be suitable for all investors.

89. Market

DEFINITION: A market is a place where people come together for the purpose of exchanging valuable goods, whether directly via barter of one type of good for another or indirectly via the sale of goods for monetary consideration.

ETYMOLOGY: The word "market" comes via Middle English and Old North French from the Latin term *mercatus,* meaning "business," "traffic," or "trade," as well as the place where the business or trade occurs, which is to say, a "marketplace."

Mercatus, in turn, is connected to the deponent verb *mercor*, meaning "to traffic in" or "to trade," and the noun *merx* (*mercis*), meaning "goods" or "merchandise."

USAGE: Markets are almost certainly as old as humanity.

Wherever there is any degree of division of labor in a society—which is to say, in all known societies—the motivation exists for people who specialize in producing one type of good to exchange the portion of their production that is in excess of their personal needs for other types of goods produced by others.

Over the course of history, direct barter has been almost entirely replaced by indirect exchange based on sales for consideration within a money-based economies.

Moreover, over time—and in recent years at an accelerating pace—many new kinds of markets have come into existence. However, it is interesting to note that the new types of markets typically exist side by side with the older ones, they do not replace them.

For example, to this day, farmer's markets—in which primary agricultural producers haul their produce into local market towns or nearby cities for face-to-face sales to customers—still exist throughout the world, including many of its most highly industrialized regions, such as Europe (the US is an outlier here).

With modernization, intermediate transactions arose in between the primary producers and the ultimate users of most goods. In the agricultural sector, this process took the form of large grocery stores, which were pioneered in the US, although they are now increasingly found in Europe and around the world.

In other sectors, the distinction between retail and wholesale businesses is much older.

Technically speaking, each such additional step in the chain between the producer and the ultimate consumer constitutes a transaction or exchange unto itself, thus creating a market of its own.

Over time, one may safely say that the overall number of such markets has proliferated exponentially. Thus, one aspect of the new forms that markets have taken historically is quantitative in nature.

However, in addition to this enormous proliferation in the sheer number of markets, we must also look at qualitatively new forms that markets have taken, especially since the industrial revolution:

For example, in addition to wholesale markets, we may distinguish the following specialized markets:

- Intermediate goods markets, for the production of goods required for the production of other goods
- Labor markets, for people to exchange their labor in exchange for a wage
- Auctions, in which goods are sold to the highest bidder
- Energy markets, in which sources of specific sources of energy (oil, gas, electricity) are bought and sold

All of the above are markets in physical, tangible goods. In addition, there are markets in non-tangible goods, including the following:

- Media markets, including newspaper, magazine, television, radio, and Internet markets
- Electronic commerce markets, in which goods are sold directly to customers via the Internet

A subset of markets in non-tangible goods is markets based on contractual obligations, also known as "financial assets." Among the many kinds of markets in financial assets, we may mention the following:

- Stock markets, for the trade in corporate stocks
- Bond markets, for the trade in corporate and governmental bonds
- Currency markets, for the trade in sovereign-state currencies
- Money markets, in global lending and borrowing
- Insurance markets, in buying and selling insurance coverage

In addition to all of the above, there are also "black markets" in a wide variety of contraband goods. In some countries, black markets constitute a significant proportion of the nation's GDP.

Finally, we ought not to leave the subject of markets without discussing their economic—or, perhaps, philosophical—dimension.

The reality of markets lies at the very foundation of all economic thought.

For example, according to the subjective theory of value first advanced by thinkers like **Carl Menger, William Stanley Jevons**, and **Léon Walras** in the late nineteenth century, and accepted by all but Marxist economists ever since, the value of a thing is determined by the equilibrium arrived at by the aggregate "forces" of supply and demand in operation within a market (which may be quite extensive geographically).

Intuitively, it is easy to understand how this can be so. For example, in an old-fashioned farmer's market, there is usually room for haggling.

The price arrived at through a process of haggling represents the equilibrium point between the desire of the seller to sell his eggs, say, at the highest price possible and the desire of the buyer to buy a dozen eggs at the lowest price possible.

If one could record and aggregate all the prices at which all the eggs are sold by various sellers at all the farmer's markets over a given geographical region, then it seems that one should in principle be able to calculate a mean price for a dozen eggs over that region.

If one did the same thing for all goods sold in all the markets in the region, then one could calculate all the mean prices for all the goods on offer in the economy in question.

This is precisely what socialism (communism) in a pure form requires of the economics commissars of socialist (communist) governments.

As **Friedrich A. Hayek** and **Ludwig von Mises** pointed out during the 1920s and 1930s, this task is inherently impossible. Even today, with the advent of supercomputers, it is still impossible.

How, then, did the economics commissars of the old USSR manage to set prices? The answer is twofold.

First, they did a notoriously poor job of it. After all, economic planning in a centralized economy must still be based on some determination of what people want.

Without market-generated prices, the commissars had nothing to go on when it came to establishing the prices of goods. So, in many cases, they simply guessed.

The result was chronic gluts in some goods and chronic shortages in others.

In all the old communist countries, the shelves of the government-run retail shops were frequently mostly empty. When shipments of goods in demand did arrive in a shop, a long line winding out the door and down the street would form immediately. Moreover, black markets were rampant.

In short, suppression of what **Adam Smith** called the "invisible hand" of the market mechanism for setting prices led to the severe dysfunction and eventually the collapse of the economies of the communist countries.

The second price-setting method that the old Soviet commissars employed was more pragmatic: They imported copies of the *Sears Catalogue* from the US and set their prices accordingly!

Thus, to the limited extent that the communist consumer economies worked, they did so only because they were parasitic on the unfettered free market of the capitalist countries.

90. Marxian Economics

DEFINITION: "Marxian economics" is the economic theory propounded by the nineteenth-century economist, philosopher, and revolutionary activist, **Karl Marx**.

The phrase is also applied to the many economists over the past century or more who have subscribed to Marx's economic doctrines.

More recently, the term "neo-Marxian economics" has begun to be used to refer to the beliefs of Marx's most-recent cohort of followers.

ETYMOLOGY: For the etymology of the word "economics," see the Glossary entry, "**economics**."

It should be noted that academics often distinguish between "Marxist economics," which consists of the principles found in Karl Marx's own books, and "Marxian economics," which is the abstract economic theory based on Marx's principles.

In other words, "Marxian economics," although broadly based on Marx's teachings, is not limited to the detailed doctrines found in Marx's books. Rather, it has been developed in different directions by various later Marxian thinkers.

The adjective "Marxist" may also be used to refer to someone committed to the violent overthrow of capitalist society, but that is a political use of the term, not an economic one.

USAGE: Karl Marx was a prolific author. However, we will ignore his journalistic and his political writings here and focus on his contributions to economics.

Marx's economic writings are mostly found in his three-volume *magnum opus*, *Capital: A Critique of Political Economy*.

The first and most-important volume of *Capital* was published (in German) in 1867. The second and third volumes were edited by **Friedrich Engels** from Marx's manuscripts —Marx having died in 1883—and published posthumously in 1885 and 1894, respectively.

Capital covers a very wide range of economic topics, but the most important of these are the following:

1. The analysis of capitalism, including the prediction of its inevitable crisis and collapse
2. The labor theory of economic value

3. The theory of so-called "surplus product" and "surplus value"
4. The distribution of surplus product and surplus value in relation to different types of economic systems
5. The theory of the so-called "class struggle" and its influence on the economy
6. The theory of "economic evolution"

Let us take a quick look at each of these topics.

(1) It is of course true that nineteenth-century capitalism, fueled by the **Industrial Revolution**, had many faults. The misery of the urban masses depicted in the novels of **Charles Dickens** was scarcely even exaggerated.

Marx extrapolated from the growing pains he saw around him to the future collapse of the entire capitalist system. This was due to a failure to appreciate the ability of capitalism to both contribute to and adapt to technological developments in a sort of positive feedback loop.

If Marx could have risen from the grave to witness the unimaginable prosperity that capitalism had created for the vast majority of people in the industrialized countries over the course of the twentieth century, he would surely have been incredulous.

Regarding Marx's prediction of the collapse of capitalism, there is little to say beyond: He got it about as wrong as it was possible to do.

(2) Regarding the **labor theory of value**, Marx swam against the current of nineteenth-century economic thought. In a nutshell, he claimed that the economic value of a good is primarily determined by the amount of labor that has gone into its production.

This idea was thoroughly debunked by the authors of the **subjective theory of value** not long after publication of *Capital*. It is now nearly universally acknowledged by economists that the economic value of a good is primarily determined by the preferences of consumers.

(3) Marx calls the difference between the sale price of a good on the market and its cost of production the "*Mehrwert*," which was translated as "surplus value." From the point of view of the capitalist—i.e., the owner of the finished good—this is simply the "profit."

What Marx is saying is that that is the wrong perspective. Instead, we should look at the surplus value from the perspective of the workers whose labor went into the production of the good.

Marx argued, on the basis of the labor theory of value, that the surplus value rightly belonged to the laborers, not the capitalist, as their contribution to the production of the good was the most important one.

This perspective, however, relies on the labor theory of value, which has been refuted as thoroughly as any social science theory can be.

(4) Marx's history of economic distribution was path-breaking in certain respects. However, in common with other historians of his time, his economic writings were tendentious by modern historiographic standards.

Though Marx cannot be faulted for not being ahead of his time, nevertheless, his historical discussions are vitiated by his limited perspective. For example, we have already observed how his predictions about capitalism were a dismal failure.

(5) Perhaps Marx's single most distinctive view was his theory of the "class struggle." He was convinced that societies are rigidly divided into hierarchical strata, which are forever locked in a violent struggle with each other.

All known human societies have been hierarchical to one extent or another. That much of Marx's analysis is true. However, the facts do not support the thesis that capitalist societies, in general, are permanently divided into hermetically sealed strata.

These same social and political facts—which basically resolve into the relatively high degree of social mobility in industrialized capitalist societies in comparison with more traditional societies—also mean that Marx's analysis of the economic influence of the class struggle is empirically unfounded.

(6) Finally, Marx's discussion of "economic evolution" has many of the same strengths and weaknesses as his discussion of the forms of economic distribution in various times and places.

Here, Marx was heavily influenced, above all, by the philosophy **G.W.F. Hegel**, but also by **Charles Darwin**, **Herbert Spencer**, and other evolutionary thinkers.

However, the application of the theory of evolution to social transformations is no longer considered to be scientifically valid.

As for Hegel, his theory of history is held, if anything, in even less esteem by today's professional historians than the Social Darwinists.

On the whole, then, it seems fair to say that Marx's influence as an economist has been slight, even if his influence as a political thinker and as an advocate of violent revolution continues unabated into the twenty-first century.

91. Mercantilism

DEFINITION: Mercantilism was a theory and practice of political economy, which operated under the premise that global wealth at any given time is a zero-sum quantity.

This means that any advantage my country obtains through international trade is your country's disadvantage, and *vice versa*.

Mercantilism was the intellectual justification which, for some two centuries during the Early Modern period, led European governments to attempt to control trade, each for its own benefit—that is, to enhance its own national wealth and influence at the expense of its neighbors'.

Many if not most European nations sought at this time to increase their own proportion of what they conceived to be the fixed quantity of world wealth. They did this by boosting their exports through subsidies and curtailing their imports through duties and tariffs.

ETYMOLOGY: The French term "*mercantilisme*" was coined in 1763 by the Marquis de Mirabeau. The term, translated into English, was popularized in 1776 by Adam Smith in *The Wealth of Nations*.

The words *mercantile* in French and "mercantile" in English both derive from the Italian *mercante*, meaning "merchant, which itself derives from the Latin past participle *mercāns, mercantis*, of the deponent verb *mercor, mercari*, meaning "to carry on trade."

USAGE: Mercantilist theory and practice flourished from approximately the sixteenth through the eighteenth centuries.

The ultimate objective of Mercantilism was to strengthen a country's reserves of gold and silver through increased exports—as opposed to diminishing them through imports—all the while promoting domestic employment.

At its core, Mercantilism prioritized the welfare of merchants and producers over those of consumers. Historically, the doctrine went hand-in-glove with the rise to power and world dominance of such firms as England's East India Company and the Dutch East India Company.

The adoption of Mercantilist theory by governments of the day ensured the protection of the economic interests of these companies as essential components of the national economic system.

Here is a checklist of the characteristics of Mercantilism:

- World trade is a zero-sum game
- A country must increase its supply of gold
- A trade surplus is necessary for national prosperity
- Protectionism is necessary to foster a trade surplus
- A country should strive to increase its population
- By supplying cheap raw materials and a captive market for finished goods, colonies help to increase national wealth

During the course of the nineteenth century, classical liberal political economy replaced Mercantilism in the financial theory and practice of most European countries.

92. Modern Monetary Theory

Modern Monetary Theory (MMT) is a controversial macroeconomic theory of recent vintage. It was invented by former hedge-fund manager, **Warren Mosler** (b. 1949), who first published the idea in his 2010 book, *The 7 Deadly Innocent Frauds of Economic Policy.*

In a nutshell, MMT says that modern national governments which are fully in control of their own currencies should view the creation of money and its injection into the economy to stimulate growth as a purely political decision that need not be constrained by economic considerations.

More specifically, Mosler argues that governments should "print money" (which is of course done today at the press of a button) without any backing in the form of government bonds or other debt instruments sold on the market.

According to the conventional understanding of the way the money supply works, if indulged in on a large scale such "free money" should have a whole suite of catastrophic consequences, from distorting the marketplace in favor of government-supported firms, which would drive their competitors out of business, to hyperinflation, leading to collapse of the currency.

With respect to market distortions, MMT's supporters typically view them as a feature, not a bug. That is to say, they are for the most part socialists who believe government officials by rights ought to be in charge of economic decision-making anyway, and not the market.

A number of socialist and progressive economists have given their public support to MMT, notably **Stephanie Kelton,** author of *The Deficit Myth* (2020). Kelton was an advisor to **Bernie Sanders** during his 2016 and 2020 campaigns for the Democratic Party's presidential nomination.

The theory is of course not entirely new (nothing is). Rather, it draws on earlier ideas of **John Maynard Keynes**, **Joan Robinson**, **Nicholas Kaldor**, **Michał Kalecki**, **Piero Sraffa**, **Abba P. Lerner**, and **Hyman P. Minsky,** among others—socialists or progressives, all.

The unexpected influence the theory has had is undoubtedly due to the 2008 financial crisis and the loss of confidence in the capitalist system that has flowed from it—events perhaps best exemplified by the cult-like following of the French socialist author, **Thomas Piketty.**

On the other hand, not all progressive economists support MMT. For example, **Paul Krugman** finds fault with the theory for a technical reason.

Krugman has pointed out that what MMT recommends—the creation of money unlinked to the issuance of debt, such as the sale of government bonds—is technically a form of *seignorage,* which is the net difference between the face value of money and its cost of production.

Since in the digital age the cost of production of money is effectively zero, the *seignorage* attached to money creation today is for all practical purposes +100%.

So, what is wrong with that?

Krugman writes:

> Do the math, and it becomes clear that any attempt to extract too much from seigniorage—more than a few percent of GDP, probably—leads to an infinite upward spiral in inflation. In effect, the currency is destroyed. This would not happen, even with the same deficit, if the government can still sell bonds.

As far as the threat of hyperinflation is concerned, MMT proponents observe that the government can always raise taxes further down the line.

That is of course true. However, the problem with this idea is that the whole point of raising taxes would be to put the brake on economic activity. After all, it is the curtailment of activity that causes the rate of inflation to fall.

In effect, MMT recommends giving inflation free rein until it begins to run out of control and then applying the brakes at the last minute to save the currency by throwing the economy into recession.

But notice that throwing the economy into recession defeats the whole purpose of MMT! Given that the main selling point of MMT was supposed to be its ability to bring about maximum productivity and provide full employment, this built-in necessity to create a recession to avoid hyperinflation would seem to be more than just a minor defect in the theory that might be fixed by a tweak or two here and there.

Remember that this necessity was created by injecting "free money" into the economy in the first place. But it is not such highly artificial "stimulation" that is the secret to economic productivity and growth. Rather, it is low taxes, reasonable regulation, and, above all, a sense of security and predictability (confidence).

Any artificial stimuli such as those recommended by MMT are likely to fail, sooner rather than later. When they do, they inevitably lead to long-term economic outcomes that are worse than they would have been if the measures had not been taken.

93. Monetarism

DEFINITION: Broadly speaking, modern governments have two levers with which to influence the economy: (1) laws affecting taxation, regulation, and spending (fiscal policy) and (2) control of interest rates and the money supply through the central banking mechanism (monetary policy).

Traditionally, fiscal policy was considered more important than monetary policy. Monetarism is the economic doctrine which holds that monetary policy is just as important as fiscal policy, if not more so.

That is, according to monetarism, government control over the interest rate and the money supply can have a significant influence over national economic output and price levels.

ETYMOLOGY: The word "monetarism" derives from the Latin word *moneta,* meaning "money."

USAGE: One of the differences between the earlier neo-classical economic consensus and the later reign of **neoliberalism**, following the Keynesian interlude of the postwar period, is the rise of monetarism during the latter period.

More specifically, monetarism is closely associated with **Milton Friedman** and the Chicago school of economics more generally, which came to international prominence in the 1970s.

Friedman basically began life as a supporter of **Keynesian economics,** then became convinced that the government should focus more on monetary policy than on fiscal policy. This would mean controlling the prime interest rate to fight recessions and the money supply to fight inflation.

One of Friedman's most famous remarks encapsulates the intellectual case for monetarism in as single sentence:

> Inflation is always and everywhere a monetary phenomenon.

Although Friedman did not approve of the Federal Reserve (the US central bank), he felt that, given that the Fed exists, its policy ought to be aimed primarily at keeping the growth of prices in line with the growth in economic output.

94. Money

DEFINITION: Money is *any medium of exchange*. The crucial word here is "medium." If I have eggs and you have bacon, we might agree to exchange a few eggs for several slices of bacon. But there's no medium of exchange here. The exchange is direct, with real goods being exchanged for real goods. Thus we might say that the exchange is "immediate" — in other words, there's *nothing mediating*the exchange.

By contrast, when money takes part in an exchange, it acts as a medium or intermediary to facilitate the exchange. Money, in many instances, acts as an instrumental good. That means it acts as an instrument to procure the real goods that we desire and that make a real difference to our lives. I can enjoy a $20 steak (a real good), but I can't enjoy a $20 bill (an instrumental good) except for the benefit I can derive from it, such as by buying steaks.

But the distinction between real goods and instrumental goods is not hard and fast. Take cigarettes. In prisoner-of-war camps in WW2, cigarettes were used as money to purchase other items (bread, jam, butter). Used in this way, as a medium of exchange, the cigarettes served as instrumental goods. But a prisoner might also simply have wanted to enjoy a good smoke, In that case, the cigarette became a real good.

Gold and silver, which have an long history serving as money, share this same duality of being both real and instrumental goods. Thus gold and silver coins, in their capacity as money, constitute instrumental goods. But as, say, metals that can be made into jewelry, gold and silver constitute real goods.

For money be useful in facilitating exchange, it needs two features: it should be a *unit of account* and a *store of value*. Unit of account just means that we can do arithmetic and accounting with money. We can count it. We can divide it. And when we divide it into parts and then put the parts back together, we get back what we started with. As a unit of account, money is also *fungible*, which means that two items of the same amount of money are interchangeable. So, if you loan me a dollar bill and I pay back the loan with a different dollar bill, we are quit.

We also like to see money serve as a store of value, the point being that money has a certain purchasing power in the present and it should retain that power in the future. As a store of value, money should, ideally, be immune to inflation and deflation. We might think that only inflation undercuts a money's ability of store value (as when a dollar buys tomorrow only half of what it buys today). But deflation is a problem as well for any form of money. If I'm a seller and the currency is deflating, then I'm losing money the longer I wait to sell.

Money comes in three traditional forms and one more recent form:

Commodity money: this is money that consists of physical stuff that has intrinsic value by being reasonably scarce. These moneys are not like air and water, which come in unlimited supplies. As commodities, they come with built-in limitations on proliferation. They are to varying degrees scarce, and their scarcity correlates with their value in exchange.

Redeemable money: This is money that gives you a claim on something of inherent value. Essentially, you can think of it as a receipt for commodity money and which allows you to redeem the receipt for a certain amount of the commodity.

Fiat money: This is money that comes into existence because the government or some other authority says it has value. It takes the form of coin or paper bills, and also as entries on bank ledgers.

Cryptocurrency: This untraditional form of money consists of cryptographic tokens transacted on a secured digital ledger (usually a blockchain) where the amount of the currency possible is strictly controlled (thus preventing proliferation of the sort that is always possible with fiat currencies).

95. Monopoly

DEFINITION: A monopoly is a market that is heavily or exclusively dominated by a single seller.

ETYMOLOGY: From the Greek words for "single" (*monos*) and "to sell" (*pōleō*). The opposite of a "monopoly"—that is, a market dominated by a single buyer—is called a "**monopsony**."

USAGE: Over the past two centuries or so, monopolies have played an important and controversial role in the history, not only of theoretical economic analysis, but also of practical government legislation.

The theoretical problem with monopolies is very simple: by exercising overwhelming domination of a given market, the monopolist undermines the efficiency-inducing mechanism of competition. In this way, a monopolistic market arguably fails to qualify as a "free market." Certainly, it is a market in which the usual mechanism for determining the optimally efficient price—meaning the price that simultaneously satisfies the requirements of the seller and the buyer as well as possible—is lacking.

On the other hand, in most cases free markets are distorted by government actions, whereas in the classic case of a monopoly under conditions of capitalism, it is a private entity that creates the monopoly condition in a given market. Here we are excluding the case of socialism, in which it is the government that creates the monopoly condition.

But if the result of competition under free-market conditions is the success and continued growth of the most efficient enterprise until it holds a monopoly on its market, then it is not clear why this should be regarded as a transgression against the free market, at least from a purely theoretical point of view.

As a further complication, it is necessary to distinguish between "natural monopolies" created endogenously by the overwhelming success of one enterprise operating within a free market and "artificial monopolies" created by some exogenous action, such as a special government privilege (price support, tax exemption, etc.) granted to one favored enterprise operating in a market but not others. The question of whether monopolies can be viewed as consistent with free-market principles applies, of course, only to natural monopolies. Artificial monopolies violate free-market principles by definition.

We are now in a position to see that the question of the legitimacy of natural monopolies from a free-market perspective is not just of theoretical interest. That is because monopolies may have unpleasant practical consequences (such as inflated prices) that warrant government intervention. The goal of such intervention would be to restore competition in the market in question. The means to that goal would be to curtail the monopolistic company's market domination through some sort of legislative action.

This practical aspect of the monopoly question has played an important role in US legislative history. The most famous of such initiatives was the Sherman Antitrust Act of 1890, which placed limits on the size and activities of the industrial conglomerates in railroads, steel, and other industries, which had come into existence over the course of the nineteenth century.

Another well-known example is the 1982 consent decree between the US government and AT&T, Inc. ("Ma Bell"), the holding company which controlled the entire network of seven regional Bell System companies ("Baby Bells"), which collectively controlled almost all long-distance telephone communications in the US. Under the decree, the seven Baby Bells became independent companies in their own right.

In a similar way, calls are being heard today to break up some of the leading Internet-based companies which function as monopolies or near-monopolies, including Facebook, Twitter, Google, Amazon, and others.

96. Monopsony

DEFINITION: A monopsony is a market that is heavily or exclusively dominated by a single buyer.

ETYMOLOGY: From the Greek words for "single" (*monos*) and "to buy" (*opsōneō*). "Monopsony" is the opposite of "**monopoly**."

USAGE: The term "monopsony" is less well known than "monopoly." However, the phenomenon itself is relatively common in modern industrial societies.

A monopsony arises primarily in a situation in which a company first creates a monopoly over a market, perhaps by virtue of some technological innovation. Then, the company decides to outsource its innovative supply needs, bringing a brand new supply chain into existence. In that case, there may be no other buyer for a given supplier's products than the original contracting company, thus creating a monopsony.

In this way, the same company that creates a monopoly over one market may create a monopsony over another one. In this respect, monopolies and monopsonies may be viewed as two sides of the same coin.

As an example, governments are said to hold a monopoly on the legitimate use of violence in society (meaning not that they sell it, but that they are authorized to use it). However, governments do not typically build weapons systems themselves. Rather, they subcontract the fabrication of the weapons they require to private companies. Those companies, then, often have no other customer for their products that the government. This type of market relationship constitutes a classic monopsony.

97. Moral Hazard

DEFINITION: "Moral hazard" is a form of "**externality**," that is, an unintended harm suffered from a market transaction by a third entity that is not a party to the transaction.

What makes moral hazard different is that the original market transaction *incentivizes* the party that causes the harm to act in the same harmful manner in the future.

Also, in the case of moral hazard, the injured party may be a party to the transaction itself.

ETYMOLOGY: The word "moral" derives, via Middle English and Middle French, from the classical Latin noun *mōs, mōris,* meaning "will," "mood," "inclination," or "custom," and the related adjective "*mōrālis,*" meaning "moral" or "ethical."

The word "hazard" derives, via Middle English, from the Middle French word *hasard,* which basically means "chance," but also has a range of extended meanings, from "occasion" and "possibility" to "accident," "danger," "risk," or "peril." The Middle French word *hasard,* in turn, derives from the Arabic word *al-zahr*, meaning "dice."

USAGE: Economic situations in which moral hazard arises are marked by what are often referred to as "perverse incentives," that is, rational motivations supplied to one of the parties to the transaction to continue engaging in the harm-causing activity in the future.

For example, when someone purchases automobile insurance, he may drive a little less carefully, raising the probability of his having an accident due to his subjective state of mind. The harm, in this case, would fall on both the insurance policy owner and the insurer which issued the policy.

None of this means that either the harms or the incentives are intended or even conscious. The claim, rather, is that economists can successfully explain the observed economic activity arising out of such situations by invoking the concepts of externality, moral hazard, perverse incentives, and so forth.

The phrase "moral hazard" dates to the seventeenth century. It originated in the budding insurance industry of the day, which explains the connection between the term "hazard" and the notion of probability (in the sense that perverse incentives increase the probability of risky behavior).

The term "moral" had a different meaning at that time, as well, having a connotation closer to the modern concepts "subjective" and "psychological" than to the concept "ethical."

Historically speaking, then, "moral hazard" originally meant "subjective probability." Thus, moral hazard pointed to the fact that perverse incentives increased the subjective (psychological) probability of an economic actor's engaging in risky behavior, that is, behavior likely to cause harm.

"Moral hazard" first became well known to the general public in the wake of the real estate bubble and subsequent financial crisis of 2008.

A part of the explanation for the bubble and the failure of many financial institutions that many economists offered at the time was that there was a widespread perception that the largest investment banks were "too big to fail," meaning that the government would step in to bail them out if necessary.

This perception was explicitly said to cause "moral hazard" for the banks. More explicitly, critics also said that the situation effectively "privatized profit" and "socialized loss."

This provided perverse incentives to the banks to engage in highly risky behavior—such as greatly relaxing the conditions on borrowers' financial qualifications in order to greatly increase the number of mortgages sold.

In recent years, the phrase "moral hazard" has begun to expand beyond the bounds of academic economics into other fields of social science.

For example, today it is not unusual to encounter claims such as that relaxing conditions on receiving welfare payments produces "moral hazard," meaning that such generosity will generate perverse incentives, which will then have the counterproductive effect of inducing more and more people to give up looking for paid work and to live from welfare.

98. Nash Equilibrium

DEFINITION: The notion of a "Nash equilibrium" is a key concept within the mathematical discipline of game theory.

Widely applied in economics, the Nash equilibrium describes the solution of a certain type of non-cooperative game involving two or more players.

A Nash equilibrium comes about in circumstances in which no player has a motivation to alter its initial strategy. In other words, all players feel that the outcome is optimal.

More specifically, even when each player learns of its opponents' strategies, all players continue to regard their initial choice as their best strategy.

ETYMOLOGY: The Nash equilibrium was introduced by mathematician **John Forbes Nash, Jr.**, in a paper published in 1950.[1]

The paper was based on work Nash was doing at Princeton University on his doctoral dissertation, entitled "Non-cooperative Games." He received his PhD in mathematics from Princeton that same year (1950).

Nash was awarded the Nobel Memorial Prize in Economic Sciences in 1994 for his work on game theory.

It is sometimes said that Nash's result was anticipated in an 1838 discussion of oligopoly by French mathematician, **Antoine Augustin Cournot**. However, Nash's work was much broader, effectively laying the foundations for the entire field of game theory.

The English word "equilibrium" is attested from the early seventeenth century.

It derives from the Latin noun *aequilibrium,* with the same meaning, from the adjective *aequilibris, aequilibre,* meaning "level." The latter word is compounded of the adjective *aequus,* meaning "equal," and the noun *libra,* meaning "a pair of scales."

USAGE: In general terms, a Nash equilibrium is a situation in which an individual gains no additional advantage by altering its actions. The solution assumes that the other players maintain consistent strategies.

A given game may possess either numerous Nash equilibria or none.

The reason why the concept of Nash equilibrium has attracted so much attention and is considered so important is that it may be applied to many fields of social science,

[1] John F. Nash, Jr. (1950) "Equilibrium Points in n-Person Games," *Proceedings of the National Academy of Sciences. USA,* **36**: 48–49.

although its utility for the discipline of economics in particular probably remains its best-known application.

Moreover, it is quite simple to determine whether a given game-theoretic solution is or is not a Nash equilibrium: simply reveal each player's strategy to the others.

If no player alters its strategy and the *status quo ante* is maintained, then the solution constitutes an instance of the Nash equilibrium.

99. Negotiable Instrument

DEFINITION: The term "negotiable instrument" refers to a writing or document that is a species of contract issued by a payor, such as a bank, which contains a promise to pay a determinate sum of money to a named payee (or else to order), either on demand or at a future date, specified or unspecified, and makes no other condition upon the payor except payment of the named sum.

ETYMOLOGY: The term "negotiable" derives from the Latin word *negotium*, meaning "business." Interestingly, *negotium* itself may be analyzed into the prefix *nec-* ("not") and the noun *otium* ("leisure").

The term "instrument" derives from the Latin word *instrumentum*, meaning "tool" or, in the plural (*instrumenta*), "equipment."

USAGE: In law, a writing or document must meet several specific requirements to be deemed a valid negotiable instrument.

- It must promise to make the payment to the payee named in the instrument, or else to order, meaning according to the named payee's instructions.
- It must promise to pay a determinate sum of money, although accrued interest may be added to the sum named in the instrument.
- It must promise to make the payment either upon demand by the payee or at a definite time.
- It must state that the payment is unconditional, meaning the payor may not be required to perform any act other than to make the payment.

There are many different kinds of negotiable instruments meeting these basic requirements. Most of them may be grouped together under the heading "unconditional promissory notes."

Another category of negotiable instrument is known as "bills of exchange."

Specific negotiable instruments we are familiar with in everyday life include bank notes, checks, certificates of deposit, stocks, and bonds.

Note that all these instruments can be traded, either with other individuals or on open markets, by assigning them to the purchaser.

Also, notice that bank notes fail to meet one of the principal formal requirements of negotiable instruments: they do not name the payee. Nevertheless, in colloquial speech they are usually included in that category.

100. Neoliberalism

DEFINITION: The term "neoliberalism" generally refers to the historical event of the turn away from the post–World War II Keynesian consensus in the Western industrial democracies, back towards the earlier *laissez-faire* consensus of the nineteenth century.

ETYMOLOGY: The prefix "neo-" derives from the Greek adjective *neos*, meaning "new," and the root "liberal" comes from the Latin adjective *liberus*, meaning "free."

USAGE: The term "neoliberalism" came into existence in the 1970s, first in the Latin American countries that attempted to roll back decades of socialist incursions in their economies in the wake of the 1973 *coup d'état* against Chile's communist **President Salvador Allende** led by **General Augusto Pinochet**.

Pinochet brought **Milton Friedman** and other American free-market economists to Chile to work as consultants, in his effort to revive his country's prostrate economy.

In line with Friedman's recommendations, Pinochet oversaw a wholesale overhaul of Chile's economy, privatizing publicly owned industries, loosening government regulations that had strangled private entrepreneurship, abolishing duties and tariffs in order to open up Chile's market to the global market, and scaling back government spending and taxation.

These policies quickly reversed decades of socialist depredations, setting off an astonishing economic boom in Chile, which had reverberations throughout Latin America.

It is important to note that the term "neoliberalism" was introduced by socialist and communist *critics* of these successful free-market policies. Thus, the word had a *pejorative* connotation right from the beginning—which continues to this day.

Neoliberal ideas—which are in essence little different from the ideas espoused by **Austrian economics**—gradually percolated out of Latin America into the wider world, where before long they swept the West.

The tenures in office of **Prime Minister Margaret Thatcher** in the UK and **Presidents Ronald Reagan** and **Bill Clinton** in the US are examples of the heyday of neoliberal consensus during the 1980s and 1990s.

However, neoliberalism's run as a victorious and uncontested policy preference was to prove short-lived.

Two events, more than any others, sounded the death knell of neoliberalism as an economic consensus. The first was the 2008 asset bubble and resulting credit crisis. The second was the sovereign-debt crisis that engulfed Greece and other small countries that were members of the **European Union (EU).**

Beginning in 2009 and culminating in 2015, the EU attempted to impose neoliberal-inspired "austerity" policies upon Greece, creating widespread unemployment, economic suffering, and political discontent.

The crisis came to a head with the Greek national elections in January of 2015, in which the progressive **Syriza** coalition was victorious. Syriza's leader **Alexis Tsipras** became Prime Minister. Tsipras's ally, the progressive economist **Yanis Varoufakis,** became Minister of Finance.

For the next eight months, Tsipras and Varoufakis battled the EU bureaucracy in Brussels, as well as the German banks who were Greece's main creditors, to obtain some breathing space for the Greek people. Their success was real, if limited.

Although Syriza fell from power in August of 2015 (it later governed for a few months in 2019, as well), the incident was historically important in two ways.

First, it created a groundswell of sympathy for the Greeks, seriously undermining the neoliberal consensus. While the EU remains officially devoted to neoliberal policies, it now treads more lightly in its economic dealings with its member states.

Second, the Greek sovereign-debt crisis was the event which, more than any other, brought "neoliberalism" in the pejorative sense into common currency among the general public that follows the news but is not expert in economic or financial affairs.

One might even argue that the rise of forthrightly socialist candidates for high office in the United States since 2016—a previously unthinkable development—is due in no small part to the 2015 donnybrook in Greece and to the resulting bad odor in which the term "neoliberalism" came to be held by millions of voters around the world.

101. Net Worth

DEFINITION: The phrase "net worth" refers to the valuation of the difference between an individual's or corporation's assets less its outstanding liabilities.

The metric of net worth plays a crucial role in assessing a company's economic well-being. It offers an invaluable snapshot of the company's present financial standing.

Occasionally referred to as "net wealth," an individual's net worth finds application in numerous financial contexts.

Specifically, net worth determines eligibility for certain kinds of investment approaches or financial instruments, such as hedge funds, structured products, or other intricate and unconventional investments.

In popular culture, the net worth of celebrities and other well-known individuals has become an object of widespread fascination, leading to investigations into such individuals' net worth and its public disclosure in the media.

ETYMOLOGY: The phrase "net worth"was probably in use by 1910.

The English adjective "net," used in the financial sense discussed here, derives from Middle English *net,* meaning "bright" or "clean," which, in turn, derives from Middle French *net,* meaning "clean." The latter ultimately derives from Latin verb *niteo, nitēre,* meaning "to shine," "to be bright," or "to glitter."

The English "net" may have also been influenced by Italian *netto,*meaning "net" in the financial sense.

Moreover, modern English word "net," in the financial sense, is allied to the adjective "neat," meaning "pure" or "free from admixture," which is also derived from Middle French *net.*

The English noun "worth" is attested from the eleventh century.

"Worth" derives, via Middle English, from Old English *weorth,* "a specified value," which is akin to Old High German *werd, "worth."*

USAGE: Net worth is calculated by deducting liabilities from assets.

An "asset" refers to anything that is owned that possesses a monetary value.

A "liability," in contrast, refers to any obligation that consumes resources, such as a loan, an account payable, a mortgage, or any of a large number of similar debts.

Net worth may be classified as either positive or negative.

A *positive net worth* implies that assets surpass liabilities, whereas a *negative net worth* means that liabilities exceed assets.

A positive and growing net worth indicates a healthy financial condition, while a diminishing or negative net worth indicates the need for emergency course correction to avoid bankruptcy.

Enhancing net worth can be achieved in either of two ways, or through a combination of them both:

- By diminishing liabilities, while maintaining or increasing assets
- By augmenting assets, while keeping liabilities constant or decreasing

The concept of net worth is widely applicable, from real entities, such as individuals and companies, to abstract statistical constructs, such as sectors and even entire nations.

Let us look more closely at the two most important of these, individual and corporate new worth:

Corporate net worth

In the business context, net worth may also be referred to as "book value" or "shareholder equity." The **balance sheet** is also recognized as a net worth statement.

A company's equity may be quantified as the difference between the total value of its assets minus the total value of its liabilities. Note that the figures on a company's balance sheet reflect historical costs or book values, rather than current market values.

Lenders examine a business's net worth to assess its financial well-being. If total liabilities exceed total assets, a creditor might think twice about the company's capacity to service a new loan.

A consistently profitable company will experience an increasing net worth or book value, provided that its earnings are not entirely distributed to shareholders as dividends.

In the case of a publicly traded company, an increasing book value frequently correlates with a rise in its stock price.

Individual net worth

An individual's net worth is calculated by subtracting his liabilities from his assets.

Individual liabilities may encompass debts like home mortgages, car loans, student loans, and credit card balances. Liabilities may also comprise obligations that necessitate payment, such as utility bills and taxes.

An individual's assets usually consist of such things as checking and savings account balances, the value of real property, a vehicle's market value, the worth of securities like stocks or bonds, and others. Net worth is what remains after liquidating all assets and settling personal debts.

Individuals with significant net worth are sometimes called "high net worth individuals" (HNWI). They constitute the key demographic for wealth managers and investment advisors.

The Securities and Exchange Commission (SEC) recognizes investors with a net worth of at least $1 million (exclusive of their primary residence) as "accredited investors." This status authorizes them to participate in unregistered securities offerings.

102. Non-Fungible Token

DEFINITION: A "non-fungible token" (NFT) is a unique, digital data file that, through **blockchain** technology, can be owned and traded on the open market.

ETYMOLOGY: The adjective "fungible" derives from the New Latin adjective *fungibilis*, which in turn derives from the classical Latin verb, *fungor, fungi*, meaning "to occupy oneself," "to perform," "to undergo," "to be affected," or "to suffer."

As an English word, "fungible" is of relatively recent origin, being first attested with this meaning in the early nineteenth century.

The word "token" derives, via Middle English, from the Old English word *tācen*, meaning "sign."

The English word "token" is akin to the Old High German word *zeihhan*, meaning "sign," and the Greek verb *deiknumi*, meaning "to show."

USAGE: The word "fungible" means "interchangeable with other physical tokens of the same type with respect to a specific purpose."

For example, US currency is fungible in that a $1 bill is interchangeable with four quarters so far as purchasing power is concerned.

Superficially, NFTs may appear to be similar to **cryptocurrency**. However, like physical currency, cryptocurrency is fungible.

Therefore, NFTs ought rather to be thought of as digital versions of unique physical objects that have traditionally been regarded as stores of value, such as autographed baseballs and other sports memorabilia, first editions of old books, Old Master paintings, and similar singular objects.

NFTs exist in the form of one-of-a-kind digital data files, which may include photographic, audio, and video elements.

The ownership and provenance of NFTs are assured through blockchain technology.

The market price at which each exchange occurs may also be included as auxiliary information associated with each block of the blockchain.

Despite the ownership and provenance authentication offered by blockchain technology, the legal system has not kept up with the growth of cryptocurrencies and NFTs.

Therefore, it must be understood that ownership of an NFT does not provide copyright or other intellectual property right protection that would be enforceable in a court of law.

NFTs have been widely criticized as an **economic bubble** and even as a type of **Ponzi scheme**.

In 2022, **Bill Gates** said he believes the economic performance of NFTs depends upon the so-called "**greater fool theory**," meaning that only a fool would buy an NFT, but the reason why the price goes up is that each seller can always find a "greater fool" to sell to.

103. Non-Zero-Sum Game

DEFINITION: A "non-zero-sum game" is a type of two-sided game—in the mathematical, game-theoretic sense of the word "game"—in which a positive outcome for one side may correspond to a positive outcome for the other side, as well

In colloquial speech, a non-zero-sum game is known as a "win-win" situation.

The opposite of a non-zero-sum game is a **zero-sum game.**

ETYMOLOGY: The phrase "non-zero-sum" derives from the fact that the sum of the outcomes of the game for the two sides may attain values other than zero.

For example, in a non-zero-sum game, if Side A achieves an outcome of $+n$, then Side B may also achieve a positive outcome, say, $+m$. The point being that, generally speaking, $n + m \neq 0$.

USAGE: In economics, it is important to remember that most situations involving production, investment, income, profit, employment, wages, and so on are non-zero-sum in nature.

Which is to say that it is perfectly possible—indeed, it is an everyday occurrence—that what makes the factory-owner better off makes the worker better off, as well.

It is relatively seldom that true zero-sum situations are encountered in everyday economic life—as opposed to the abstract theory and the political rhetoric surrounding economic decisions and policy-making.

For further discussion, see the article **zero-sum game**.

104. Obamanomics

DEFINITION: "Obamanomics" is a colloquial term referring to the economic policies pursued by the administration of US **President Barack Obama** between 2009 and 2017.

USAGE: When Barack Obama assumed office in January of 2009, he inherited the effects of the worst international economic collapse since 1929.

The financial crisis had erupted about four months earlier, in September of 2008, when a growing worldwide recession that began in 2007 culminated in the simultaneous failure of dozens of financial institutions, notably, Lehman Brothers, the fourth-largest investment bank in the US at the time, which filed for bankruptcy protection on September 15, 2008.

The underlying reason for the Great Recession (as it came to be called) and the 2008 crisis is much debated. However, many observers attribute it to an unsustainable asset bubble in real estate prices that had been encouraged by various federal banking policies.

All in all, it is estimated that the financial crisis wiped out some $10 trillion in economic output.

The outgoing administration of President George W. Bush had already intervened to bail out some banks and to inject money into the economy in a desperate effort to turn the recession around.

In short, Obama inherited an economic shambles when he took the oath of office on January 20. 2009.

Upon the advice of his Secretary of the Treasury, **Timothy Geithner**, Federal Reserve Chairman **Ben Bernanke**, and others, Obama decided to double-down on Bush's bail out–stimulus approach to the crisis.

Accordingly, Obama sent a legislative package to the US Congress, which came to be known as the **American Recovery and Reinvestment Act of 2009**. This Act provided an overall stimulus package with a price tag of some $830 billion, including a bailout for the US automobile industry to the tune of $13 billion.

While Obama's policies did save many of the nation's largest industrial and financial institutions and did put the US economy on the road to recovery, it came at a high cost in trust of the country's institutions, over and above the cost to the country's balance sheet.

The criticisms of Obamanomics may be divided into three categories.

First, there is the empirical fact that, while Obama's policies were undoubtedly successful in the short term, in that they prevented the emergency from spinning further out of control, leading to many more bankruptcies and a much deeper recession, over the longer term they were not in fact very successful.

That is to say, the recovery during Obama's two terms in office was anemic by the criterion of historic recoveries. The growth rate in the gross national product (GDP) on the day Obama left office eight years later, January 20, 2017, was just 1.7%.

Second, there is the theoretical criticism by advocates of the free market, who see Obamanomics as a gross and harmful increase in government spending, regulation, and taxation.

Such critics argue that in the long run it would have been better to forgo the stimulus and the bail outs, since—even though the recession would have been deeper—it would have been shorter and the subsequent recovery would have been far more robust.

For the free-market critics, though, the worst thing about Obamanomics was that it set a terrible precedent. It essentially "privatized sucsess" and "socialized failure," thus amounting to a massive exercise in inflating moral hazard beyond all previous bounds.

Finally, critics argued that Obamanomics badly exacerbated the already-growing economic inequality plaguing US society.

For example, between 2007 and 2010, there were nearly four million foreclosures on American homes, while the immensely wealthy and powerful financial institutions that had made these bad loans in the first place almost all walked away from the crisis having been made whole.

Thus, in addition to being a terrible precent, as already mentioned, Obamanomics also represented a gross violation of simple justice.

105. Offshore

DEFINITION: As an adjective, the colloquial term “offshore” refers to any subsidiary entity of a company that is located outside the recognized political borders of the nation in which the company is situated.

As a verb, the term refers to the company’s action of setting up such a subsidiary entity abroad.

USAGE: The term “offshore” is used in a variety of contexts, from petroleum engineering to alternative power generation.

However, in the economic/financial sense of the term that is our primary concern here, “offshore” refers to the practice of a company’s transplanting a portion of its operations outside the legal jurisdiction in which its main operations are situated into a foreign jurisdiction.

The reason for offshoring operations is that the business expects the foreign legal jurisdiction will be more favorable to its operations in some way or other (see below).

Since the term “offshore” is an English word that originated in the US, it is most often used to refer to American-based companies that engage in the practice of offshoring. But it applies equally well to any company, located in any country anywhere, that engages in the practice.

There are a host of legal nuances regarding the legal jurisdictions of companies engaging in business operations in multiple countries.

Here, we will only look at the distinction between two most-fundamental types of offshoring: namely, for wage reasons and for tax reasons.

The first type of offshoring is a subset of the practice of “**outsourcing**.”

In outsourcing, a larger company engages a smaller company to carry out a portion of its operations as an outside contractor. When the outside contractor is located in another country, the instance of outsourcing becomes an instance of offshoring.

The main economic motivation for this type of offshoring is to get the needed work done at a lower cost. For this reason, such contractors will naturally be located in countries with a much-lower wage structure.

Familiar examples of this type of offshoring are the *maquiladores*(relatively low-tech manufacturing facilities) located in Mexico and elsewhere in Latin America; the human-resource and software-writing contractors located in India; and the hi-tech manufacturing operations located in China.

The other type of offshoring has a name of its own: "tax havens."

These are jurisdictions which offer an extremely favorable tax environment to foreign companies which open subsidiary operations on their soil.

Some small countries and territories—notably, the Cayman Islands, the British Virgin Islands, Bermuda, Singapore, Mauritius, and others—have specialized in attracting such subsidiary operations to their shores.

Such tax havens are perhaps what the term "offshore" most readily brings to mind.

106. Oligopoly

DEFINITION: An oligopoly is a market that is dominated by a small number of sellers.

ETYMOLOGY: The word "oligopoly" derives from the Greek adjective *oligos*, meaning "a little (not much)" or "few (not many)," and verb *pōleō*, meaning "sell."

USAGE: In theory, markets with several sellers ought to be competitive. After all, an oligopoly is not a **monopoly**. In a purely rational world, one might expect that even two or three sellers would suffice to form a perfectly free market.

In practice, however, human beings are not perfectly rational economic actors.

Or perhaps it would be more accurate to say that they will attempt to bend the rules of the game in their own favor, wherever possible.

Specifically, companies that enter into an oligopoly negotiate among themselves over prices. This practice is called "price fixing."

Why would a company enter into a price-fixing agreement, rather than compete head-to-head with its competitors, letting the invisible hand of the free market set the final price?

Because prices fixed by companies entering into an oligopoly are typically much higher than the prices that emerge from a truly competitive market.

To paraphrase the philosopher **Bertrand Russell**, oligopolies possess all the advantages of theft over honest toil.

Thus, when there are only a few economic actors present in a given market, the temptation to oligopoly is always present.

Moreover, due to decades of mergers and buy-outs, the number of economic actors in many, if not most, modern markets has been drastically reduced.

In other words, we are now living in the age of oligopoly.

107. Oligopsony

DEFINITION: An oligopsony is a market that is dominated by a small number of sellers.

ETYMOLOGY: The word "oligopsony" derives from the Greek adjective *oligos*, meaning "a little (not much)" or "few (not many)," and the verb *opsōneō*, meaning "buy."

USAGE: An oligopsony from one point of view is often an **oligopoly**from the opposite point of view.

For example, the vast majority of the world's primary cocoa production is bought by just three multinational companies.

By the same token, nearly all the world's processed chocolate is sold by these same three companies and their subsidiaries.

108. Open Market Operations

DEFINITION: The phrase "open market operations (OMOs)" refers to the purchase and sale of securities on the open market by the US Federal Reserve ("the Fed").

The Fed undertakes OMOs to control the amount of money held in reserve by American banks collectively.

The Fed buys Treasury securities when it wishes to increase the money supply and sells them when it wishes to decrease the money supply.

Open market operations enable the Fed to fine-tune the federal funds rate. The Fed's adjustments then ripple through various short-term and long-term interest rates, as well as foreign exchange rates.

For this reason, OMOs create the potential for shifts in the volume of money and credit accessible within the economy, which, in turn, impacts a variety of significant economic phenomena, including commodities and services pricing, output and unemployment rates, and similar factors.

ETYMOLOGY: The phrase "open market operations" seems to have been introduced around 1923, along with the practice it describes.

The English adjective "open" derives from Middle and Old English words with the identical form and meaning. The Old English word is akin to Old High German *offan,* also meaning "open."

The English noun "market" (used here adjectivally) derives, via Middle English and Old North French, from Latin *mercātus, mercātūs,*meaning "trade," "traffic," or "business," as well as the place where the trade or business occurs (i.e., a "marketplace").

Mercātus, in turn, is connected to the deponent verb *mercor, mercari,*meaning "to trade" or "to traffic in," as well as the noun *merx, mercis,*meaning "goods" or "merchandise."

The English noun "operation" derives, via Middle English *operacioun,*from Middle French *opération,* which, in turn, derives from the Latin noun *operatio, operationis,* with a similar meaning.

Operatio, for its part,is connected with the past participle *operātus* of the deponent verb *operor, operari,* meaning "to work," "to labor," or "to be busy."

Operatio may also be connected directly with the noun *opus, operis,*meaning "work," "labor," or "a finished piece of work."

USAGE: To grasp the concept of open market operations, it is first of all essential to understand how the Federal Reserve, the United States's central bank, puts the government's monetary policy into action.

The Fed's ultimate goal is to preserve the stability of the US economy and to prevent out-of-control price inflation or deflation. The Fed's Board of Governors is the entity tasked with achieving these aims and thus with determining the federal funds rate target.

The federal funds rate is the interest rate at which depository institutions make short-term loans to each other.

This ongoing circulation of funds accomplishes two purposes:

- It allows banks to generate earnings on surplus funds held in their Federal Reserve balances
- It allows banks to maintain the reserves necessary to satisfy customer demand

The federal funds rate functions as a benchmark, which exerts influence over a wide array of other interest rates, ranging from savings deposit rates to home mortgage rates to credit card rates and more.

In summary, open market operations represent one of the principal instruments by means of which the Fed maintains the federal funds rate at or near its predetermined target.

109. Option

DEFINITION: The term "option" refers to a financial tool whose value is contingent upon the value of underlying assets, such as stocks, indexes, and exchange-traded funds (ETFs).

An options contract provides the purchaser with the choice of either buying or selling, the choice hinging on the underlying asset, depending upon the specific kind of contract.

Options differ from futures in that the holder is not obliged to buy or sell his asset but may do as he chooses.

Options contracts always designate an expiration date by which the option must be exercised.

The indicated price on an option is referred to as the "strike price."

Options are commonly bought and sold via retail, including online, brokers.

ETYMOLOGY: The concept of purchasing the right to buy a commodity at some point in the future is already attested in Antiquity.

Options, under earlier appellations, were in common use during the late Renaissance origin of modern banking and the Early Modern beginnings of modern industry and commerce. The English word "option" itself is attested from the early seventeenth century.

The English noun "option" derives, via French, from Latin *optio, optiōnis,* meaning "choice" or "option." *Optio,* in turn, derives from the verb *opto, optare,* "to elect," "to select," or "to elect."

USAGE: Options involve a buyer and a seller, with the buyer offering a premium in exchange for the privileges authorized by the contract.

As financial instruments, options exhibit a good deal of versatility.

"Call options" authorize the holder to purchase the asset at a predetermined price within a specified period, while "put options" authorize the holder to sell the asset at a predetermined price within a specified period.

In the case of call options, one might say that a bullish buyer is matched with a bearish seller, while in the case of put options, a bearish buyer is matched with a bullish seller.

Traders and investors engage in the purchase and sale of options for various reasons.

First, engaging in options speculation enables a trader to maintain a leveraged stance in an asset with lower expenditures compared to acquiring shares of the asset.

Second, investors employ options to hedge against (mitigate) the risk exposure of their portfolios.

Third, the holder of an option may sometimes have the potential to generate earnings by purchasing call options or assuming the role of an options writer.

Fourth, options also present a straightforward avenue for investing in certain circumstances, such as, for example, oil.

In all cases, options traders should closely monitor their options' daily trading volume and open interest level (the number of options or futures contracts held by traders in active positions at a given time), which are significant data for making astute investment choices.

Calls versus Puts

A call option entitles its holder, but without creating any obligation, to purchase the underlying security at a pre-determined price called the "strike price"—regardless of market conditions when the option is exercised—whether on or before the expiration date.

The value of a call option increases as the price of the underlying asset goes up (calls exhibit a "positive delta"). In other words, a call is tantamount to a bet that the underlying security will increase in price.

Note that a long call has a limitless potential for gain (if the value of the underlying security continues to rise), while the maximum potential for loss remains capped (at the strike price).

Unlike the case with call options, a "put" entitles its holder, but without creating any obligation, to sell the underlying security at the strike price before or on the expiration date.

The value of a put increases as the price of the underlying asset goes down (puts exhibit a "negative delta"). In other words, a put is tantamount to a bet that the underlying security will decrease in price. Thus, a put essentially constitutes a short position in the underlying security.

Note that a long put has an inherently limited potential for gain (established by the strike price) and a potential for loss that is limited to the whole value of the strike price (if the value of the underlying asset drops to zero).

However, like short positions, puts may be desirable because they function as insurance, establishing a lower limit on price and enabling investors to mitigate risks in their positions.

110. Outsource

DEFINITION: To "outsource" is for one company to hire a second, external company to perform a business activity ordinarily carried out by one of the first company's internal departments.

ETYMOLOGY: The verb "outsource," and the noun "outsourcing," derive, via Middle English, from the Old English word *ūt,* meaning "out," which is akin to the Old High German word *ūz,* with the same meaning.

The word "source" derives, via Middle English and Middle French, from the Old French verb, *sourdre,* meaning "to rise" or "to spring forth, which in turn derives from the classical Latin verb *surgo, surgere,* meaning to "to rise," "to get up," "to stand up," "to spring up," or "to arise."

The practice we now call "outsourcing" was originally referred to as "outside resourcing." The term "outsource" is thought to have been created—most likely sometime around 1980—as a telescoped form of this phrase.

USAGE: The practice of outsourcing—as opposed to the term itself—has its origins in the upheaval in business and management practices which followed upon the economic boom in the wake of World War II.

Some of the first business functions to be outsourced were such things as payroll processing, claims processing, auxiliary (non-core) manufacturing functions, and customer service or call center support, among others.

If the companies to which a business function is outsourced are located in a foreign country, we speak of "**offshoring**," which is a subset of outsourcing.

While outsourcing is primarily a practice of the private sector, in recent decades a wide variety of government functions have begun to be outsourced, as well, including notably, prisons and various forms of security and quasi-military operations, from personal protection of public officials to the provisioning of government army units deployed in conflict zones.

111. Paper Money

DEFINITION: The phrase "paper money" has a wide sense and a narrow sense. In both senses, paper money is a form of **negotiable instrument** that is a species of unconditional promissory note.

ETYMOLOGY: the word "money" derives, via Middle English and Middle French, from the Latin word *moneta,* meaning "money."

USAGE: In its narrow sense, "paper money" refers to "banknotes" (or "bills") that are a form of **money** that is legally a species of unconditional promissory note.

Bank notes are issued by banks, possess a face value denominated in the currency of the jurisdiction in question, and are payable to the bearer of the note on demand.

The last-named condition distinguishes bank notes from other kinds of unconditional promissory notes, which ordinarily require that a payee be named on the instrument.

In its broad sense, "paper money" refers to any form of paper negotiable instrument or promissory note. An example would be paper receipts and IOUs issued by wholesalers to suppliers to avoid the expense of transporting and storing heavy **coins.**

Such promissory notes existed long before banknotes. The first paper money, in the wide sense, dates from the Tang Dynasty (618–907 AD) in China—which is not surprising, seeing that the Chinese invented both paper and the printing press.

The Chinese invention filtered into Europe during the Middle Ages. The **banks** which grew up in the later medieval and Renaissance periods, beginning in northern Italy, made use of very similar promissory notes.

However, the issuance of paper money in the narrow sense of banknotes soon became primarily the prerogative of the central banks of nation states.

Thus, the first true bank notes date mostly from the seventeenth century, when the first central bank of a nation state came into being in Sweden: namely, the *Sveriges Riksbank,* which was founded in Stockholm in 1668.

From that date until 1971, bank notes were fully convertible into gold. This meant that government banks were required to exchange their bank notes for an equivalent amount of gold.

In 1971, **President Richard M. Nixon** took the US off of the gold standard. Subsequently, bank notes could no longer be exchanged for gold.

The practical effect of this policy was that one of the most important restraints on government spending was removed.

In the third decade of the twenty-first century, a strong move is afoot to abolish paper money and transition to an all-electronic system of economic exchange.

Is it an accident hat such a system would greatly facilitate the totalitarian control of the populace by government?

Who would have thought that paper money would turn out to be one of the last weapons in the defense of human freedom?

112. Paradox of Value

DEFINITION: The "paradox of value"—also known as the "water–diamond paradox"—is the counterintuitive fact that the most valuable goods for human life and well-being, such as water, often have little or no exchange or market value, while goods with very high exchange or market value, such as diamonds, often have little or no value for human life and well-being.

ETYMOLOGY: The word "paradox" derives from the Greek word*paradoxos*, meaning "contrary to opinion," "unexpected," "strange," or "marvelous." The word *paradoxos*, in turn, is composed of the prefix*para-*, meaning "beside" or "beyond," and *doxa*, meaning "opinion."

The word "value" derives, via Middle English, Middle French, and Vulgar Latin, from the classical Latin verb *valeo, valēre*—more specifically, fromthe feminine of the past participle, *valuta*—meaning "be strong," "be vigorous," or "prevail." Thus, the root meaning of "value" was originally "strength, "vigor," or "predominance."

USAGE: The paradox of value was first noted in passing by the Greek philosopher **Plato** in his dialogue ***Euthydemus*** in the early fourth century BC.

Later authors who mention it include the Polish astronomer **Nicolaus Copernicus**, the English philosopher **John Locke**, and the Scottish economist **John Law**.

The "Father of Economics," **Adam Smith**, attempted to resolve the paradox of value by distinguishing between two different kinds of value, which he styled "use value" and "exchange value."

Here is how he expressed the matter in his 1776 classic, *The Wealth of Nations*:

> What are the rules which men naturally observe in exchanging them [goods] for money or for one another, I shall now proceed to examine. These rules determine what may be called the relative or exchangeable value of goods. The word VALUE, it is to be observed, has two different meanings, and sometimes expresses the utility of some particular object, and sometimes the power of purchasing other goods which the possession of that object conveys. The one may be called "value in use"; the other, "value in exchange." The things which have the greatest value in use have frequently little or no value in exchange; on the contrary, those which have the greatest value in exchange have frequently little or

> no value in use. Nothing is more useful than water: but it will purchase scarcely anything; scarcely anything can be had in exchange for it. A diamond, on the contrary, has scarcely any use-value; but a very great quantity of other goods may frequently be had in exchange for it.

Smith then attempted to explain "exchange value" in terms of what later became known as the **labor theory of value**, writing:

> The real price of every thing, what every thing really costs to the man who wants to acquire it, is the toil and trouble of acquiring it.

In other words, in Smith's view, diamonds are worth more than water in "exchange value" because of the labor involved in mining and cutting them.

However, this cannot be whole story, because one can easily imagine circumstances in which someone would readily exchange a handful of diamonds for a canteen full of water.

Those circumstances, however, would have to include an immediate environment in which water was scarce—such as being marooned in the desert. In such an environment, one might think of the transportation of water to that location as being labor-intensive. Therefore, it might seem that the labor theory of value was correct, after all.

But scarcity and the amount of labor required to produce a thing or bring it to a particular location are two different concepts.

It is true that the much greater scarcity of diamonds than water is at the root of the paradox of value. However, scarcity is only a necessary condition for the paradox, not a sufficient one.

To understand the full story, including the sufficient condition for the paradox to occur, one has also to take into account the subjective state of mind of the individual consumer.

For this, we must turn to the **subjective theory of value**.

According to this theory—pioneered in the second half of the nineteenth century by **Carl Menger**, **William Stanley Jevons**, and **Léon Walras**—the value of goods is largely, if not wholly, determined by the preferences of individual consumers.

To illustrate: No matter how much loving labor a writer puts into writing a novel, if no one else wants to read it, it has no market value.

Analogously, if a man is dying of thirst in the desert, diamonds have no value to him, no matter how much labor went into their mining and cutting.

Contrariwise, if a man lives next to a river or a freshwater lake, water will be so plentiful that he can simply take it for granted. Thus, while water continues to have great fundamental value to him—it remains necessary to his very existence—circumstances are such that he is not conscious of this value.

So, it is not the case—as Adam Smith supposed—that there are two kinds of value: "use value" and "exchange value."

Rather, it is the case that, while the value of a thing is based on the subjective preference of the individual consumer, part of that subjective preference itself is constituted by the degree of scarcity or abundance of the thing.

113. Poison Pill

DEFINITION: A “poison pill” is one of several defensive tactics for resisting a hostile corporate takeover that are available to the management of the target company.

ETYMOLOGY: The phrase “poison pill” is a colloquial way of referring to what is technically known as a “shareholder rights plan.”

USAGE: A hostile takeover situation arises when one company’s bid to take over another one is substantially higher than the market price and yet is rejected by the target company’s management team.

Traditionally, the principal means by which a bidding company attempts to take over a company against the wishes of its management is by going over the heads of management and negotiating directly with shareholders to acquire a voting majority of shares.

The concept of the shareholder rights plan, or poison pill, was invented by the mergers and acquisitions attorney **Martin Lipton** in 1982.

In a nutshell, what Lipton did was to devise language to be added to a company’s bylaws which states that in the event an outside bidder purchases a given percentage of shares (typically, 20%), the existing shareholders would be offered additional shares for purchase at a discount.

The idea was that the shares purchased by the bidding company would be diluted in such a way that it would be unable to accumulate a controlling interest in the target company.

The colloquial name by which such shareholder rights plans became known derived from the fact that a hostile bidder typically lacks access to the target company’s bylaws. Thus, it would have no way of knowing in advance that its effort to buy up shares in the target company would trigger the discount for existing shareholders.

In this way, the bidding company would, in effect, have swallowed a pill that ended up poisoning the purchase it hoped to make.

There are numerous refinements to the concept of the shareholder rights plan—various flavors of poison pill, if you will—including “preferred stock plans,” “flip-ins,” “flip-overs,” “back-end rights plans,” and “voting rights plans,” which are variations on the theme just outlined.

The poison pill tactic was used extensively during the 1980s and 1990s by such famous “corporate raiders” as **T. Boone Pickens** and **Carl Icahn.**

Quite recently (spring of 2022), the concept of the poison pill has been back in the news in connection with **Elon Musk**'s much-discussed hostile takeover bid against Twitter.

However, in recent years shareholders have increasingly balked at incorporating poison pills into their company's bylaws, mainly because they have an economic interest in seeing their company sold at an above-market price—thus inflating the value of their shares—even against the wishes of management.

114. Ponzi Scheme

DEFINITION: A "Ponzi scheme" is a form of financial fraud which operates by paying dividends to past investors entirely out of funds obtained by attracting new investors.

ETYMOLOGY: The phrase "Ponzi scheme" is derived from the name of the Italian-born con man, Charles (Carlo) Ponzi (1882–1949).

While Ponzi did not invent the scheme named for him, he was the first to become famous for his association with such a scheme.

This association was due to the large scale of his operations in the US during the 1920s and to the sensational press coverage of the economic damage done to famous wealthy investors in the wake of the failure of his schemes.

USAGE: A Ponzi-style investment, by definition, is one which is based on no other source of economic value than the promoter's ability to attract investment itself.

This ability may be based either on the promoter's charm and personal connections or on outright misrepresentation.

An instance belonging to the latter category would be a claim to the effect that investors are purchasing a share in some entity that generates economic value, such as a gold mine, when no such entity exists.

In either case, so long as new dupes prepared to invest in the Ponzi scheme can be found, the financial venture can continue to grow and flourish, providing generous returns on investment to early investors.

Sooner or later, however, the liability owed to earlier investors must outrun the income stream generated by new investors, causing the entire financial venture to collapse.

Ponzi schemes are often considered to be inherently fraudulent and, strictly speaking, that is correct.

However, so long as there is no actual misrepresentation of the source of their financing, Ponzi schemes may be difficult to distinguish from certain legitimate investment ventures.

The underlying problem is that many legitimate forms of investment share certain features with Ponzi schemes, such as bandwagon effects and susceptibility to **bubbles**.

Like all economic bubbles, Ponzi schemes work by exploiting the "**greater fool theory**"—the notion that even though a financial venture works by attracting dupes, or "fools," so long as a "greater fool" can be found, all will be well.

The trouble with Ponzi schemes is that their formal structure is such that they could only succeed over the long term if human potential for foolishness was infinitely great.

But the essence of economic wisdom is the recognition of **scarcity**—which is another name for the finiteness of the human condition.

115. Present Value

DEFINITION: The concept of "present value" refers to the worth at the present time of expected future receipts—whether a sum of money or source of cash flow—assuming a given rate of return.

To calculate the present value of expected future receipts, one must discount the expected receipts at an assigned discount rate. The greater the discount rate, the smaller the present value of the future receipts.

The most important factor in accurately assessing present value is the correct determination of a suitable discount rate.

ETYMOLOGY: Most historians trace the origin of the concept of "present value" to work by the American economist Irving Fisher published in his 1930 book *The Theory of Interest*. However, others argue that the basic idea is already present in the *Liber abaci* [Book of Calculation] by Fibonacci (Leonardo Pisano), published in 1202.

The English adjective "present" derives, via Middle English and Middle French, from the Latin present participle *praesens, praesentis,*from the verb *praesum, praeesse,* meaning "to be before,"

The English noun "value" derives, via Middle English and Middle French, from the Vulgar Latin noun *valuta,* meaning "value," which is the feminine form of the adjective *valutus* ("valued"). The Vulgar Latin forms derive from the classical adjective *validus,* meaning "strong," and verb *valeo, valēre,* meaning "to be strong."

USAGE: It is a basic principle of economics—which derives from an essential feature of human nature—that a given sum of money has a higher subjective value if one obtains it today than if one must wait until, say, next week to obtain it.

Put differently, a given sum of money that is expected to be obtained in the future does not have the same subjective worth as the very same amount of money received today.

That is why the *present value of future receipts* is a *discounted*amount. Namely, it is the amount of receipts that an individual would subjectively consider to be equivalent, if it was obtained today, to the amount of receipts expected in the future.

Opportunity Costs

In addition to the fundamental human preference for the present over the future, there is a further economic reason why money in hand today has a greater value than money expected in the future (especially, the relatively distant future).

The reason is that one may invest money obtained today so that one will have a larger amount of money (principle plus interest) in a year's time than one would have if one simply received the principal amount in a year's time.

This additional amount of money that one would forgo by waiting a year to receive the principal amount is a type of "opportunity cost."

For this reason, the concept of present value should incorporate any opportunity costs that may accrue over a given time period.

Inflation

Inflation consists in the gradual rise of prices for goods and services as time passes.

The money you possess at present entitles you to purchase certain goods at their present prices. However, if it expected that the prices of those goods prices will increase in the future, reducing the buying power of your present quantity of money.

Therefore, it may be foreseen that money left unspent today will decrease in value in the future by an amount linked to the rate of inflation.

The Discount Rate

The concept of the "discount rate" refers to the rate of return on an investment used in computing present value.

Essentially, the discount rate represents the opportunity costs incurred by an investor if it decides to defer its receipts, in inflation-adjusted terms, to the future, as opposed to receiving the same amount today.

The discount rate combines the element of opportunity cost with an applicable interest rate, systematically amplifying future value in a commensurate manner.

On the other hand, the discount rate may be used to calculate the present value of expected future receipts of a given amount to be obtained on a certain date.

Thus, the term "discount rate" alludes to the process of reducing future value to present value. It creates a sort of parity between the larger future and smaller present amounts of money, taking into account the opportunity costs and inflationary erosion associated with waiting for the larger future amount.

The Present Value Formula

For these reasons, the present value of a future amount of money must take into account the potential opportunity costs and inflation rate.

This may be achieved quantitatively by means of the following mathematical formula:

Consider the following case:

An investor must choose between receiving an amount *FV* in *n* years' time and a somewhat higher amount today.

The question is: How much, exactly, must it receive today to make the trade-off worthwhile?

Or, in other words: What is the present value of *FV*, *n* years from now, assuming a given rate of return on investment and inflation rate.

Here is the formula (where r = discount rate; and n = number time periods involved):

Present Value = Future Value / $(1 + r)^n$

Let us take a concrete example.

Suppose that the future principal to be delivered in the future is $5,000; the discount rate (i.e., the rate of return in inflation-adjusted dollars) is five percent; and the number of time periods involved is two years.

Then,

Present Value = $5,000 / $(1 + .05)^2$

Present Value = $5,000 / (1.1025)

Present Value = $4,535.15

Thus, the individual in question must receive at least $4,535.15 today if he is wait two years to receive a principal of $5,000 plus five-percent interest.

This calculation effectively showcases the idea of the *time value of money.* It also emphasizes the rationale for supplementary interest based on risk.

In summary, money held today holds greater significance than an identical amount in the future due to the passage of time.

The calculation of discounted or present value holds great significance in various financial evaluation contexts. Instances include net present value, bond yields, and pension commitments, all of which are based on present value assessments.

116. Price Elasticity of Demand

DEFINITION: The "price elasticity of demand"—sometimes shortened to just "elasticity of demand"—refers to a metric that measures the way in which changes in the unit price of a product affect changes in demand for the product (consumption).

Mathematically, price elasticity of demand may be defined as follows:

Price Elasticity of Demand = Percentage Change in Quantity Demanded ÷ Percentage Change in Unit Price

This formula just represents the intuitively obvious fact that as the unit price of a product decreases, demand for the product increases, other things being equal, and *vice versa.*

The psychological principle of human nature underlying the formula is the fact that buyers love a bargain.

ETYMOLOGY: The English word "price" derives from Middle English "*pris*," which in turn derives from Old French and, ultimately, from the Latin noun *pretium* ("money," "price").

The English abstract noun "elasticity" is first attested from the mid-seventeenth century. It derives, of course, from the adjective "elastic," which derives from the New Latin *elasticus.* The Latin adjective, in turn, derives from Late Greek *elastos,* meaning "beaten" or "ductile," a past participle from the verb *elaunō, elaunein,* meaning "drive" or "to set in motion" in classical Greek, and "to beat out" in Late Greek.

The English noun "demand," which is attested from the fourteenth century, derives, of course, from the related verbal homonym. The latter derives from Middle English *demaunden,* which may be traced back through Middle French *demander* and Medieval Latin *demando, demandare,* meaning "entrust" or "commit."

USAGE: In addition to demand, supply possesses its own elasticity, called, naturally enough, the "price elasticity of supply."

The same formula that applies to the price elasticity of demand applies to this metric, as well:

Price Elasticity of Supply = Percentage Change in Quantity Supplied ÷ Percentage Change in Unit Price

This equation represents the intuitively obvious fact that as the supply of a product increases, its unit price decreases, other things being equal, and *vice versa.*

The psychological principle underlying this formula is the fact that sellers do not want to be stuck with unsold inventory.

Economists commonly take both of these metrics into consideration when they are attempting to prospectively determine (or retrospectively explain) which goods will be produced at what unit price.

However, since the two equations are mathematically identical, we can just as well focus on the price elasticity of demand alone for present purposes.

Price Inelasticity

One of the most interesting discoveries that economists have made in exploring the price elasticity of demand is that not all goods are created equal. Rather, certain goods exhibit high *price inelasticity.*

The "price elasticity" of a given product means that changes in its unit price do *not* affect demand for the product in the ways in which that one would have expected.

Another way of putting the same point is to say that, no matter whether the price of the product in question goes up or down, the amount of it demanded remains about the same.

For example, take the case of gasoline, diesel, jet fuel, and other similar fuel products. Individual automobile owners, long-haul truck drivers, and the airline companies continue to purchase the fuel they require in about the same quantities, regardless of any fluctuations in price, either up or down.

Certain goods, on the other hand, display an unusually high degree of elasticity, leading to significant shifts in demand in response to even modest price changes.

In short, a product is considered elastic if the demand point shifts significantly from its initial position in response to variations in its price.

Conversely, if the quantity doesn't deviate from its previous point very much following a change in its price, the product is considered inelastic.

Unsurprisingly, the elasticity of demand holds great interest for marketing professionals. In fact, creating inelastic demand for the products they promote might be viewed as their primary purpose.

117. Prime Rate

DEFINITION: The phrase "prime rate" is short for the expression "prime lending rate," meaning the **interest** rate at which banks lend money to their best customers—that is, their customers with an excellent or "prime" credit rating.

While, generally speaking, the prime rate is set by the marketplace (borrowers seeking the lowest rate they can find), it is also strongly influenced by the **federal funds rate**, which is set by the US Federal Reserve System, better known as "the Fed."

ETYMOLOGY: The word "prime" derives, via Middle English, from the Latin word *prīmus*, meaning "first."

The word "rate" derives, via Middle English, Middle French, and Medieval Latin, from the Latin deponent verb *reor, rēri*, meaning "to reckon." More specifically, "rate" derives from the past participle, *ratus*, of the aforesaid verb, meaning "reckoned," "determined," or "fixed."

USAGE: The prime rate serves primarily as a benchmark or index for use in the calculation of interest rate changes in several categories of short-term, variable-rate consumer loans, notably adjustable-rate mortgages (ARMs) and other variable-rate loans (see below).

The prime rate is also the basis for the calculation of many privately funded student loans.

Perhaps the largest category of variable-rate consumer loans consists of those with interest rates that are tied directly to the prime rate, plus a fixed amount known as "the margin" or "the spread."

The familiar categories of consumer products which are structured in this way include most credit card lines of credit and home-equity loans and lines of credit.

In the US, the prime rate has been historically set around three percentage points above the federal funds rate. Some of the most important foreign countries have analogous institutions, such as the UK's London Inter-Bank Offered Rate (LIBOR).

Before 2008, it was common practice in the US for the *Wall Street Journal* (*WSJ*) to update its published prime rate when 23 out of the 30 largest banks in the US changed their prime rates.

However, since the financial crisis of 2008, and partly in recognition of the fact that fewer banks now control the majority of all banking assets, the *WSJ* now publishes a prime rate reflecting the rates posted by 70 percent of the ten largest banks in the US.

118. Pro Rata

DEFINITION: The phrase "*pro rata*" refers to a proportionate allocation of something, usually, in the financial context, of funds.

Essentially, "*pro rata*" signifies the allocation of something in parts or portions that are proportionate according to some criterion, such as ownership.

For example, when something, such as dividends or interest, is due to be distributed to individuals on a *pro rata* basis, it means that the distribution will be divided up according to some metric, which in this case will be each individual's proportionate share of the principal.

While *pro rata* calculations can be applied to determine suitable divisions within any whole, they are commonly employed in the domains of finance, business, and law.

ETYMOLOGY: English use of the Latin phrase "*pro rata*" is attested from the late sixteenth century.

It derives directly from the classical Latin phrase, *pro ratā* (*parte*).

The preposition *pro* means, in this sense, "according to" or "in proportion as."

The modifier *ratā*—meaning "reckoned," "determined," "fixed," or "settled"—is the feminine, ablative case, past participle of the deponent verb *reor, rēri,* meaning "to reckon."

The word *ratā* is in the ablative case because *pro* governs that case and it is feminine because the noun it is understood to modify—namely, *parte,* meaning "part"—possesses that grammatical gender.

The word *ratā* also appears in classical Latin in the form of the ablative absolute *ratā parte*, with the same meaning as *pro ratā*.

USAGE: The phrase "*pro rata*" signifies the principle that every individual or entity obtains its fair portion relative to the entirety.

Note that, in this context, at least, the word "fair" does not necessarily mean "equal," but rather "just" or "merited," meaning "correct according to a given standard or criterion."

Pro rata calculations are applicable in various domains. A common example is distributing dividends according to the size of one's share in the ownership of the whole company.

Thus, the concept of "pro rata" presupposes a whole that must be divided and a criterion according to which a fair (i.e., just) proportionate distribution may be determined.

Likewise, *pro rata* calculations can be employed to distribute the appropriate segments of an annual interest rate over a shorter duration.

As an example of the use of *pro rata* in a non-financial context, consider the insurance industry. Here, the phrase "*pro rata*" may be used to determine the premium amount payable for a portion of the full term covered by a policy.

Similarly, *pro rata* calculations may be involved in such things as tax bills, which may be assessed over only a portion of a whole term (typically, a year).

Finally, the concept of "*pro rata*" is also used to calculate the portion of a distribution from a qualified retirement account—such as an IRA, an SEP, or a 401(k)—which becomes subject to taxation, accounting for the mixture of funds that have been contributed before and after taxes.

For example, consider an individual holding a 401(k), 20 percent of whose funds are contributed pre-tax and 80 percent post-tax. As a result, any withdrawals made will be have to be composed of 20 percent taxable funds and 80 percent funds not subject to taxation.

119. Public Choice Theory

DEFINITION: "Public choice theory" is the name of a subdiscipline of political economy, which studies the working of the political system using the traditional analytical tools of economic theory.

ETYMOLOGY: The word "public" derives, via Middle English and Middle French, from the Latin adjective *publicus,* meaning "belonging to the people" or "public," which is itself connected to the noun, *populus,* meaning "the people."

The noun "choice" derives, via Middle English, from the Old French verb, *choisir,* meaning "to choose." *Choisir* is of Germanic origin, being connected to the Old High German verb, *kiosan,* also meaning "to choose."

The word "theory" derives from the Greek verb *theōreō* , meaning "to look at," "to view," or "to observe," and the associated noun *theōria,* meaning an "act of viewing or observing," "contemplation," or "reflection."

"Theory" is first attested in English towards the end of the sixteenth century.

USAGE: It has been observed that public choice theory "rests on the homely but important observation that politicians are, after all, no different than the rest of us."

Nevertheless, it took many decades before political economists gradually came to see that economic theories could be extended beyond the marketplace and applied to the behavior of government officials.

Hitting just the highlights of this history, we may observe that the roots of public choice theory are often said to lie in the 1890s in the work of the Swedish political economist, **Knut Wicksell.**

It was not until the 1950s, though, that the foundations of the modern approach to public choice were laid, notably, by **Kenneth J. Arrow** in his 1951 book *Social Choice and Individual Values,* by **Anthony Downs** in his 1957 *An Economic Theory of Democracy,* by the Scottish economist, **Duncan Black**, in his 1958 *Theory of Committees and Elections,* and by **Mancur Olson** in his 1965 *The Logic of Collective Action.*

The culmination of the foregoing body of research—which transformed scattered observations and insights into the systematic and highly sophisticated field of public choice theory as it exists today—is usually held to have been constituted by the work of Nobel laureate **James M. Buchanan**, beginning in the 1960s and extending over many decades.

In 1962, working together with his colleague **Gordon Tullock**, Buchanan published what many regard as his *magnum opus, The Calculus of Consent.*

This landmark study introduced important novel concepts and distinctions, such as, notably, the one between long-term ("constitutional") and short-term ("political") decisions, which constrain the choices and behavior both of the public and of government actors themselves.

Another important conceptual breakthrough introduced by the book, and studied by Buchanan, along with Tullock and other colleagues, over the following decades, was the insight that government actors may have interests that diverge from the stated function of their office.

For example, an official within the government welfare bureaucracy might well act in support of the bureaucratic interests of his own department out of self-interested motives, while disregarding the question of whether the department was doing more harm than good to the public.

Later researchers—especially, the political philosophers **Geoffrey Brennan** and **Loren Lomasky**—have studied the ways in which government actors may be influenced by "expressive" motives, as opposed to strictly rational or utilitarian ones.

Another fertile and revealing area of public choice theory has been the investigation of the manifold ways in which bureaucracies create perverse incentives, which result in government officials' often being far more responsive to the wants and needs of well-heeled special interest groups than to those of the general public.

Finally, public choice theory has successfully raised the consciousness of economists, government officials, and the public at large regarding the widespread phenomenon of "rent-seeking" in government service.

The term "rent-seeking" is defined by economists as the practice of seeking to increase one's share of an already-existing pool of wealth without contributing anything of value to the pool oneself.

Most examples of rent-seeking in government involve the sale of a government actor's influence within a given bureaucracy to third parties who must deal with the said bureaucracy.

Rent-seeking by government officials may take various forms, from implicit to explicit *quid pro quo* arrangements involving perquisites, payments in kind, kickbacks, or outright bribes.

Even in political systems in which overt bribery is rare, other forms of rent-seeking may still be quite common.

Structurally, rent-seeking is basically a form of protection racket. Indeed, it is really little more than a polite name for a protection racket that happens to be tolerated by the powers that be—if only because it is so hard to stamp out.

120. Qualified Opinion

DEFINITION: The phrase "qualified opinion" refers to an independent auditor's report accompanying a company's audited financial statements.

A qualified opinion expresses the independent auditor's belief that the financial information supplied by the company was in some way inadequate or that a significant disagreement arose about the application of generally accepted accounting principles (GAAP).

However, it is important to note that the problems outlined in a qualified opinion are not pervasive or overly serious.

Qualified opinions may also be rendered when the footnotes accompanying a company's financial statements do not furnish sufficient disclosures.

ETYMOLOGY: Legally mandated independent auditing can be dated back to the 1840s in New England; however, America's modern system of auditing, including qualified opinions, dates only from the 1930s.

The English adjective "qualified" is attested from the sixteenth century. The word derives from the Middle French verb *qualifier,*meaning "to qualify" or "to describe," and Medieval Latin, *qualificare,* meaning "to judge," "to define," "to describe," or "to qualify." The Medieval Latin verb, in turn, derives from the classical Latin adjective *quālis, quāle,* meaning "of what kind," "such," "such as," or "like."

The English noun "opinion" is attested from the fourteenth century. It derives, via Middle English and Middle French, from Latin noun *opīnio, opīnionis,* meaning "opinion," "conjecture," or "supposition," which is related to the deponent verb *opīnor, opīnari,* meaning "to believe," "to suppose," or "to conjecture."

USAGE: One of principal reasons why qualified opinions are issued is because, for certain transactions, a company's financial records deviate from GAAP.

The issuance of a qualified opinion in such a case implies that the departure from GAAP is not widespread. Independent auditors possess the professional discretion to interpret how much latitude may be given to applying the concept of "pervasive" in a given set of circumstances.

However, for an error to be considered non-pervasive, representation of the overall financial state of the company created by the error must not be factually inaccurate or impact the decision-making of users who might potentially rely upon the financial statements.

A qualified opinion can also arise when the information provided by a financial statement is inadequate, in the sense that it prevents an auditor from acquiring the evidence necessary to substantiate the statement's claims. In the absence of thorough transaction validation, an unqualified opinion cannot be provided.

Additional reasons for a qualified opinion's being issued include insufficient information in the financial statement's footnotes, uncertainty surrounding quantitative estimates, or the absence of a cash flow statement.

Qualified opinions are presented in the third and last section of an independent auditor's report.

The first part of the auditor's report spells out the responsibilities of the company's management with respect to the formulation of financial statements and the maintenance of internal controls.

The second section describes the obligations of the auditor.

In the third section, the auditor furnishes an assessment of the company's internal controls and accounting records. This assessment can take the form of an unqualified opinion, a qualified opinion, an adverse opinion, or a disclaimer of opinion.

A qualified opinion affirms that the financial statements of a corporate client are fairly represented, except for a designated problem area. In their qualified opinions, auditors commonly employ qualifying language such as "with the exception of the following" in their report. Such language indicates that the auditor lacks sufficient information to confirm specific components of given financial transactions.

It is very important to stress that a qualified opinion does neither represents a dire assessment of a business's financial performance nor suggests that it is concealing or distorting information in its financial statements. Rather, a qualified opinion means that an auditor is unable to provide an entirely flawless report.

Issuing a qualified opinion means that the auditor acknowledges the overall accuracy and truthfulness of the company's financial statements. Nevertheless, such an opinion pinpoints specific aspects of those statements that the auditor considers problematic.

121. Quant

DEFINITION: The term "quant" is a colloquialism for a type of individual working in the field of finance and investment planning, who chiefly employs quantitative (mathematical, especially statistical) methods of analysis in his work.

ETYMOLOGY: The root "quant" derives from the English word family that includes the verb "quantify," the noun "quantity," and the adjective "quantitative."

All these words derive from the Latin interrogative adjective,*quantus*, meaning "how big?" or "how much?" An interrogative noun and a relative pronoun are then derived from the neuter form of the adjective, *quantum*.

USAGE: The quantitative theories used by quants in their day-to-day work were mostly invented by academic economists in the period following World War II.

However, the theories in question did not percolate into the fields of finance and investment until a couple of decades later.

By the 1980s, quantitative methods were beginning to become more common and more widely accepted on Wall Street and elsewhere.

The tag "quants" began to be applied to young, mathematically sophisticated recruits to the fields of finance and investment during that same decade, but did not become widely known to the general business press–reading public until the early 2000s.

In 2004, Emanuel Derman's wrote *My Life as a Quant: Reflections on Physics and Finance*, which helped to make the formerly recondite slang expression "quant" into a widely recognized buzz word.

Among the many subfields of finance and investment management which constitute the primary domain of quants, we may mention the following types of financial products:

- fixed-income derivatives
- interest-rate derivatives
- credit derivatives
- "exotic" derivatives
- real options
- employee stock options

From a mathematical point of view, the most important factor underlying the expected performance of these financial products is the interest rate.

The two main models used in the quantitative analysis of interest rates are known as the “short-rate model” and the “Heath–Jarrow–Morton (HJM) framework.”

122. Quantitative Easing

DEFINITION: Quantitative easing (QE) is a **monetarist** doctrine which recommends fighting recessions by injecting money into the economy by means of central bank purchases of government bonds and other financial assets according to specific criteria, namely:

- The purchases must involve riskier, longer-term bonds
- They must involve a commitment to a predetermined time
- The amounts involved must also be pre-determined
- The amounts involved must be very substantial

USAGE: Monetarist policy in general involves buying financial assets from commercial banks and other financial institutions. The purpose of making such purchases is twofold: to increase the money in circulation and to lower the interest rate (by raising the price and lowering the yield of financial assets).

The goal of QE was to stimulate the economy without causing inflation to spike.

What makes QE distinct from traditional monetary intervention through ordinary open-market operations is the four controlling criteria listed above.

QE was originally used in 2008, when the standard instruments employed by proponents of ordinary monetarist policy had become ineffective due to very low interest rates.

QE has been criticized for putting most of the increase to the money supply into the pockets of the stock- and bond-holding class, thus worsening income inequality.

The possibility of a different form of QE has been discussed, which might be used in the future without producing this unwanted effect. Namely, checks could simply be sent directly to citizens.

This type of QE goes by the name “helicopter money,” after the tongue-in-cheek suggestion made by **Milton Friedman** that the Fed simply dump bags of currency out of a helicopter.

123. Quasi Contract

DEFINITION: The phrase "quasi contract," also known as a "contract implied in law," refers to judicial ruling that serves as a resolution for disagreements between two parties who have no formal contract.

Unlike an ordinary legal contract, a quasi contract does not derive from mutual agreement. Rather, it is established by a court's decision to settle a dispute in favor of one party rather than another.

ETYMOLOGY: The concept of a "quasi contract," if not the phrase, is already attested in Roman law, where it has been inferred from the well-known Roman legal principle which states: "*nēmo dēbet locuplētari ex aliēnā iacturā* [no one ought to be enriched by another's loss]."

During the Middle Ages, the idea of quasi contract emerged as an explicit legal concept. Known by the Latin phrase "*indebitatus assumpsit* [being indebted made the promise]," this principle is essentially identical to that of a quasi contract.

The principle of a quasi contract is also firmly established in the English common law tradition.

The English adverb "quasi"—meaning "in some sense" or "to some degree"—is attested from the seventeenth century. It derives from the Latin adverb *quasi,* meaning "as if," "as it were," or "approximately."

The English noun "contract" is attested from the fourteenth century. It derives—via Middle English *contracten* and Middle French *contracter,* meaning "to agree upon"—from the Latin past participle *contractus,* of the verb *contraho, contrahere,* meaning "to draw together," "to collect," or "to unite."

USAGE: In essence, a quasi contract is an *ex post facto* judicial ruling aimed at rectifying a situation in which one party to a dispute is judged to have taken unfair advantage of the other. It is meant to serve the function of a contract drawn up before the fact, when such a contract is missing.

For example, a quasi contract might be enforced in a situation in which one party receives goods or services it did not explicitly solicit or contract for in writing.

Nevertheless, upon accepting the goods or services, the buyer creates a legal obligation, or implied contract, to pay the seller that provided the goods or services.

A quasi contract may be said to enforce such an implied contract.

This legal doctrine serves as a method of compelling one party to a dispute to compensate the other *as though* a regular written contract or agreement between the parties existed.

In other words, the defendant's responsibility to adhere to his obligations created by a transaction is interpreted as implicitly mandated by law. Historically, quasi contracts have been primarily used to enforce restitution for damages incurred by the plaintiff.

Once a quasi contract has been established by a court of law, the latter issues a directive which compels the defendant to provide restitution to the plaintiff.

This restitution, called "*quantum meruit*" in Latin (meaning "the amount deserved") is computed based on the extent to which the defendant was unfairly benefited.

This type of legal contrivance is also sometimes referred to as a "constructive contract." The reason is that it is "constructed" by a judge in cases where no pre-existing contract exists between the parties involved.

124. Raider

DEFINITION: The colloquial term "raider"—short for "corporate raider"—refers to a corporation or its leadership team which participates in the effort to take over another corporation against the will of its current management.

Such an effort is known as a "hostile takeover."

ETYMOLOGY: The word "raid" derives, via Scottish English, from the Old English word *rād*, meaning "ride" or "raid."

"Raider" is a metaphor which alludes to historical raiding societies, such as the Vikings and others.

USAGE: Corporate raiders operate according to the following process.

The first step is to buy a large stake in a target corporation, ideally a majority share.

The second step is for the raider corporation to use its newly acquired shareholder voting rights to put through certain measures that are ostensibly designed to increase the target company's share value. However, these measures actually make it easier for the raider to acquire the target company against the wishes of its current management.

Such measures may range widely, from replacing the target company's top management with executives more sympathetic to the raider, to downsizing the target company's operations, to liquidating the company altogether.

The era of corporate raiders stretched from the 1970s through the 1990s.

In the twenty-first century, the practice has declined due to the invention of new means of legal defense on the part of target companies' management teams.

These measures include such strategies as **poison pills**, golden parachutes, and taking on increased levels of debt.

125. Rainmaker

DEFINITION: The colloquial term "rainmaker" refers to an individual in the higher echelons of the business world who comes to a new employer, bringing with him many new clients.

More specifically, the term tends to be applied to such individuals who seem able to bring in new clients of unusual kinds or from unexpected places, that their new company might never have known about without the services of the rainmaker.

ETYMOLOGY: The term is presumably an allusion to the Native American ritual dance known as a "rain dance," which is performed during a drought to persuade the heavens to bring forth rain.

The basic point of the term is to highlight the fact that the new business brought to a company by a "rainmaker" seems to come from some hidden or mysterious source.

USAGE: In the business world, rainmakers are highly prized because, by definition, they generate substantial new business for the new company they join, and thus additional cash flow for the company.

Since this new business usually comes from outside established business channels, the rainmaker has an unusually close personal relationship with his clients. For this reason, his services are not easily replaceable by anyone else.

Although rainmakers are usually most highly valued for bringing clients from hidden or non-traditional markets, sometimes their talent may lie more in the ability to convince current clients to spend more money.

Thus, the term "rainmaker" has a certain elasticity.

On the other hand, a rainmaker is nearly always a key figure in the organization he joins—that is, a highly compensated principal or executive, as opposed to a salesman.

More recently, the term "rainmaker" has begun to be used beyond the bounds of the business world, for example, in the field of political fund-raising.

126. Random Walk

DEFINITION: A "random walk" is a mathematical function on an abstract space, which describes a path through the space consisting of a sequence of steps such that each subsequent step is randomly related to the prior step.

ETYMOLOGY: For the etymology of the word "random," see the Glossary article "**randomness.**"

The noun "walk" derives, via Middle English, from the Old English verb *wealcan*, meaning "to roll," "to toss," or "to journey about."

The term "random walk" was coined by the mathematician **Karl Pearson** in 1905.

USAGE: Random walks on one-dimensional spaces, known as a "Markov chains," play various roles in theoretical physics.

Random walks on two-dimensional spaces play a role in physics and chemistry, for instance, in the representation of Brownian motion.

Random walks on three-dimensional spaces may play a role in biology, as well, notably in the study of protein folding, of animal locomotion, and other phenomena.

In economics, random walks have a variety of uses. Probably the best known of these is economic "random walk theory."

Economic random walk theory is a mathematical model of the performance of certain markets, notably, the stock exchange, which hypothesizes that changes in stock prices are causally independent of each other, and so related via a random walk.

Economic random walk theory provides a mathematical justification for the common-sense belief that future stock price changes cannot be inferred from past changes.

In other words, the notion of a random walk supports what everybody already knows: namely, that yesterday's increase in a stock's price is no guarantee that the price will increase tomorrow.

127. Randomness

DEFINITION: In everyday parlance, "randomness" is the unpredictability of some individual event or the overall disorder, or patternlessness, of a sequence of events.

In mathematics, there are more precise definitions of "random" stemming from the fields of statistics and probability.

In statistics, a variable is random if it may assume any possible value ("outcome") within a given probability (or "event") space.

This definition, in turn, permits the calculation of a probability distribution for outcomes within the space.

ETYMOLOGY: The adjective "random" derives, via Middle English and Middle French, from the Old French verb *randir*, meaning "to run."

The English and the French words are also akin to the Old High German verb *rinnan*, meaning "to run."

USAGE: From the definitions presented above, it may be seen that even though individual random events are unpredictable, the frequency of different outcomes within the space ("trials") may be predictable.

Perhaps the most common illustration of this combination of the randomness of individual events with the knowability of the probability of those events is the case of dice.

Each individual roll of the dice, of course, produces a purely random outcome.

However, the narrowly delimited space of possible outcomes determined by one or two, fair, six-sided, regular polygons (cubes) makes it a trivial matter to calculate the probability distribution of those outcomes.

The concept of randomness has numerous uses in the mathematical modeling of economic phenomena.

One of the most important of these is the notion of a "**random walk**."

128. Reaganomics

DEFINITION: The term "Reaganomics" refers to the economic policies pursued by the administration of US **President Ronald Reagan** between 1981 and 1989.

Synonyms for "Reaganomics" that were in use at the time by its supporters included "**supply-side economics**" and "free-market economics," while its critics preferred such pejorative phrases as "trickle-down economics" and "voodoo economics."

USAGE: The historical context of Reaganomics was the new administration's need to respond to the economic crisis of the late 1970s, which was characterized by high inflation together with simultaneous low or negative growth—the era of so-called "stagflation."

Reaganomics consisted of four essential policy initiatives:

- Reducing government spending
- Reducing federal income and capital gains tax rates
- Reducing government regulations on business activity
- Tightening the money supply to bring inflation under control

The principal question surrounding Reaganomics—How successful was it?—is still hotly debated by historians of economics.

Conservative economists answer "yes," pointing primarily to the economic growth which finally kicked in about two years into the Reagan administration, reversing the prior recession and leading to one of the longest peacetime economic expansions in US history.

Progressive economists answer "no," pointing to a variety of things.

First and foremost is the growth in income inequality in the US, which began during the Reagan years and continues to the present.

Also, while Reagan's tax cuts and tight money policy appear to have had their intended effects, it has been argued that the first point listed above—reducing government spending—was never effectively put into practice.

In fact, Reagan's heavy spending on advanced weapons systems within the context of the competition with the Soviet Union led to enormous budget deficits, which were not offset in any meaningful way by increased tax revenues, as supply-side advocates had predicted.

As a result, net government spending ballooned during the 1980s, leaving the US with a deficit three times larger on the day that President Reagan left office than on the day he took the oath of office.

Finally, critics stress that the overall size of the government continued its steady growth during the Reagan years.

On the other hand, in response to all these criticisms, supporters of Reaganomics also point to the so-called “misery index.”

Defined as the inflation rate plus the unemployment rate, the misery index shrank from 19.33 at the beginning of the Reagan administration to 9.72 at its end.

This is the greatest economic improvement, as measured by the misery index, on record for any US president since **Harry S. Truman**—and perhaps the single greatest vindication of Reaganomics.

129. Regulatory Capture

DEFINITION: The phrase "regulatory capture" refers to the phenomenon of a government regulatory agency—or one or more its individual officers—coming under the influence of the corporate or other private entity it is charged to regulate.

ETYMOLOGY: The adjective "regulatory," as well as the related noun "regulation" and verb "regulate," derive, via Late Latin, from the classical Latin noun *rēgula*, meaning a "straight length," a "ruler," a "pattern," a "model," or a "rule."

"Regulate" and its related forms entered the English language during the seventeenth century.

The word "capture" derives, via Middle French, from the Latin noun *captūra*, meaning a "capture of prey," the "prey" itself, or "gain."

Captūra, in turn, derives from the past participle *captus*, of the verb *capio, capere*, meaning "to take" or "to seize."

USAGE: Regulatory capture is a deep-seated pathology of advanced liberal democracies.

While superficially akin to such openly criminal behavior as bribery, it often involves *quid pro quos* that are more subtle and hard to prosecute.

One of the most common forms of *quid pro quo* taken by modern regulatory capture is the so-called "revolving door" between the personnel of regulatory government agencies and the corporations they were formerly charged with regulating.

In other words, companies have subtle ways of signaling that, so long as they receive favorable treatment from an individual regulator, the latter will be welcome to join the company, or sit on its board of directors, when he or she retires from government service.

The economic subdiscipline of **public choice theory** studies regulatory capture and related pathological situations characteristic of modern governance.

The field offers persuasive reasons for understanding why such behavior occurs, as well as why it is extremely difficult to stamp out.

130. Retained Earnings

DEFINITION: The phrase "retained earnings" (also known as "plow back") refers to the amount of profit a company has left after paying dividends to shareholders, as well as its income taxes and its direct and indirect costs.

Thus, retained earnings represent the portion of a company's equity that can be used for investment in new equipment, in marketing, or in research and development.

The term "retained" in the phrase "retained earnings"—a crucial concept in the field of accounting—points to the fact that these earnings have been kept within the company, rather than being distributed to shareholders as dividends.

Hence, when a company either incurs losses or distributes dividends, retained earnings will fall, whereas when new profits are generated, retained earnings will increase.

ETYMOLOGY: The phrase "retained earnings" likely arose sometime in the early twentieth century. It is well attested by 1930.

The English adjective "retained," from the verb "to retain," is attested from the fifteenth century. It derives from Middle English *reteinen* or *retainen,* which derives from Middle French *retenir,* with the same meaning. The Middle French verb, in turn, derives from the Latin verb *retineo, retinēre,* meaning "to hold back," "to keep," "to reserve," or "to maintain."

The English noun "earnings" is attested from the seventeenth century. It derives from the noun "to earn," which derives from the Middle English verb *ernen* and, ultimately, the Old English verb *earnian,* both with essentially the same meaning.

USAGE: Retained earnings may be defined by the following formula:

$RE = PRE\ (+\ NI\ or - NL) - (C + S)$

where:

RE = retained earnings

PRE = previous RE

NI = net income

NL = net loss

C = cash dividends

S = stock dividends

Note that the notion of "retained earnings" encompasses the previous earnings a company has accrued, excluding any dividends disbursed in the past.

To gain a deeper understanding of the insights that the concept of retained earnings may provide, the following choices encompass many of the ways in which a company can use its excess funds. For instance, the first option (dividend payments) results in earnings leaving the company's financial books permanently.

The remaining options preserve earnings for internal use within the company. It is these investment and financing actions that constitute the company's retained earnings.

- Generated income may be distributed, in whole or in part, to shareholders through dividend allocations
- Income may be channeled into expanding current business operations, such as hiring additional sales representatives or increasing production capacity
- Income may be invested in the introduction of a new product or product line, such as a refrigerator manufacturer diversifying into air conditioner production or a chocolate cookie manufacturer launching strawberry- or lemon-flavored products
- Income may also be allocated for potential mergers, acquisitions, or partnerships that hold the promise of enhanced business opportunities
- Income may be used to facilitate share buyback initiatives
- Income may be directed toward repaying any outstanding business loans or other debts

In these ways, retained earnings embody reserved funds that a company's management may reinvest back into the business. When presented as a portion of total earnings, retained earnings are also referred to as the "retention ratio," which is equivalent to one minus the dividend payout ratio.

While the final option of repaying debt also results in funds exiting the business, it does influence the business's financial records—such as reducing future interest payments. This option makes the funds eligible to be included in retained earnings.

131. Return on Investment

DEFINITION: The phrase "return on investment (ROI)" refers to a metric for assessing the effectiveness or profitability of an investment.

Additionally, ROI is useful for comparing the efficiency among various investments.

However, the primary aim of ROI is to provide a quantitative measure of the profit generated by a specific investment compared to its initial cost.

To compute ROI, the profit from an investment is divided by its cost. This result is presented as a percentage.

ETYMOLOGY: Both the concept and the phrase "return on investment" were introduced in 1914 by DuPont Company executive Frank Donaldson Brown.

The English noun "return" is attested from the fourteenth century. In the verbal form, it derives from Middle English *retournen* and Middle French *retourner*, from the particle *re-*, meaning "back" or "again," and the Medieval Latin verb *tornare*, meaning "to turn on a lathe," which itself derives from the noun *tornus*, meaning "lathe."

The English preposition "on" derives from Middle English *an*, and the same form in Old English. The latter is akin to Old High German *ana*.

The English noun "investment" is attested from the seventeenth century. It derives from the verb "to invest," which derives from Medieval Latin *investire*, meaning "to clothe."

USAGE: Return on investment may be calculated using the following formula:

$ROI = (CIV - COI) / COI$

where

ROI = return on investment

CIV = current investment value

COI = cost of investment

Note: the term (CIV – COI) equals the *profit* on the investment, which is a distinct concept from ROI.

The term CIV ("current investment value") refers to the earnings obtained from the sale of the relevant investment.

Since ROI is expressed as a percentage, each such calculation may be compared in a straightforward fashion with returns from other investments, facilitating the evaluation of different kinds of investments in relation to each other.

For example, consider the following case: Anna allocated $2,000 to Red Country Company in 2022 and sold the shares one year later for a cumulative sum of $2,400.

To compute the ROI for Anna's investment, we plug these values into the formula given above:

ROI = (2400 – 2000) / 2000

ROI = 400 / 2000

ROI = .2

ROI = 20 percent

The popularity of ROI calculations is due to their simplicity and adaptability. In essence, ROI can serve as a basic indicator of an investment's profitability.

ROI calculations may be performed in a wide variety of investment contexts, including stock purchases, physical plant expansion, or real estate transactions.

The computation itself is not difficult, and its broad applicability makes it relatively easy to understand.

When an investment's ROI is in positive, it generally indicates a solid investment. However, there may still be alternative opportunities for investment available that would have a higher ROI.

In this way, ROI may provide cues which may assist investors in choosing the most favorable investment.

Conversely, a negative ROI, which suggest a net loss, should obviously be avoided by investors.

132. Scarcity

DEFINITION: The term “scarcity” refers to a situation in which the supply of a good is insufficient relative to the demand.

ETYMOLOGY: The noun “scarcity” and the related adjective “scarce” derive, via Middle French, from the Old North French adjective *escars*.

Escars is believed to derive from *excarpsus*, a Vulgar Latin deformation of the classical Latin past participle, *excerptus*, of the verb *excerpo, excerpere*, meaning “to pick out” or “to separate.”

Excerpo, in turn, is composed of the preposition *ex*, meaning “from” or “out of,” and the verb *carpo, carpere*, meaning “to pluck,” “to select,” “to choose,” “to separate,” or “to divide.”

USAGE: Scarcity is a fundamental concept of economic theory. This is because it refers to one of the fundamental phenomena governing human action and human life more generally.

Let us unpack that claim.

First, it is necessary to appreciate that scarcity is a relative concept. This is because a good can only be “scarce” if it is valued in the first place and according to the consensus **subjective theory of value**, the value of a thing derives from the subjective preferences of consumers.

On the other hand, there are (at least) two kinds of value-relativity that must be distinguished.

First, there are the preferences that consumers would have for certain goods, if all else were equal, but which might well change under different circumstances.

For example, consumer Y might have a distinct preference for ice cream, but if the price of gasoline goes up, one might be prepared to go without it. In other words, ice cream has a value for consumer Y only relative to cheap gasoline.

Let us call this type of relative value “derived value.”

In contrast to derived values, there are preferences that consumers would have for certain goods under almost any conceivable set of circumstances.

For example, consumer Y will have an equal preference for clean water no matter what the price of gasoline happens to be.

The value is still relative. It is relative to consumer Y’s preference.

It is just that consumer X and consumer Z and, indeed, all other imaginable consumers are likely to share this same preference.

The reason that all consumers will share this preference is that it is relative to human nature itself—the need that all human beings have for water in order to sustain life.

Let us call this type of relative value "basic value."

The existence of basic values is a direct result of human materiality, or finitude.

That is the reason why scarcity is one of the most fundamental concepts of economic science.

Of course, most goods are not basic; they are derived.

For these types of goods, the concept of scarcity is still central to economic thinking. In fact, it is presupposed by the fundamental economic concepts of supply and demand.

Which brings us back to our original definition of "scarcity": any situation in which the supply of a good does not meet the demand for it.

133. Short Selling

DEFINITION: The phrase "short selling" refers to the investment or trading practice of profiting from the anticipated decrease in the price of a stock or other type of security.

Short selling involves initiating a position by borrowing shares from a bank or other lending institution and selling them immediately on the open market, with the contractual obligation of returning the shares to the bank (and thus of buying them back) by a specified due date.

In essence, the short seller is betting that the shares he sold (and owes to the bank) will decline in value during the intervening time period.

If they do, then the short seller will pay a smaller amount to buy the shares back than he received when he sold them. This means he will be able to pocket the difference between the two prices (less the bank's lending fee).

However, if the short seller bets wrong, and the shares increase in value, then the short seller—who is still under contractual obligation to return the shares to bank by the due date—must buy them back anyway at the higher price.

Since he has to pay out more money now than he received when he sold the shares earlier (because their price is now higher), he loses money on the deal.

It is important to note that short selling is highly risky because the possibility of loss is theoretically boundless (seeing that, theoretically, the price of the shares could rise practically without limit).

For this reason, short selling is a sophisticated strategy best suited for adept traders and seasoned investors.

ETYMOLOGY: The origin of short selling has been traced to the Dutch businessman, Isaac Le Maire, a major shareholder of the Dutch East India Company, in 1609.

The English adjective "short" derives, via Middle English, from Old English *scort.*

The English gerund "selling," from the verb "to sell," derives from Middle English *sellen* and Old English *sellan,* which is akin to Old High German *sellen,* meaning "to sell," and Old Norse *sala,* meaning "sale."

USAGE: Short selling may serve as a speculative tool for traders, while investors or portfolio managers might employ it as a safeguard against potential losses when taking a long position in the same or a related security.

Short selling is a form of speculation which involves significant risk and thus represents an advanced trading approach.

On the other hand, hedging, which involves establishing a counteracting position to mitigate exposure to risk, is a more widespread strategy.

To initiate a short position, an investor or trader must possess a margin account, which typically involves paying interest on the value of the borrowed shares for the duration of the position.

Regulatory bodies, such as the Financial Industry Regulatory Authority (FINRA), are responsible for enforcing regulations concerning registered US brokers and broker-dealer firms.

Additionally, entities like the New York Stock Exchange (NYSE) and the Federal Reserve (the Fed) have established minimum thresholds for the maintenance margin—the mandated level for the margin account.

If the value of an investor's account falls below this maintenance margin, he will need to put additional funds into the account. Otherwise, the broker might choose to liquidate the position.

134. Silk Road

DEFINITION: The phrase "Silk Road" refers to the main overland trading route across the Eurasian landmass that connected China to the Mediterranean Basin during much of recorded history.

ETYMOLOGY: The phrase "Silk Road" derives from the Chinese expression *sichou zhilu,* which means exactly that: "silk road."

USAGE: Some 4000 miles in length, the Silk Road largely followed a network of much shorter and older local trading routes, some dating back to Neolithic times.

The Chinese portion of the Silk Road was officially inaugurated under the Han Dynasty (202 BC–220 AD).

The Silk Road as a whole continued to function as the primary trade route between Europe and East Asia for approximately 1500 years, until the sixteenth century, when European maritime trade began to supplant the overland route.

Looked at from the European perspective, the jumping-off points for the Silk Road were the cities of Constantinople, Antioch, and Cairo—the first under Byzantine control until the Ottoman takeover in 1453, and the latter two under Muslim control following the Arab conquests in the seventh century.

The routes leading inland from these three main port cities converged at the ancient Syrian oasis town of Palmyra.

From there, the Silk Road led eastward to Babylon (later, Baghad) in Mesopotamia, across northern Persia (Iran), and through Transoxiana (modern Central Asia, or "Turkestan"), to the far-western region of China now occupied by the so-called Xinjiang Uygur Autonomous Region, and sometimes referred to as "East Turkestan."

From the city of Kashgar, in western Xinjiang, the route split into two paths skirting the Taklamakan Desert along its northern and southern reaches. The divided routes reunited at Anxi, now a ghost town in eastern Xinjiang, just south of the Gobi Desert and near the starting point of the Great Wall.

From Anxi, the Silk Road ran south and east to the old central-Chinese city of Chang'an (modern Xi'an) in modern Shaanxi Province, where it split once again into an eastern path leading to Yangzhou on the East China Sea and a northeastern path leading to Beijing.

Much of the journey was very arduous, as the route passed over some of the harshest desert terrain on the planet. Most trading parties passing back and forth along the Silk Road took the form of camel caravans and a good many of the resting places along the way were oases.

However, the value on the European market of the many luxury goods produced only in East Asia—especially silk (whence the trading route's name)—was such that traders of various nationalities were willing to invest considerable capital into sending trading parties along portions of the Silk Road.

In the earlier centuries, Chinese-based trading parties would meet up with Arab intermediaries at various resting places along the way, with Europeans trading mainly with the Arabs at points in the Near East and in the Mediterranean Basin.

Finally, during the High Middle Ages, individual European trading parties began to travel the entire length of the Silk Road. The best-known European who traveled to China by this route was the Venetian trader **Marco Polo**.

The book that Polo wrote about his journey, now known as *The Travels of Marco Polo,* fired the imagination of the European reading public for centuries.

135. Spoofing

DEFINITION: Spoofing is a type of fraudulent manipulation of the algorithmic trading of futures, stocks, and other financial products. The manipulation consists in placing an order to buy or to sell with the intent to cancel the order before it can be filled.

The purpose of spoofing is to create the illusion that the demand for a product is greater or less than it really is. This illusion, then, will tip the market in the direction desired by the spoofer.

The spoofer can then profit from the movement of the market in the direction he desires by putting through an order he does intend to fulfill.

ETYMOLOGY: The word “spoof” was the name of a type of hoax invented in 1933 by the English music hall entertainer and comedian, **Arthur Roberts**.

The word seems to have been appropriated for financial use sometime around 2008.

USAGE: It took time for **Security and Exchange Commission (SEC)**investigators to become aware of spoofing and for rules to be put in place clarifying its illegal status.

For technical reasons, it has also proved difficult for prosecutors to succeed in bringing prosecutions for spoofing to successful conclusion.

However, in August of 2022, after a three-week trial, two traders working for **J.P. Morgan** were convicted of securities fraud for spoofing by a federally empaneled jury in Chicago, Illinois.

The pair were scheduled for sentencing in 2023.

136. Statement of Changes in Equity

DEFINITION: A *statement of changes in equity* (also known as a *statement of shareholder equity*) shows the changes in a company's equity over the course of a given period of time.

The statement of changes in equity usually provides information about such such types of financial transactions and results as new share issuances, share buybacks, dividends, and the company's earnings for the time period in question.

137. Stock

DEFINITION: The word "stock" is short for "capital stock," which signifies an ownership share in a corporation or other commercial enterprise.

ETYMOLOGY: The word "stock" derives, via Middle English, from the Old English word *stocc*, meaning "stick," which in turn is connected to the Old High German word *stoc*, with the same meaning.

The original meaning of "stick" mutated over time to assume such new meanings as a "stump," a "block of wood," the "trunk of a tree," a supply or inventory of goods, as in "livestock," and, finally, "capital."

USAGE: To own a "stock" is to own a piece, part, or share in a business.

The management of companies—mainly in the legal category of "corporation"—may decide to "take the company public" by offering shares on the open market.

Such an offering is also known as an "equity issue." The purpose of an equity issue is to raise capital.

Purchasers of stock, known as "stockholders," own a fractional share of the issuing company.

That is, if the Acme Widget Company issues 100 shares of stock, which are all purchased, and if Mr. Jones buys 10 shares, then Jones owns 10/100, which is to say ten percent, of Acme Widget.

This has two consequences for Jones:

- He will be entitled to receive ten percent of any distributions or profits ("dividends") paid by the company to its shareholders
- He has ten votes to cast in any election or other vote on policy within the legal competency of the shareholders

Public stock companies trace their origin back to the Roman Republic. However, they became economically highly significant during the rise of capitalism in northern Italy during the Age of Exploration.

In 1602, the Dutch East India Company issued shares of capital stock which could then be traded on the Amsterdam Stock Exchange. This innovation greatly expanded the market for shares, because they could be liquidated on the open market much more easily.

During the twentieth century, the nature and complexity the many types of publicly traded stocks expanded exponentially.

The two most basic kinds of stock are “common stock” and “preferred stock.”

In spite of what one might think from the terminology, it is common stock which affords the greater privileges, permitting both dividends and voting rights.

Owners of preferred stock, in contrast, may receive dividends, but do not have voting rights.

A more recent and sophisticated type of security connected to stocks is known as a “derivative.”

A derivative is any **negotiable instrument** which is based on an underlying asset that consists of stocks.

Among the many different kinds of derivatives, we may mention “futures” and “options.”

A stock future is a contract which obliges one party to buy stock upon a future date (the contract’s “maturity”), and the other party to sell on the same date, regardless of the prices prevailing on that date.

In the technical jargon of the financial industry, the futures buyer is said to be “long” (with an obligation to buy), while the seller is “short” (with an obligation to sell).

In contrast, an option is the right (*note*: not the obligation) to either buy or sell stock in the future at a price fixed in advance.

A right to buy is also known as a “call” option, while a right to sell is known as a “put” option.

138. Strategy

DEFINITION: A "strategy" is a general plan laying out a sequence of steps aimed at achieving an overall goal.

The term "strategy" is best understood in contrast to the term "**tactics**," which are the specific actions required to realize the individual steps of the strategy.

ETYMOLOGY: The word "strategy" derives from the Greek word *stratēgos*, meaning "general," which itself derives from the words *stratos*, meaning "an army encampment," and *agō*, meaning "to lead."

USAGE: As indicated by its etymology, the primary original context of the term "strategy" was military. Essentially, strategy is the practice of generalship.

However, warfare and soldiering have long been a rich source of metaphors that have been exported to many other fields of other human endeavor.

One of the most notable of these is the science of economics.

In economics, the notion of "strategy" has been applied in a variety of ways.

First, strategy is well-nigh ubiquitous in the economy due to the fact that all business firms exist to achieve some purpose. Therefore, firms must have a strategy, understood as a general plan for attaining their goals.

For example, if a company's goal is to sell as many widgets as possible, it will need a strategy to set out its general vision of what specific steps it must take to achieve its general or overall goal.

Thinking about a company's goals in such terms is sometimes referred to as "strategic management."

The word "strategy" is often used in more limited contexts, as well.

For example, the term is widely used in the field of marketing, which is the attempt to maximize the number of consumers aware of a company's products and to optimize the efficacy of the messages used to influence those customers.

These ambitious goals lend themselves naturally to strategic planning, which is often called "marketing strategy."

It is interesting to note that the word "strategy" is sometimes replaced by a near-synonym, "policy."

For example, the phrase "economic policy" refers to the general strategy employed by a government to achieve its broad economic goals.

Similarly, government strategies with respect to a particular sector of the economy may also be termed "policies."

For example, a government's strategy for extending financial subsidies or protection from foreign competition to the firms in a particular industrial sector is often called an "industrial policy."

139. Subjective Theory of Value

DEFINITION: The subjective theory of value is the idea that the economic value of a thing is determined by the subjective preferences of the buyer and the seller as revealed through the autonomous operation of the free market.

USAGE: The subjective theory of value was developed independently in the 1860s and 1870s by three different economists: the Englishman **William Stanley Jevons**, the Austrian **Carl Menger,**and the Frenchman **Léon Walras.**

It effectively replaced the earlier labor theory of value of **Adam Smith, David Ricardo,** and other founders of classical economics. Only **Karl Marx** and his followers have continued to reject the subjective theory in favor of the labor theory.

The shift from the labor theory of value to the subjective theory was one of the most important elements in the construction of modern economic analysis. Much of our modern understanding of supply and demand and the functioning of the market stems directly from the subjective theory of value.

One of the reasons why it was so difficult for economists to arrive at the subjective understanding of value was the widespread belief that "science" has to rest upon entirely "objective" foundations.

However, it is precisely the fact that the apparently objective labor theory of value is profoundly mistaken, while the self-avowedly subjective theory of value is essentially correct, which demonstrates that the social sciences rest upon an entirely different metaphysical foundation from that of the natural sciences.

The metaphysical foundation of the social sciences is human agency. The existence of human agency, in turn, implies that human actions exhibit objective purpose, value, intention, and meaning. (See Ludwig von Mises, *Human Action* [1949].) Therefore, there is a sense in which the "subjective theory" is a bit of a misnomer.

Rather, the existence of human feelings, needs, desires, wishes, and interests (in short, "preferences")—together with human free will—is itself an objective fact about the universe of which human beings form a part.

140. Supply

DEFINITION: In economics, the word “supply”—construed as a noun—refers to the goods of all types which individuals or businesses firms are prepared to make available for sale on the open ***market*** at a particular time and place.

ETYMOLOGY: “Supply” derives, via Middle English and Middle French, from the Latin verb *suppleo, supplēre,* meaning “to fill up.”

USAGE: “Supply” may refer to anything that may be offered for sale, such as raw materials, value-added goods, **labor**, or any other valuable or scarce resource.

More technically, “supply” in the strict economic sense is defined in relation to a specific market in a particular good.

Then, relative to that market, the supply is the amount of the good a given supplier is willing to sell at a specific price and which the supplier is capable of producing within a fixed unit of time, other factors being equal.

The supply of labor is calculated in a slightly different way. Relative to a given labor market, the labor supply is the amount of time per fixed unit (usually, week, month, or year) that individual laborers participating in that market are willing to spend working at a given wage.

Economists frequently graph supply against other economic factors. For example, in the case of the labor market, one might plot the supply of labor against the level of the wage being offered.

Presumably, one would find that the supply of labor would increase as a function of the wage being offered.

From this empirical discovery, one would then be able to infer the following general principle:

The more money a worker makes, the longer he is willing to work.

If this conclusion seems too obvious to justify all the heavy economic theorizing, such is the nature of social science. In the best cases, it usually confirms common sense.

Nevertheless, “supply” is an important concept that does allow us—especially, in conjunction with its complement, “demand”—to make many useful inferences about the way the economy works that go beyond common sense.

Good examples of such insights are the "law of supply" and the concept of "economy of scale."

The so-called "law of supply" states the counterintuitive principle that an increase in the price of some goods—of certain types and within certain limits—will result in an increase in their supply.

One might naively think that the higher the price of a good, the fewer the number of consumers who will purchase it, leading the supplier to cut back production of the good. What the law of supply shows is that the truth, at least for most consumer goods, is just the opposite.

Namely, receiving a higher price will influence a supplier to produce more of the good. That much is in fact just common sense. But, then, the principle known as "**Say's Law**" kicks in.

Say's Law states that "supply creates its own demand," meaning that in most cases supply increases will lead to an increase in demand, as well—thus preventing demand from falling in the case under consideration in the way one might expect.

As for the notion of "economy of scale," this is just the observation that as the supply of a good increases, its cost-per-unit decreases, so that it is cheaper (on a per-unit basis) to produce more of a thing.

This, too, is an insight attributable to the science of economics, although not so much to economic theory as to the systematic empirical investigation of the workings of the economy.

If the concept of "economy of scale" seems intuitively obvious to us today, that is only because it is a discovery of political economy that has been very widely disseminated beyond the boundaries of the academic economics profession for a very long time—in fact, ever since the pioneering work of **Adam Smith** almost 250 years ago on the relation between the division of labor, production (supply), and profit.

141. Supply Chain

DEFINITION: The phrase "supply chain" refers to the network of individuals and businesses engaged in the physical production of a commodity and its transportation to consumers.

The nodes in this chain begin with the miners or other producers of raw materials and end as the completed product reaches the consumer (which may be a business), via a retail outlet, the US mail, or a private delivery service.

Supply chain management plays a central role in modern commerce. Businesses strive to optimize the efficiency of their supply chains, because doing so reduces expenses and improves competitiveness.

ETYMOLOGY: It appearsthat the British logistician and business consultant Keith Oliver coined the terms "supply chain" and "supply chain management." He first used these phrases in a public forum in an interview he did for the *Financial Times* on June 4, 1982.[1]

The English noun "supply" is attested from the fifteenth century. The associated verb derives, via Middle English *supplien,* from Middle French *soupleier* and, ultimately, from Latin *suppleo, supplēre,*meaning "to fill up," "to make complete."

The English noun "chain" is attested from the fourteenth century. It derives, via Middle English *cheyne* and Middle French *chaiene,* from Latin *catena,* all with the same meaning.

USAGE: A supply chain encompasses all the stages essential for delivering a finished product or service to the customer.

These stages encompass everything from extracting and refining raw materials, to transporting raw materials to production facilities, to conveying completed products to distribution centers or retail outlets or public or private delivery services for eventual distribution to the end consumer.

Thus, supply chains may consist of such entities as producers, suppliers, factories, storage facilities, transportation enterprises, distribution hubs, and brick-and-mortar or online retail establishments.

---

[1] Arnold Kransdorff, "High Stock Levels—Not the Answer to Volatile Demand," *Financial Times,* June 4, 1982.

Sometimes, the concept of "supply chain" is given an even wider interpretation, encompassing all of the above-mentioned activities and entities, plus such additional activities as research and development, product design, financing, marketing, and customer service.

Supply chain management—that is, the effort to optimize supply chains for efficiency—has the potential to reduce a company's overall expenses, thereby enhancing its profitability.

The considerable importance of supply chains may be brought home by emphasizing the following fact: The failure, or temporary disruption, of a single link within a supply chain may have cascading effects on the entire production process, leading to avoidable excess costs.

There are numerous different forms of supply chain models. A given company's choice of model will depend upon its organizational framework and particular requirements.

The following are some common examples:

Continuous Flow Model: Suited for enterprises manufacturing largely uniform products, which enjoy substantial demand and require little or no alterations. The absence of significant fluctuations permits efficient production scheduling and exacting inventory management. Under this model, managers must continually replenish raw materials to avoid production bottlenecks.

Fast Chain Model: Suitable for enterprises capitalizing on current trends. In order to effectively leverage prevailing trends, companies employing this model must move quickly from concept to prototype, to production, and, ultimately, to distribution to the consumer. A prime example of an industry making use of this type of supply chain model is the fast fashion sector.

Flexible Model: Companies that manufacture seasonal or holiday merchandise often use the model. Such companies experience periodic surges in demand for their products, followed by long fallow periods of little to no demand. This model ensures that companies will be able to begin production quickly when the time is right and—equally importantly—to shut down production efficiently when demand falls off. Thus, for companies involved in seasonal businesses, profitability depends upon the ability to accurately forecast raw material, inventory, and labor needs.

142. Supply-Side Economics

DEFINITION: "Supply-side economics" refers to a controversial macroeconomic theory advanced in the late 1970s in response to the combination of high inflation and low or negative growth ("stagflation") prevailing at that time.

ETYMOLOGY: The proponents of supply-side economics held that the most important factor driving economic activity is productive capacity—that is, the *supply* of goods and services—and not consumer demand.

USAGE: Supply-side advocates accordingly recommended policy measures designed to stimulate productivity as the best way out of the stagflation quagmire.

These measures, which were adopted in part beginning in 1981 by the incoming administration of **President Ronald Reagan**, included lowering taxes, repealing duties and tariffs, and abolishing unnecessary regulations on business formation and activity.

Immediately after the Reagan administration's implementation of supply-side policies, there was a difficult period of economic pain as the economy adjusted. However, after a couple of years, Reagan's policies produced sustained economic growth and increased employment, as predicted by the theory.

It is important to note that, as we have described it so far, supply-side economics scarcely differs from classical free-market economic thinking.

Indeed, the idea that economic growth is primarily a function of the supply of goods and services on offer in the marketplace was already expressed in the early nineteenth century by the French economist **Jean-Baptiste Say**, whose insight was later dubbed "Say's Law." Say's Law basically says that "supply creates its own demand."

What made the supply-side economics of the 1970s and 1980s controversial was not so much its central classical-liberal ideas as the additional claim that the tax-rate cuts it recommended would pay for themselves through the extra taxes generated as a byproduct of economic growth.

This claim, which was based on the **Laffer curve** devised by American economist **Arthur Laffer**, has not been widely accepted by the academic economic profession. Given that the federal deficit ballooned by around $100 billion during Reagan's eight years in office, it seems hard to argue with the academy's skepticism on this point.

143. Tactics

DEFINITION: The word "tactics" refers to the particular actions required to achieve some specific goal or to implement some limited plan.

More specifically, tactics may be understood as constituting a sequence of actions that are instrumentally required to achieve a general, or overall, goal.

In this way, the term "tactics" is best understood in contrast to the term "**strategy**," which refers to a general plan consisting of a number of subsidiary steps.

ETYMOLOGY: The term "tactics" derives, via the New Latin word *tactica*, from the Greek word *taktika*, meaning "military tactics," which in turn derives from the verb *tassō*, meaning "to arrange" or "to put in order."

USAGE: Obviously, the word "tactics" (like the word "strategy") has its roots in the context of military affairs—a field of human endeavor which has contributed metaphors to many other fields.

One such field is economics.

There are two schools of thought about the relation between economics and tactics.

On the one hand, all business firms possess the goal of being profitable, that is, of being successful and remaining in existence.

Wherever an overriding goal can be identified, a strategy will be required to lay out a general plan for achieving the goal.

Finally, wherever a strategy exists, tactics must be employed to see to it that the individual steps specified by the strategy are realized.

On the other hand, tactics—which are actions aimed at attaining limited and instrumental goals—are by their very nature amenable to economic analysis in a way that strategies are not.

Those who take the second view believe that tactics may be studied scientifically because tactical goals are determined causally by a strategy.

However, on this view, strategy itself is not amenable to scientific analysis because strategic goals are not determined by any higher-level cause, but rather by values.

And values—so the argument goes—cannot be rationally discussed.

However, in the absence of strategy, the concept of tactics is fundamentally incoherent.

144. Tariff

DEFINITION: A tariff is a tax imposed by one country on the goods and services imported from another country, with the aim of protecting the first country's industry, of raising revenue, or of influencing the other country's policies.

Why do countries use tariffs?

Most nations face economic constraints due to their natural resources and their capacity to manufacture goods and services.

For this reason, in the vast majority of cases, a country must resort to international trade to acquire the goods its people want but which cannot be provided domestically.

Even though most nation states find themselves in the same position, international trade is not always conducted harmoniously among the countries of the world.

The factors which may lead to discord among international trading partners include policy differences, competing geopolitical interests, among others.

Tariffs provide one tool that governments may use to cope with trading partners with whom they have disagreements.

ETYMOLOGY: The English noun "tariff" is attested from the late sixteenth century. It derives, via Italian *tariffa,* from the Arabic *ta'rīf,* meaning "notification."

USAGE: The purpose of tariffs is to limit imports.

In essence, tariffs raise the cost of goods and services purchased from foreign nations, thus making them less attractive to domestic consumers.

It is important to note that a tariff may impact both the exporting and the importing nation.

This is obvious in the case of the exporting nation: If consumers in the country imposing the tariff are deterred from buying imported goods due to increased prices, then this, of course, has a direct negative impact on the exporting country.

However, if consumers in the importing country persist in purchasing the imported goods subject to the tariff even at the higher price, then the effect of the tariff will essentially be to increase the cost of living of the country that put the tariff in place.

There are two categories of tariffs:

- A *specific tariff* is a specified amount imposed on all goods in a certain category, for instance, a $1,000 tariff on automobiles imported from certain countries.

- An *ad-valorem tariff* is a percentage of the price of an imported commodity, for example, six percent of the declared value of television sets imported from certain countries.

Reasons for Imposing Tariffs

1. *To raise revenues:* Tariffs may serve as a means of generating government revenue. Such tariffs are referred to as "revenue tariffs" and are not intended to limit imports.

2. To protect domestic industries: Governments may use tariffs to provide an economic advantage to specific industries to safeguard companies and employment opportunities.

3. *To protect domestic consumers:* Tariffs may be used to render certain imported products prohibitively expensive, not to protect domestic producers, but rather to protect domestic consumers from potentially dangerous products—for example, ones imported from countries with lax safety standards.

4. *To protect national interests:* Tariffs may also serve as an extension of foreign policy. For example, country A might impose tariffs on Country B's principal export to exert influence on Country B to change its international behavior.

145. Trust

DEFINITION: The term "trust" refers to a legal entity endowed with distinct and separate rights; it is thus akin to an individual or a corporation.

A trust has the following structure: One party (the "trustor"), such as a bank or a court, confers upon a second party (the "trustee") the authority to possess title to and oversee property or assets on behalf of a third party (the "beneficiary").

Trusts are created for a variety of reasons. They may be initiated to furnish legal safeguards for the assets of the trustor, guaranteeing their allocation in accordance with predetermined intentions. They are also formed to protect the interests of beneficiaries who are minors.

Trusts can be very useful, having the capacity to streamline processes, to reduce paperwork, and, occasionally, to lessen inheritance (estate) taxes.

Trusts may also function as a closed-end fund structured as a public limited company.

ETYMOLOGY: The English noun "trust" is attested from the thirteenth century.It probably derives, via Middle English, from Scandinavian, possibly Old Norse *traust*, meaning "trust." It is also likely akin to Old English *trēowe*, meaning "faithful."

USAGE: The trustors, whether individuals or commercial or legal entities, who are authorized to establish trusts are also known as "settlors."

The function of the settlors is to determine the allocation of a beneficiary's assets to one or more trustees, and to subsequently manage and safeguard said assets on the beneficiary's behalf.

The regulations governing a trust depend upon the purpose for which it was established, as well as upon particular features of the law in the jurisdiction where the trust is established.

For example, within certain legal jurisdictions beneficiaries are allowed to assume the role of trustees—that is, an individual who is the beneficiary of a trust may also serve as a trustee administering the trust.

The point of establishing a trust is to specify how the beneficiary's finances should be supervised and allocated during his or her lifetime, or posthumously. Such a legal arrangement may be helpful in avoiding some taxes, or the entire probate process, for an estate.

In addition, a trust may be used to control the way an inheritance is distributed to the beneficiary. It may also be used to shield assets from creditors.

Further, a trust provides a method for protecting the interests of a beneficiary who is underage or otherwise unable to oversee his financial affairs himself—such as for medical reasons.

Once a beneficiary is judged to be capable of independently managing his assets, the trust may be dissolved, with its assets reverting to the direct control of the former beneficiary.

While there are various kinds of trusts, each one falls within one or more of the following broad categories:

1. ***Living or testamentary trusts:*** A "living trust," also called an "*inter-vivos* trust," involves an arrangement where an individual's assets are placed within a trust for his or her personal use and advantage throughout his lifetime.

A living trust's administration is overseen by a designated trustee, who is responsible for managing the trust and for transferring assets to the beneficiary upon the trustor's demise. On the other hand, a "testamentary trust," also known as a "will trust," outlines the allocation of a beneficiary's assets subsequent to the trustor's passing.

2. ***Revocable or irrevocable trusts:*** A "revocable trust" permits the trustor to make modifications to, or to dissolve, the trust during his lifetime. An "irrevocable trust," in contrast—as its name suggests—cannot be modified after it is established.

Living trusts may fall into either the revocable or irrevocable category. Testamentary trusts typically adopt an irrevocable nature when they are first established, although they may become revocable through a will while the trustor is still alive. Irrevocable trusts, due to their unalterable nature, facilitate the reduction or total avoidance of estate taxes.

3. ***Funded or unfunded trusts:*** In a "funded trust," the trustor contributes assets during his lifetime, whereas an "unfunded trust" comprises only the trust agreement, without the transfer of any assets.

Unfunded trusts may either be endowed with assets after the trustor's death or else remain without funding. Since the assets in an unfunded trust are vulnerable to risk—which it is the purpose of the trust to mitigate—it is important to ensure adequate funding.

146. Underclass

DEFINITION: "Underclass" is a recently invented term, which refers to an age-old phenomenon: namely, that part of the population of most societies, in all times and places, which is either unable or unwilling to work for a living and lives on the charity of other individuals or of private or public institutions.

ETYMOLOGY: The term "underclass" was invented during the second half of the twentieth century by English-speaking social scientists.

The term corresponds, more or less, to the older German term "*Lumpenproletariat,*" which derived from the Latin word *prōlētarius,*meaning a member of the lowest layer of Roman society, and the German word, *Lumpen*, meaning "rags."

The Latin word "*prōlētarius*" was taken up by Karl Marx. Within his analysis of the social structure of capitalist society in which economic class predominated, Marx used the corresponding German word id *Proletariat* to indicate the laboring class (which, however, does not correspond to the meaning of the original Latin word).

"*Lumpenproletariat,*" then, means "the proletariat in rags." This is as vivid and descriptive a way as any of indicating the socioeconomic reality referred to by the English word "underclass," as well.

USAGE: In more traditional societies, the underclass is largely composed of individuals who have suffered misfortune of one sort or another, and cannot work for a living. For example, in the Bible there is a great emphasis on helping "widows and orphans."

In such societies, the "social safety net" originally consisted primarily of one's extended family and, later on, of institutions like temples, churches, and mosques.

In more recent times, people have tended to look to their government to help the members of the underclass.

For this reason, in part, the notion of the underclass has become a major subject of public discussion among politicians, economists, and many others. Such discussions tend to be quite controversial.

When it comes to economic analysis, the fundamental question has tended to be the following:

- Is the existence of the underclass primarily due to prevailing economic and social structures?

- Or is the existence of the underclass primarily due to the behavior of the individual members of the underclass themselves?

Progressive economists tend to believe that the underclass could be eliminated (and full employment attained), if only the capitalist system could be modified to operate more fairly.

Conservative economists tend to believe that the underclass is a permanent fact of human life because it is a permanent potentiality of human nature.

Conservatives tend to agree with progressives that in the modern world it is appropriate for the government to provide a social safety net. They merely hold that recipients of public largesse be restricted to victims of misfortune who have become a member of the underclass through no fault of their own.

Conservatives point out that the fewer the conditions that are imposed on the recipients of public largesse, the more individuals there will be who seek handouts in the future. In other words, strict conditions on the safety welfare net are necessary to counteract the moral hazard it essentially poses.

Progressives reject all such reasoning about moral hazard as "blaming the victim." Because they believe the underclass is due to structural factors, not to individual behavior, they refuse to distinguish between members of the underclass who are the victims of circumstances and those who are the victims of their own lack of virtue, addiction, or other failings of character.

To revert to an older vocabulary, conservatives wish to distinguish within the underclass between the "deserving poor" and the "undeserving poor."

Progressives believe such a distinction to be unwarranted and morally retrograde.

147. Underground Economy

DEFINITION: The "underground economy," also known as the "black market," is a clandestine market in which exchanges or transactions are illegal for one (or both) of two basic reasons.

The first reason is that the goods or services offered for sale are illicit (prohibited by law) in themselves. Common examples are the sale of illegal drugs and prostitution.

The second reason is that the goods offered for sale, while not illicit in themselves, are exchanged under illicit conditions. A common example is the sale of alcohol or cigarettes on which the appropriate taxes have not been paid.

USAGE: The concept of the underground economy is complementary to—and partially overlaps with—the notion of the "illegal economy."

The illegal economy embraces more than just illicit market transactions. It also encompasses the production or other provision of inherently illegal goods or services.

Thus, for example, middle- and higher-level individuals engaged in the primary manufacture or importation of illegal drugs are deemed a part of the illegal economy. As individuals, they could not be properly counted as a part of the underground economy in the sense of the black market, since they are not directly involved in any market transaction.

On the other hand, the local drug dealer who sells directly to consumers might be deemed a part of either the underground economy or the illegal economy, or both, depending upon the nature of the accounting being made.

Other common examples of typical underground economy transactions and activities include human trafficking (transportation of individuals under illegal conditions), loan-sharking and illegal currency transactions (loaning money or exchanging currency at other than legally approved rates), and tax evasion (fraudulent reporting of taxable income).

What all these transactions have in common is the illicit way in which legally sanctioned transactions or activities are conducted.

Other common examples of illegal economy activities include the production and sale of certain kinds of illegal weapons, the extraction and sale of biological organs for transplantation, counterfeit currency, and the piracy of medicines, books, music, films, and other forms of intellectual property. In all these cases, the goods offered for sale are inherently illegal.

Perhaps the clearest example of the difference between the underground economy and the illegal economy is the difference between illicit currency exchange—which involves the exchange of the legal tender of two countries at an unapproved rate—and the sale of counterfeit currency.

Yet another set of terms of related interest is the following:

- White market—the legal exchange of legal goods
- Black market—the illegal exchange of legal or illegal goods
- Gray market—the ambiguously legal exchange of legal goods that are sold under unforeseen, unauthorized, or unofficial—though not strictly illegal—conditions

Money earned from black markets is often referred to as "black money." Black money often takes the form of cash.

The existence of black money has spawned an entire industry, known as "money laundering," whose aim is to make black money disappear into a larger pool of legally acquired money.

The connection between black money, money laundering, and cash has led to a political movement for the elimination of cash from the economy, in favor of some such system as **Centralized Bank Digital Currency**.

148. Unearned Income

DEFINITION: The phrase "unearned income" refers to any earnings that do not result from services rendered, commonly known as "employment."

This definition contrasts with "earned income," which signifies earnings received for services rendered.

Unearned, also known as "passive," income can take various forms, such as interest from savings accounts, stock dividends, bond yields, rents, and alimony.

ETYMOLOGY: The concept of unearned income was already adumbrated by **Jeremy Bentham** in the 1790s. However, the phrase itself seems to have been coined by **John Stuart Mill** in 1865 in his book *Principles of Political Economy*. It was popularized by **Henry George** in his 1879 book *Progress and Poverty.*

The English adjectives "unearned" and "earned," from the verb "to earn," are attested from around the eleventh century. The verb "to earn" derives from Middle English *ernen* and Old English *earnian,*both with the same meaning.

The English noun "income" is attested from the fourteenth century. It is composed on the preposition "in" used as a prefix and the verb "to come."

"In" is attested from the eleventh century. It derives from identical Middle English and Old English forms. The Old English word *in* is akin to Old High German *in,* with the same meaning.

The English verb "to come" is also attested from the eleventh century. It derives from Middle English *comen* and Old English *cuman,* which is akin to Old High German *queman,* all meaning "to come."

USAGE: The Internal Revenue Service (IRS) defines earned income as wages, salaries, tips, and self-employment earnings. It should be noted that unearned income is ineligible for contribution to individual retirement accounts (IRAs).

Taxation of earned income and unearned income differs due to the inherent distinction between them.

In addition, tax rates on different sources of unearned income may differ to a considerable degree. For example, most sources of unearned income are typically exempt from payroll taxes, and no source of unearned income is subject to employment-related taxes, such as Social Security and Medicare contributions.

Types of Unearned Income

1. *Interest:* Interest and dividend earnings stand out as the prevailing categories of unearned income. Earnings acquired through these means are categorized as unearned income, with the associated tax classified as unearned income tax.

Among the types of income-generating sources subject to taxation as ordinary income are checking and savings deposit accounts, certificates of deposit (CDs), and loans. However, exemptions exist, such as the interest accrued from municipal bonds, which is not subject to federal income tax.

2. *Dividends:* Dividends, which constitute income derived from investments, may be subject to either standard tax rates or the more-favorable long-term capital gains tax rates.

Investments typically generate dividends that are disbursed to shareholders on a regular basis. Dividends may be distributed to investment accounts on a monthly, quarterly, semi-annual, or annual basis.

The taxation of dividends depends on whether they are categorized as ordinary or qualified:

- *Ordinary dividends*, which are the prevalent type of dividends disbursed to investors by companies, are subjected to regular tax rates.
- *Qualified dividends*, in contrast, are subject to the more-advantageous capital gains tax rates. To qualify for this status, dividends must meet several additional conditions.

Other Sources of unearned income include:

- Retirement accounts, including pensions, 401(k)s, and annuities
- Inheritances
- Property income
- Gifts
- Alimony
- Unemployment compensation
- Welfare benefits
- Social Security benefits
- Veterans Affairs (VA) benefits
- Lottery winnings

149. Unemployment Rate

DEFINITION: The term "unemployment" refers to the state of affairs in which an individual is actively seeking paid work but cannot find anyone willing to hire him.

The "unemployment rate" is calculated by dividing the number of unemployed individuals (as defined in the previous paragraph) by the total number of individuals available for participation in the labor force.

The unemployment rate is a crucial gauge of a country's economic well-being. Indeed, it is one of the most-used metrics for the assessment of the real state of an economy.

The unemployment rate is also widely used by governments in calculations related to the provision of various services, such as determining the eligibility of individuals to receive payments out of unemployment insurance funds.

ETYMOLOGY: The number of unemployed persons began to be reported in census figures during the latter part of the nineteenth century. However, the phrase "unemployment rate" probably originated in economic research efforts undertaken during the Great Depression in the early 1930s by the Census Bureau and the Works Progress Administration (WPA).

The English nouns "unemployment" and "employment" are attested from the fifteenth century. The related verb "to employ" derives from Middle English *emploien* and Middle French *emploier,* meaning "to use" or "to employ." The French verb derives from the Latin verb *implico, implicare,* meaning "to enfold," "to entwine," "to entangle," or "to involve."

The English now "ratio" is attested from the seventeenth century. It represents a direct borrowing of the Latin noun *ratio, ratiōnis,*meaning, in the relevant sense, "a reckoning," "a computation," or "a calculation."

USAGE: The unemployment rate serves as a pivotal economic indicator, as it represents workers' ability to obtain profitable employment and participate in the economy's productive output. The higher the number of unemployed workers, the lower the overall economic output.

It is important to realize that the definition of unemployment economists use (as mentioned above) excludes individuals who have left the labor force due to factors like disability, pursuing advanced education, or retirement, or who have simply given up looking for work.

It is also worth noting that unemployed individuals must of course continue to eat and generally sustain a minimum level of consumption to meet their basic needs. This fact implies that an economy with a high unemployment rate must experience reduced output of goods and services, without a corresponding decrease in the necessity for essential consumption.

For this reason, sustained, elevated unemployment rates may indicate significant economic turmoil and potentially result in social and political unrest.

In contrast, a very low unemployment rate indicates that the economy is most likely operating close to its maximum potential, fostering wage expansion, and gradually improving living standards.

Nonetheless, excessively low unemployment may also serve as a warning sign of an economy that is overheating, leading to inflationary forces and challenging circumstances for businesses that would like to hire more workers.

While the definition of unemployment is clear, economists divide unemployment into many different categories.

The two broadest categories are voluntary and involuntary unemployment.

When unemployment is voluntary, it means that a person left his job of his own accord in search of other employment. When it is involuntary, it means that a person was fired or laid off and must now look for another job.

150. Valuation

DEFINITION: In economics, the "valuation" of a thing is its estimated market value, as understood by the **subjective theory of value**.

In the realms of real estate and expensive equipment, the valuation of a piece of property is often called "an appraisal."

ETYMOLOGY: The word "valuation" derives, via Middle English, from the Middle French word *valuer*, "to value" or "to evaluate."

USAGE: Since the middle of the nineteenth century, nearly all economists (apart from Marxists) have been in agreement that the value of a scarce good on the open market is determined mainly by the preferences of consumers.

For most purposes, economists believe it is far better to allow the market to set the price of a thing than it is to set a price in ignorance of the market price.

However, for some purposes it is simply not possible to wait to see what the market price of a commodity will turn out to be. Therefore, some sort of provisional best-guess estimate must be made based on whatever information is available.

The types of situations in which valuations are necessary have to do mainly with the legally required periodic specification of the value of some form of property—notably, real estate—for some government purpose.

One of the best-known examples of such periodic valuations is the appraisal of real estate.

This form of valuation must often be performed on a regular basis (usually, every so many years) for the purpose of estimating a property owner's tax liability.

This, in turn, may be necessary so that the taxing authority is able to prepare a bill or statement to be sent to the property owner in a timely manner, or in accordance with a regular schedule.

151. Venture Capitalist

DEFINITION: The phrase "venture capitalist"—often abbreviated "VC"—refers to an investor who, in return for an equity share, provides funds to entrepreneurs whose young businesses show promise of significant growth.

VC investors may aid both start-ups and smaller firms with growth potential but which lack entry to the stock market.

ETYMOLOGY: The American businessman and investor Arthur Rock is credited with having coined the phrase "venture capitalist" in the 1950s.

The English noun "venture" is attested from the fifteenth century. The related verb derives, via Middle English *venturen,* from Middle French *aventuren,* which is related to the noun *aventure,* meaning "adventure." The latter derives from Vulgar Latin *adventura,* which, in turn, derives from the Latin past participle *adventus* of the verb *advenio, advenire,* meaning "to come to" or "to happen."

The English word "capitalist" derives, of course, from the noun "capital." In the relevant economic sense, "capital" is attested from the seventeenth century.

The noun "capital" derives, via Middle English *capitale,* from French or Italian *capitale,* meaning "chief" or "principal." The latter words ultimately derive from the Latin adjective *capitālis, capitāle,* meaning "relating to the head," which, in turn, is from the noun *caput, capitis,*meaning "a head."

USAGE: Typically organized as limited partnerships (LPs), venture capital firms have partners who invest in the VC fund. A committee is then appointed that is responsible for making investment choices.

When promising start-up and other emerging companies are selected by this committee, the firm's capital is used to finance them in return for a substantial equity share.

Contrary to popular assumption, venture capitalists do not typically finance startups from the very beginning.

Rather, they aim to invest in companies that have started generating revenue and need additional funding to bring their concept to the market.

The VC fund acquires a share in these companies, supports their expansion, and aims to achieve a significant **return on investment**when they cash out.

Venture capitalists commonly search for businesses offering a distinctive product or service, possessing a capable management team, and likely to enjoy a robust competitive edge and so substantial market prospects.

VCs also target sectors they are well-acquainted with and aim for a significant ownership stake in the company, enabling them to shape in its expected growth trajectory.

The reason why VCs are willing to assume the inherent risk of investing in promising start-up and young enterprises is because they have the possibility of reaping substantial returns if the companies take off and become successful.

In short, VC firms often direct investments towards enterprises or projects that traditional banks or capital markets tend to avoid due to the significant inherent risk.

For this reason, venture capitalists experience high rates of failure due to the unavoidable unpredictability associated with new and untested companies.

The pooled funds from which VC firms draw their resources for investment may derive from a variety of sources, including pension funds, insurance firms, corporate pension funds, foundations, and affluent individuals.

The VC firm acts as general partner, while the remaining corporations and individuals become limited partners. All partners hold an ownership share in the fund proportional to their investment. Nevertheless, the VC firm decides upon the allocation of funds.

Managers of venture capital funds receive compensation through management fees and carried interest, while around 20 percent of the profits are allocated to the firm responsible for overseeing the private equity fund.

The remaining portion is distributed among the limited partners who have invested in the fund. In addition, general partners typically receive an extra two percent fee.

152. Vertical Integration

DEFINITION: The phrase "vertical integration" refers to a business tactic which enables a company to optimize its operations by directly controlling multiple phases of its production process.

Vertical integration makes it possible for a company to dispense with external contractors or suppliers.

ETYMOLOGY: The phrase "vertical integration" appears to have been coined sometime around the turn of the twentieth century by industrialist **Andrew Carnegie.**

The English adjective "vertical" is attested from the sixteenth century. It derives, via Middle French and Late Latin, from the classical Latin adjective *verticalis,* which is connected to the noun *vertex, verticis,*meaning "eddy," "whirl," "crown of the head," "head," or "pole star."

The noun "integration" is attested from the early seventeenth century. The connected verb "to Integrate" is derived directly from the Latin past participle *integratus,* from the verb *integro, integrare,*meaning "to make whole."

USAGE: Generally speaking, the supply chain usually begins by procuring raw materials and ends by selling the end product to the customer.

A company is said to be "vertically integrated" when it establishes control over two or more of the stages in the development and sale of a product or service. This may include either purchasing or creating its own suppliers, manufacturers, distributors, or retail outlets, as opposed to outsourcing these functions.

This may proceed in various ways. For example, companies may vertically integrate by purchasing their suppliers, by buying warehouses and fleets of vans to control the distribution process, or by investing in the retail end of the process by such means as opening brick-and-mortar stores or websites.

The reason for all these types of vertical integration is to streamline the production process so that the company may operate more efficiently.

On the other hand, all of these activities require a significant capital investment for such things as building facilities and recruiting additional skilled personnel and management. Moreover, vertical integration leads to the expansion of both the scale and the intricacy of the company's operations.

For these reasons, vertical integration may carry considerable risk, as well as opportunity for savings through the greater efficiency of its operations.

There are two chief types of vertical integration: backward and forward.

Backward Integration

"Backward integration" refers to shifting ownership and control of its products to a previous point within the supply chain or the production process.

This type of vertical integration is appropriately termed "backward," seeing that companies often aim to purchase companies situated at the origin of a supply chain, such as a raw material distributor or supplier.

For example, take the case of a furniture manufacturer. In a bid to optimize operations, the manufacturer might attempt to purchase the distributor from which it has been receiving its raw materials—in this case, wood.

Forward Integration

"Forward integration" refers to obtaining control over a later point within the supply chain or the production process.

For example, in the case of the furniture manufacturer, forward integration might involve taking over the distribution process or the sale of its finished products. This might occur in several ways.

For instance, the manufacturer might merge with a retailer to acquire the capability of launching its own stores. The purpose of such a merger would be to generate higher revenue per product.

Forward integration is less frequently employed in vertical integration than backward integration. This is mainly due to the fact that the farther along the supply chain a company is located, the more difficult it is for a company located earlier along the chain to acquire it.

For instance, major retailers situated at the end of a supply chain usually possess substantial cash flow and significant purchasing influence. Instead of these retailers being purchased, they frequently have the financial resources to initiate acquisitions themselves.

153. Wealth Effect

DEFINITION: The phrase "wealth effect" refers to the change in spending habits that usually accompanies a change in an individual's perception of his wealth.

ETYMOLOGY: The word "wealth" derives from the Middle English word *welthe*, which also means "wealth." The word *welthe*, in turn, is connected, via the Middle English *wele*, to the Old English *wela*, meaning "weal." *Wela*, in turn, is connected to the Old English *wel*, meaning "well."

The word "effect" derives, via Middle English and Middle French, from the past participle, *effectus*, of the Latin verb *efficio, efficere*, meaning "to do," "to make," "to produce," or "to bring about."

USAGE: It is, of course, little more than common sense that if one feels richer, then one will spend more (and, indeed, if one feels poorer, then one will spend less).

However, the wealth effect is mainly discussed by economists in relation to the specific case in which an increase in one's perceived wealth—and so, in spending—leads, in turn, to wider effects on the economy as a whole.

With respect to this specific case, there are several points worth making.

The first is to note that the wealth effect is, by definition, determined by a change, not in some objective measure of an individual's wealth, but rather in an individual's subjective *perception* of his own wealth.

Now, obviously, if someone gets a raise at work, he will become richer by any objective measure. Therefore, it is not surprising that he will *feel* richer, as well, and so is likely to spend more.

However, if property values in someone's town or neighborhood rise, then, even though the homeowner does not have access to a larger income stream, he may feel richer by virtue of owning a more-valuable property. And this *feeling* may then lead him to spend more money.

This is one important aspect of the wealth effect. Here is another.

If consumer spending goes up, then that spending will act as a stimulus to the economy as a whole.

Obviously, the impact of one individual's spending will be quite small. However, if the wealth effect is widespread enough, the cumulative impact may be considerable.

This is one of the reasons why political leaders are notorious for exaggerating how well the economy is performing. The wealth effect helps to explain this striking fact.

If people believe they are likely to get a raise or the value of their stock portfolio is likely to increase, then the wealth effect may kick in.

If it does, then those individuals might well spend more money due to such rosy prognostications. In this way, the exaggerations would become retroactively justified—a self-fulfilling prophecy.

Another aspect of the wealth effect involves the distribution of the increased spending. Namely, if a person feels wealthier and spends more money, the money is likely to be spent on different things than it would have been otherwise.

For example, money that would have been spent on fast food may be spent in a fancy restaurant, instead.

Finally, it is necessary to note that the wealth effect is somewhat controversial within the academic discipline of economics.

Some economists say the wealth effect is not empirically observable from the statistical data.

Other economists stress that the wealth effect is both psychologically intuitive and long accepted historically.

To date, there has been no widely accepted resolution to this debate, but it seems safe to say that the majority of economists believe the wealth effect exists.

154. Working Capital

DEFINITION: The phrase "working capital," sometimes also known as "net working capital" (NWC), refers to the difference between a company's current assets and its short-term liabilities.

Current assets encompass things like the cash a company has in the bank, its accounts receivable (unpaid customer bills), its inventories of raw materials and finished products, and other assets that are expected to be liquidated (turned into cash) within a period of one year or less.

Short-term liabilities encompass accounts payable (unpaid supplier statements), wages, taxes payable, and the portion of long-term debt owed to banks or other companies that falls due within a year.

Working capital serves as a widely utilized metric for assessing the near-term well-being of an organization.

ETYMOLOGY: The phrase "working capital"is attested from around the turn of the twentieth century.

The English present participle "working," from the verb "to work," derives, via Middle English *werken* or *worken,* from Old English *wyrcan,* meaning "to bring about," "to effect," "to fashion," "to forge," or "to create."

The English noun "capital" derives, via Middle English *capitale,* from either Italian or French *capitale,* meaning "chief" or "principal." *Capitale* ultimately derives from the Latin adjective *capitālis, capitāle,* meaning "relating to the head," which, in turn, is from the noun *caput, capitis,* meaning "head."

USAGE: Assessments of working capital are calculated from the assets and liabilities recorded on a company's balance sheet.

By focusing on its imminent debts—and counterbalancing them with its most readily available assets—a company can gain a deeper insight into its liquidity status for its immediate future.

As well as a metric of a company's short-term financial health, working capital is also a measure of its operational efficiency. If a company has substantial positive NWC, then it could have the potential to invest in expansion and grow the company.

On the other hand, if a company's NWC is negative—that is, if current assets are smaller than its short-term liabilities—then it may have trouble growing or paying back creditors, or even be at risk of bankruptcy.

The amount of working capital a company possesses generally depends upon its industry.

Certain sectors characterized by lengthier production cycles might necessitate a greater amount of working capital to offset their limited capacity for rapid inventory turnover, which hinders quick cash generation.

Conversely, retail enterprises that serve thousands of customers on a daily basis may be able to expedite the generation of short-term funds, thus reducing their need for working capital.

To compute working capital, deduct a company's current liabilities from its current assets.

Working Capital = Current Assets – Short-Term Liabilities

Working capital is often stated as a dollar figure. For example, say a company has $10,000 in current assets and $4,000 in short-term liabilities.

The company is therefore said to have:
$10,000 – $4,000 = $6,000
of working capital.

This means the company has $6,000 at its immediate disposal if it needs to raise money for some reason.

Note that in the case of publicly traded firms, these data may typically be found in publicly disclosed financial statements.

However, in the case of privately held companies, the relevant financial information might not be immediately accessible.

It's important to recognize that negative working capital is not inherently bad. Its impact may be either positive or negative, depending upon the particular business and whether and how fast the company is growing.

On the other hand, a persistent state of negative working capital may potentially lead to unfortunate consequences.

155. Work-in-Progress

DEFINITION: The phrase "work-in-progress" (WIP)—also known as "work-in-process"—refers to partially finished goods awaiting completion. The term is used mainly in the context of supply chain management.

WIP refers to the cost of raw materials, labor, and overhead that went into the production of items situated at different stages of the production process.

On a company's balance sheet, WIP shows up as a component of the inventory asset account.

After completion of the production process, the costs associated with WIP are transferred to the finished goods account and, eventually, to the cost of sales.

The basic purpose of WIP is to avoid spending more money on individual nodes in the supply chain than is necessary.

ETYMOLOGY: The phrase "work-in-progress" appears to have originated during the 1950s within the context of a Japanese management movement aimed at reducing overhead and streamlining supply chain production developed by Toyota Motor Company. The movement was given the name "**lean thinking**" in 1988 by Hyundai Motor America president and CEO, **John F. Krafcik**, when he was a graduate student at MIT.

The English noun "work" is attested from around the eleventh century. It derives, via Middle English *werk* or *work*, from Old English *werc* or *weorc*. The latter is akin to Old High German *werc*.

The English preposition "in" derives from the same form in Middle English and in Old English. The Old English word, in turn, is akin to the same form in Old High German and in Latin. Thus, the form *in* in all four languages is identical to the modern English form, with the same meaning.

The English noun "progress" is attested from the fifteenth century. It derives, via Middle English, from the Latin past participle *prōgressus* from the deponent verb *prōgredior, prōgredi*, meaning "to go forth," "to go out," "to go forward," "to proceed," or "to advance."

USAGE: The notion ofWIP refers to the flow of manufacturing costs from one location within a production supply chain to another.

The WIP balance represents all the costs of production incurred for goods upon which work has begun but not yet ended.

That is to say, the WIP is a component of a company's balance sheet, which reflects only the value of those products that are in an intermediate stage of production.

The production costs included in WIP may represent such things as raw materials, the labor used in making goods, and allocated overhead.

However, WIP excludes the value of raw materials not yet incorporated into an item for sale, as well as the value of finished products being held in inventory pending future sales.

For example, take a plastic pail manufacturer. During the process of manufacturing pails, plastic moves from the category of raw material to that of material used in production.

Next, wages paid to the employees who the operate the molding equipment which presses the bulk plastic into the shape of pails fall into the category of labor costs.

Since the pails are not yet finished, for the time being these costs count as WIP.

Then, when the pails are finished, the costs are moved from the category of WIP to that of finished goods (both accounts are considered part of the inventory).

When the pails are finally sold, these costs are moved from the category of inventory to that of "cost of goods sold" (COGS).

In other words, an item in inventory is designated as work in progress when human labor and raw materials have been invested in it, but it is not yet classified as a finished good. That is, while some essential tasks have been completed, others remain to be done.

The classification of WIP may vary according to distinct accounting approaches which may be adopted by different companies.

Therefore, investors need to differentiate between the method a company uses to measure its work in progress and the way it handles other inventory categories. For this reason, it may not be proper to compare one company's WIP classification with another's.

For instance, the apportionment of overhead by two different companies might rely on factors such as labor hours versus machine hours.

WIP is recorded as an asset on the balance sheet. Thus, the conventional accounting approach involves minimizing the WIP inventory before mandatory reporting occurs. This is all the more necessary given the complexity and labor-intensive nature of estimating an inventory asset's completion percentage.

156. Xenocurrency

DEFINITION: The term "xenocurrency" refers to a currency that is used outside of the national boundaries of the country that issued it.

In the US, xenocurrency is usually called "foreign currency." However, that usage assumes a provincial US perspective.

The term "xenocurrency" may be applied with equal validity to any country whose currency is traded in other countries.

ETYMOLOGY: The term "xenocurrency" seems to have been introduced by the **Austrian school** economist Fritz Machlup in 1974.

The English term "xenocurrency" is compounded from two component parts:

1. The Greek adjective *xenos,* meaning "foreign";
2. The English word "currency" is attested from the turn of the eighteenth century; the related adjective "current" derives, via Middle English *curraunt,* from the Old French present participle *curant* of the verb *courre,* meaning "to run," which, in turn, derives from the Latin verb *curro, currere,* also meaning "to run."

USAGE: Even though the term "xenocurrency" was introduced in the first place precisely to avoid taking a US-centric point of view for granted, it has fallen out of favor more recently.

This is probably due to the general aura of negativity attached to the Greek root *xeno–* among modern people, who have not had the benefit of a classical education and who recognize the root only from the pejorative term "xenophobia."

Whatever the reason, the fact is that the ethnically neutral term "xenocurrency" is now used relatively infrequently, while the ethnocentric term "foreign currency" has regained its former status as the preferred term for referring to currencies that circulate widely outside their borders.

This is doubly regrettable in that, when the term "foreign currency" is employed by an American national, the US dollar is naturally assumed to be meant. How, then, is one supposed to refer to the euro, say, or the Japanese yen?

It is important to note that investing in xenocurrencies carries some risk due to their inherent complexity, including volatility and uncertainty surrounding conversion rates. How so?

For one thing, risk arises when deposits are made in a strengthening domestic currency market, because reconversion of the invested funds back to the native currency may result in lower returns or losses.

On the other hand, investments in a weakening domestic currency may have the opposite effect, leading to higher profits.

These types of uncertainties and risks are commonly referred to as "foreign currency effects."

Political risks may also play a role in xenocurrency investments. For example, in a crisis a nation's government might impose limitations on the quantity of xenocurrency that travelers are allowed to take out of the country.

Moreover, in some contexts, the term "xenocurrency" may be used as a synonym for the euro. Similarly, the phrase "xenomarket" is sometimes used interchangeably with "eurocurrency market."

The eurocurrency market denotes a financial market where trading involves xenocurrency. This market may consist of participating banks, mutual funds, hedge funds, and multinational corporations.

Such lending institutions turn to the eurocurrency market in an attempt to bypass interest rate limitations, tax regulations, and other regulatory constraints that frequently apply to domestic banking, especially in the US.

157. Yankee Bond

DEFINITION: The phrase "Yankee bond" refers to a debt instrument issued by a foreign (that is, non-US) government or corporation, which is denominated in US dollars and is traded within the territory of the US.

ETYMOLOGY: The origins of the phrase "Yankee bond" are uncertain.However,one plausible theory attributes the phrase to the London-based investment bank **S.G. Warburg & Co.**, which was engaged during the 1960s in facilitating the issuance of US dollar-denominated bonds by non-US entities for sale in the US.

The English proper noun "Yankee" is attested from the eighteenth century. Its origins are unknown.

The English common noun "bond" is attested from the twelfth century. Its economic sense is closely connected to the basic sense of "restraint," "fetter," "band," or "cord."

"Bond" derives, via Middle English *bond* or *band*, from Old Norse *band*. The latter is akin to the Old English verb *bindan*, meaning "to bind."

USAGE: Despite their foreign origin, Yankee bonds are subject to regulation by the US Securities and Exchange Commission (SEC), under the provisions of Securities Act of 1933.

Yankee bonds are commonly released in "tranches," that is, distinct segments of a broader debt issuance or structured financial plan. The various tranches may carry different maturity dates, interest rates, and levels of risk.

Yankee-bond offerings may be quite substantial in size, some reaching as high as $1 billion.

Yankee bonds may also take the form of certificates of deposit (CDs). These are CDs issued within the US by a branch or agency of a foreign bank.

Yankee bonds may present a mutually beneficial opportunity both for those issuing the bonds and for investors.

Among the principal potential benefits of Yankee-bond issuers is the chance to secure more affordable financing capital. This is especially true if comparable US bond rates are considerably lower than the prevailing rates in the foreign company's home country.

The enormous scale of the US bond market, as well as the active engagement of US investors trading in it, also bestow an advantage upon the issuer, especially if the bond offering is of a substantial size.

A major advantage for US investors presented by Yankee bonds is that such bonds frequently offer higher yields than the yields available on comparable, or even lower-rated, bond issues from US issuers.

Another potential advantage is the fact that Yankee bonds offer investors a chance to diversify their bond portfolio with international investments.

Yankee bonds also offer US investors the advantage of investing in foreign corporation bond issues made in the foreign company's home country. Since Yankee bonds are denominated in US dollars, investing in them virtually eliminates the currency risk commonly associated with foreign bond investments.

Looked at from the other point of view, Yankee bonds may be advantageous for the foreign issuing company for several reasons.

While US regulatory requirements might initially pose some challenges for foreign issuers in terms of obtaining approval for their bond offering, the lending conditions in the US could still be less strict overall than those in the issuer's own country.

This means that, in spite of the challenges, the greater maneuverability US conditions may provide to the issuer may make Yankee bonds attractive on balance.

In 2003, so-called "reverse Yankee bonds" emerged on the market.

These bonds are typically of very high quality. They are issued by US corporations in foreign (non-US) markets and are denominated in a currency other than the US dollar.

Reverse Yankee bonds are also subject to mandatory registration with the SEC.

158. Year-over-Year

DEFINITION: The phrase "year-over-year," sometimes abbreviated as "YOY," refers to a commonly used quantitative method of analyzing two or more recurring, financially relevant variables on an annualized scale.

YOY analysis has several advantages for evaluating a company's economic performance, including assessing whether its financial situation is growing, standing still, or shrinking.

ETYMOLOGY: The phrase "year-over-year" cannot be traced to an exact origin. However, it undoubtedly evolved along with the growth in publicly traded stocks, transparency in financial statements, improved financial analyses, and the accounting profession, more generally, over the course of the late nineteenth or early twentieth century.

The phrase likely originated in Britain, as the idiomatic American equivalent would be "year-to-year."

The English word "year" is attested from around the eleventh century. It derives, via Middle English *yere,* from Old English *gēar,*which is akin to Old High German *jār,* with the same meaning.

The English preposition "over" is also attested from the eleventh century. It derives, via Middle English, from Old English *ofer,* akin to Old High German *ubar.*

USAGE: A year-over-year analysis of a company's growth compares its recent financial performance with comparable data for the same time one year earlier.

These annualized figures will likely be more indicative of the true status of a company's financial well-being than, say, a shorter, a month-to-month comparison would be.

To illustrate how YOY works, take the case of Company A, a widget-maker. Company A's financial reports might indicate that during the month of December of 2022, its net widget sales stood at $11,000 and that during the month of December of 2021, they amounted to $10,000. This shows that widget sales are up by ten percent for period between January 1, 2022, and January 1, 2023.

If one did a similar analysis on the two or three years prior to 2021 and found similar results of a YOY increase of around ten percent, one would be entitled to conclude that Company A is in a strong financial position.

Note that there is some flexibility in the nature of the variable chosen for year-over-year comparison: in addition to sales-by-month, sales-by-quarter are also frequently selected for YOY analysis.

One of the chief advantages of year-over-year comparisons is the way they help to provide a picture of a company's financial position that is not skewed by such factors as seasonality.

For many if not most businesses, sales and profit levels, as well as various financial metrics, may fluctuate throughout the year in a predictable way, due to seasonal effects on demand.

For example, it would make little sense for retailers which are strongly affected by year-end holiday shopping to compare their sales month-to-month. All that would do would be to track the seasonal change in demand for their product, which is something that is already known.

Similarly, if an investor compares a company's performance sequentially (that is, during consecutive quarters), he or she might be misled by passing trends due to transient changes in the company's management, in market conditions, etc.

What is needed is some means of offsetting seasonality and other transient effects. And that is just what YOY analysis provides.

Comparing a company's last-month or fourth-quarter performance across at least two different years is desirable precisely because it takes into account the total change in sales over the entire intervening year, thus wiping out any effects from seasonality.

159. Yield

DEFINITION: "Yield" is a form of **interest** that functions as a term of art used by the financial industry.

Like all forms of interest, yield is an amount of money that is earned after a set period of time on a principal amount that an investor has loaned to another individual or institution.

However, the term "yield" usually refers to the interest earned on specific kinds of financial instruments.

More specifically, "yield" most often signifies the earnings on fixed-income securities (certificates of deposits, bonds, and real estate investments), on stocks (common, preferred, and convertible), or on annuities.

ETYMOLOGY: The word "yield" derives from the Old English word *gieldan*, meaning "to pay," which is related to the Old High German word *geltan*, with the same meaning.

USAGE: The yield on a security must not be confused with changes in its market value.

The yield on a security, and the increase in its market value, if any, are separate and complementary components of the total earnings generated to an investor by a security.

There is a considerable technical vocabulary associated with the concept of "yield."

Some of the best-known of these terms are the following:

- ***Coupon rate*:** the interest on a fixed-income security, expressed as a percentage of the security's principal amount ("par value"). The coupon rate is also known as the "nominal rate."
- ***Current yield*:** the interest on a fixed-income security, expressed as a ratio between the security's annual interest payment at the coupon rate (the "coupon payment") and its current market price.
- ***Yield-to-maturity*:** an estimate of the total rate of return anticipated to be earned by an investor over the life of a security. It is composed of all of a security's estimated coupon payments, plus the original principal.
- ***Par yield*:** the current yield of a security under the assumption that its current market price is equal to its par value. A security's par yield is also known as its "nominal value."

160. Zero Bound

DEFINITION: The phrase "zero bound," or "zero lower bound," refers to a monetary policy in which a central bank decreases short-term interest rates to zero.

The purpose of a zero-bound monetary strategy is to stimulate the economy by encouraging borrowing, spending, and investing.

The advisability of a zero bound policy is highly disputed. Even if it can be justified by its stimulative effect, a central bank must nevertheless exercise caution in implementing this approach, by, among other things, employing other measures to stimulate or revive the economy, as well, even if they are unconventional or controversial.

Thus, zero bound should only be considered in connection with relatively dire economic stagnation, when all other, more-conventional stimulative measures have failed.

ETYMOLOGY: The phrase "zero bound" probably goes back to the 1930s, when it was discussed as a theoretical possibility by Depression Era–policymakers. It was first implemented as actual policy by the US Federal Reserve in March of 2020.

The English word "zero" is attested from the early seventeenth century. It derives from either Middle French *zéro* or Italian *zero,*which both derive from Medieval Latin *zephirum*, which itself derives from Arabic *ṣifr*, all meaning "zero."

The word *zephirum*, the Medieval Latin version of the Arabic *ṣifr*, was coined by the Italian mathematician Fibonacci (Leonardo of Pisa) in his *Liber abaci* [Book of Calculation] in 1202.

The English noun "bound," in the mathematical sense derived from the closely related noun "boundary," is attested from the thirteenth century. It derives, via Middle English, from Old French *bodne,* which, in turn, derives from Medieval Latin *bodina.*

USAGE: The phrase "zero bound" means the lower bound that interest rates may fall to, given that, while negative rates (meaning the owner pays the bank to hold his money for him) are theoretically possible, they are not usually practicable, at least in the context of a national government's monetary policy.

Central banks manipulate interest rates in two main ways: either by reducing the prime rate (which is used as a benchmark by all other banks) to stimulate a stagnating economy or else by raising the prime rate to cool off an overheating economy.

Logically, there is no upper limit to how high the central bank can raise interest rates. However, there is a lower bound and that is obviously zero (once again, ignoring negative rates).

Assuming that interest rates ought not to be allowed to fall into negative territory, it may be presumed that once interest rates reach the zero bound, or approach very near to it (as with 0.1 percent rates, for example), then monetary-policy adjustments elsewhere in the system will be required to sustain or economic stability.

Perhaps the best-known substitute for further interest-rate cuts within a government's monetary-policy toolkit is what is known as "**quantitative easing**" (QE). Quantitative easing is thus an adjunct to a zero-bound policy.

Quantitative easing involves the implementation by a central bank of an extensive program of the repeated purchase of assets, usually including Treasury bills and government bonds.

The goal of QE is not only to keep short-term interest rates (those of financial instruments with terms of one year or less) low, but also to reduce longer-term rates.

If successful, the combined policies of zero bound and quantitative easing may succeed in stimulating the economy by putting in place the requisite incentives to motivate increased borrowing.

The long-term sustainability of these novel and drastic policies, however, remains highly contentious.

161. Zero-Sum Game

DEFINITION: A “zero-sum game” is a type of two-sided game—in the mathematical, game-theoretic sense of the word “game”—in which a positive outcome for one side corresponds to an equivalent but negative outcome for the other side.

In colloquial speech, a zero-sum game is known as a “win-lose” situation.

The opposite of a zero-sum game is a **non-zero-sum game**.

ETYMOLOGY: The phrase “zero-sum” derives from the fact that the sum of the outcomes of the game for the two sides always equals zero.

For example, in a zero-sum game, if Side A achieves an outcome of $+n$, then Side B must achieve an outcome of $-n$. And, of course, $+n + -n = 0$.

USAGE: The classic example of a zero-sum situation is cutting up a cake.

To make the zero-sum character of dividing up a cake apparent, we need to make two assumptions:

- a specified number of pieces—say, corresponding to the number of guests at a party
- a rule for cutting the pieces—namely, that they should all be of the same size

It is clear that if we divide the cake by the specified number of pieces—let us call this number z—and impose the constraint that all the pieces be of the same size, then the size of each piece will be fixed by the basic rules. Let us call this fixed size m.

Given these assumptions, then, if one piece $> m$ by some fixed amount j, then the recipient of that $m + j$ sized piece of cake is by definition the “winner” in a zero-sum game.

The definition also allows us to calculate exactly the size of each of the remaining $z - 1$ pieces, always assuming equality.

Since each piece will clearly be $< m$ by some amount $k < j$, each of the other guests at the party will receive an $m - k$ sized slice of cake.

More exactly, each of the other guest will get a slice of cake of a size determined as follows:

$$m - k = (zm - (m + j)) / (z - 1)$$

This may seem like much ado about very little when it comes to dividing up a cake.

However, in political economy, the notion of a zero-sum game is very important because it is often lurking in the background of bitter policy disputes as an unexamined presupposition.

For example, the very language in which policy proposals are couched—especially, in terms of the words "distribution" or "redistribution"—rest upon the unspoken assumption that we are talking about a zero-sum game.

Thus, progressives tend to look upon income, not as something earned through human effort, but as something that is just there—representing a fixed amount of money at any given moment in time.

Since this fixed amount of money will not be equally "distributed"—which is simply to say that some people will be have more money than others—it will be argued that justice demands "redistribution," which amounts to taking money away from some people and giving it to others.

In short, progressives see economic output as a sort of big cake or pie. Indeed, sometimes the actual language of someone's not getting his "fair share of the pie" is even used.

To be sure, if it were true that the economy was a zero-sum game, then such a way of speaking and thinking would make sense.

But it is not true.

In fact, the assumption underlying progressive rhetoric about "redistribution" is demonstrably false.

The consequences of the economic activity of hundreds of millions of individuals simply bears no resemblance to a zero-sum game.

Not only is it possible that the fortunes of all those who are productively engaged in economic activity rise or fall together. It is the usual case.

162. Zombie Company

DEFINITION: The term "zombie company" refers to a business firm that generate barely sufficient revenue to sustain its operations and meet its debt obligations but lacks the wherewithal ever to pay off its debts completely.

Since zombie companies are barely able to cover essential expenses, such as rent, wages, and debt service, they do not have any extra funds left over for investment.

Therefore, they have no ability to expand the company's operations, other than by borrowing money. Indeed, zombie companies rely heavily on banks for financial support. Although banks are essentially lifelines for zombie companies, the down side is that zombies are likely to face elevated borrowing costs.

In any case, zombie companies are vulnerable to potential crises, such as market disruptions or periods of weak performance, which could push them toward insolvency.

Zombie companies are also known as "the living dead" and, if publicly traded, their shares may be termed "zombie stocks."

ETYMOLOGY: The phrase "zombie company" was coined in Japan during the 1990s —a period sometimes referred to as the "lost decade," which was marked by the bursting of a massive asset price bubble in that country's financial sector.

The English word "zombie" is attested from the mid-nineteenth century. It most likely derives, via Haitian Creole, from a language of the Bantu family. For example, it is akin to the Kikongo word *nzambi,*meaning "god."

The English noun "company" is attested from the thirteenth century. It derives, via Middle English *companie,* from Old French *compagnie,*which is formed from *compain,* meaning "companion." The latter word derives from Late Latin *companio* with the same meaning.

USAGE: Not infrequently, zombie enterprises experience setbacks or ultimately go bankrupt due to the substantial expenses involved in debt service or in other activities necessary in some business sectors, such as research and development.

Zombie companies may face limitations in terms of funds for capital infusion that would enable investment with a view to expansion.

If a zombie company is so large that its collapse might have widespread adverse repercussions throughout the economy, causing political embarrassment for the government of the day, then it may be considered "too big to fail" and the government may step in to save it. This was the case with some of the institutions that were bailed out during the 2008 financial crisis.

Since it may be safely assumed that many zombie companies will have difficulty in meeting their financial obligations, such firms may come to be regarded as risky prospects for investment. This assessment may, in turn, lead to downward pressure on a zombie company's stock price.

In the middle of a financial crisis, politicians feel immense pressure to "do something," which accounts in part for bailouts to keep afloat companies that may be too large or otherwise ineffective and struggling. Most economists maintain that it would have been more beneficial for the economy as a whole if such underperforming companies had been allowed to fail.

It was in this context that the phrase "zombie company" resurfaced in 2008—this time in the US, in response to the federal bailout payments to the failing companies that came to be bundled together in the form of the Troubled Asset Relief Program (TARP).

Although the risk to the US economy from zombie companies is thought to remain low, their numbers have been augmented by years of lenient monetary measures such as extensive borrowing, historically rock-bottom (**zero bound**) interest rates, and quantitative easing (QE).

Economists contend that these policies preserve inefficiencies while impeding innovation. productivity, and growth. In future, under different market conditions, it is likely that zombie companies will find it increasingly challenging to fulfill their fundamental obligations due to rising interest rates and the mounting cost of servicing their debts.

For this reason, zombie companies will likely be among the earliest casualties of any downturn in the market or change in monetary policy in the direction of a more restrictions.

On the other hand, if current market conditions and government policies continue, solid and thriving enterprises might experience unwarranted restrictions on their credit opportunities and so might not weather an economic downturn as well as they otherwise would.

www.ingramcontent.com/pod-product-compliance
Lightning Source LLC
LaVergne TN
LVHW060026210926
848481LV00013B/3798